The Case of the Sexy Jewess

THE CASE OF THE SEXY JEWESS

Dance, Gender, and Jewish Joke-Work in US Pop Culture

Hannah Schwadron

OXFORD
UNIVERSITY PRESS

Oxford University Press is a department of the University of Oxford. It furthers
the University's objective of excellence in research, scholarship, and education
by publishing worldwide. Oxford is a registered trade mark of Oxford University
Press in the UK and certain other countries.

Published in the United States of America by Oxford University Press
198 Madison Avenue, New York, NY 10016, United States of America.

Library of Congress Cataloging-in-Publication Data
Names: Schwadron, Hannah, author.
Title: The case of the sexy Jewess : dance, gender, and
Jewish joke-work in US pop culture / by Hannah Schwadron.
Description: New York : Oxford University Press, [2018] |
Includes bibliographical references and index.
Identifiers: LCCN 2017018845| ISBN 9780190624194 (cloth : alk. paper) |
ISBN 9780190624200 (pbk. : alk. paper) | ISBN 9780190624231 (oxford scholarship online)
Subjects: LCSH: Jewish women—United States—Social life and customs. |
Jewish women in popular culture—United States. |
Jews in popular culture—United States. | Jewish women comedians—
United States—History. | Jewish women—Humor. | Stand-up comedy—
Social aspects—United States. | Black swan (Motion picture : 2010) |
Angel, Joanna— Appreciation. | United States—Ethnic relations.
Classification: LCC E184.36.S65 S39 2018 |
DDC 305.48/8924—dc23
LC record available at https://lccn.loc.gov/2017018845

9 8 7 6 5 4 3 2 1

Paperback Printed by Sheridan Books, Inc., United States of America
Hardback Printed by Bridgeport National Bindery, Inc., United States of America

CONTENTS

ACKNOWLEDGMENTS

The work of writing this book has been a significant project of imagining for whom I am writing, how, and why. So first, I want to thank my students. I am writing now for you. What you have said you care about most has generated the very questions at the core of this book: *Why performance? And why now?* In the process of putting this book together, your voices have resonated throughout. As we often discuss, theorizing dance and social meaning is always both personal and political and as urgent as it is difficult. Certainly performance writing feels as if it is a task of smoothing out and over ideas that don't or won't stay fixed. It assigns language to the aftereffects of thought, of articulation and argumentation, and again in the name of cohesion. This is especially difficult when performance itself commands attention in the very now moment of rapture, the wow of anxious watching and being watched from the sideline seats of sensory overload, or the unnamable visceral impact of a screened event. Know this and find conviction there: that writing is a play in its own right, of desire and identification, projection and misrecognition, in which the work of representation is a practice in getting closer to the real of experience and the politics of often too deeply felt personal premises.

Rethinking the text for undergraduate and graduate students, practiced scholars across related disciplines, and all others who may be invested in thinking about Jewishness, gender, sexuality, and humor has been an exercise in collaboration with many contributors. First, I can thank Marta E. Savigliano, who taught me how to think on dance and politics in the popular realm. As the supervisor of my doctoral research and the guide of the dissertation upon which this book is built, her mentorship has continued to influence its critical stakes. She taught me that writing should provoke rather than answer, and that when it comes to sexy plays with self-display, especially when they are funny, it is never easy or obvious to know what laughter brings. Other mentors of my research deserve huge thanks, including Jeff Tobin, who prompted me to create chapter 4 on *Black Swan* and inspired the book's link to psychoanalysis. Anthea Kraut pushed for theorization of race rooted in movement, tuning the research to the body and its unique work of representation.

Linda Tomko guided my thinking on period-whiteness, helping me contextualize the historical specificity of shifting race and gender values in the context of ethnic assimilation. She also attended every conference at which I presented a paper on this research, and when we were sitting together on one plane ride back to Riverside, commented that my face is my "self-reflexive capacity," inspiring the focus of my writing on ideas about such a face ever since. Priya Srinivasan is the mentor mentioned at the beginning of chapter 2, who hails me as a funny girl with her "Hello Gorgeous" greetings when we talk on the phone and who encourages me to grow more resilient at every turn. She stops listening when I go on too long, and because of that, I both think more quickly and react less to life's dulling dramas. Susan Rose, the final member of my doctoral committee and the chair of my MFA thesis committee, has since become a life coach and a best friend. Studying and performing in her improvisation-based dance company throughout the first several years of writing this book helped me discern the "it" from the "not it" as an improvisation practice in paying attention. She has taught me to fight passionately for the things that deserve it, but then not to care too much if they don't work out. The result is a writing and performance life that is both more intentional and more flexible.

My father, Terry Schwadron, deserves special mention as key reader and book mentor. I have tested theories of contemporary American Jewishness against his understanding as himself a writer and a musician, as well as the son of a Holocaust survivor, the husband of a Jewish dancer, and the father of three Jewish artists. It is he who has asked me when I mean "ethical" or "ethnical," as if the two terms were nearly interchangeable. This has helped me remember where I am from. My mother, Patch Schwadron, supplied the inspiration for my analysis of Jewish Swans, having herself danced many ballet roles in the Boston Ballet and then learning the *Funny Girl* soundtrack word for word. She continues to teach me how to be loud, unafraid of failure, and full of life. My sister, Julia Schwadron, is easily the funniest woman I know and the greatest impersonator of all, if also the most insightful social theorist. On top of that, the stunning intensity of her paintings is a meditation on a life of questioning that models a way to be profoundly Jewish, feminist, and deeply human without needing to claim any one of those titles. My brother, Louis Schwadron, inspired my life in performance, stealing hearts on stage as a child and ever since with cosmic lyricism and generosity that is nothing short of rabbinical. Throughout this writing, he delivered a regular supply of YouTube links to the everyday absurd, delighting in the balance of the bizarre and the beautiful. To know how funny something is, he has reminded me at key points, is to know how truly serious it is.

Writing groups with Rachel Carrico and Anusha Kedhar have helped clarify the scope of the book, while championing an academic process that is rooted in real relationships of support. I also owe enormous thanks to my Tallahassee lifeline, modern languages professor, Jeannine Murray-Román, who has acted as book doctor on chapter drafts in process, reading the manuscript in full and noting patterns while thinking with me throughout. The generous eyes of Melissa Hudson Bell, J. Dellecave, Michelle Timmons Summers, Alicia Cox, Kate Alexander, and Cesar Lopez carried me through drafts of the writing at many points in the process.

The privileged opportunity to join the Mellon funded Dance Studies in/and the Humanities Summer Fellows Program provided me with the chance to workshop my writing with a host of senior and emerging dance scholars, with the additional feedback of thomas f. defrantz, Sherril Dodds, Susan Foster, Susan Manning, Janice Ross, and Rebecca Scheider, as well as the insightful Sarah Wilbur, Joanna Dee Das, and Ninoska M'bewe Escobar. The keen editorial eyes of Jen Atkins, Sally Sommer, Tricia Young, Rebekah Kowal, Gerald Siegmund, Clare Croft, and Jennifer Fisher provided a wealth of feedback on versions of chapters while preparing excerpts for essay publication. I'm especially grateful for the insight on material in progress that has come from my colleagues and friends in Jewish dance studies, Hannah Kosstrin and Rebecca Rossen.

For the production stages of this book, I thank editor Norman Hirschy at Oxford University Press, who has encouraged the project since his initial readings of chapter drafts and whose warm sense of humor has helped create a home for my writing on comedy and dance. I also thank assistant editor Lauralee Yeary, whose generous guidance on the stages of this book's submission offered key support and also welcome cheer, as well as Production Editor Alphonsa James who has carried the book through its final production phases. Oxford University Press arranged for anonymous readers who have lent an astute sense of how to enhance the book, from proposal to full manuscript reviews, and I am thankful for their rich feedback.

Time and funds to conduct research for the book and complete its various writing phases have come from Florida State University and the University of California, Riverside. At FSU, the significant First Year Assistant Professor Award, as well as the prestigious Arts and Humanities Project Enhancement Award, helped me with necessary support for the academic and choreographic research of this study. At UCR, the Dissertation Year Fellowship and the Graduate Mentorship Research Fellowship funded opportunities for me to focus on research and writing. Multiple travel grants at both institutions allowed me to share my work with professional academic audiences as well as public dance audiences and provided the opportunity to build important relationships with members of the Congress of Research on Dance/Society of Dance History Scholars, Popular Culture Association, Performance Studies International, Dancing Under Construction, the American Jewish Historical Society, and Conney Project on Jewish Arts. I am especially lucky to be a returning member of the Conney Project's Jewish Choreographer's workshop, where I have had the pleasure of working closely with Judith Brin Ingber, Naomi Jackson, Karen Goodman, Hasia Diner, Sophia Levine, Jessie Zarritt, and Rebecca Pappas on questions of dance and Jewish identity through performance.

Many other creative collaborations have contributed to the choreographic development of this research, including projects workshopped over three years of Field Studies performance lab in New York City with Melissa Hudson Bell, Ilana Goldman, Ann Mazzocca, Amanda Waal, Rachel Carrico, Crystal Sepúlveda, Marilyn Maywald, Cydney Watson, Alfonso Cervera, Irvin Gonzalez, Dasha Chapman, Adanna K. Jones, Anusha Kedhar, Chelsea Rector, Rebecca Pappas, Rachel Thorne Germond, Trent D. Williams, and Jeannine Murray Román. Additional performance projects with Susan Rose, Sue Roginski, Priya Srinivasan, Natalie Zervou, Malia Bruker, Aboubacar Camara, and Ircamar Garcia have inspired my continued choreographic experimentation with ideas core to this book and are helping point to new directions this research can take. I also thank my growing list of collaborators in Hamburg, Germany, who have helped me with research aspects of this work in the sites of my own Jewish family history: Inge Mandos, Klaus Weber, Maria Milkyway, Mahdi Nagisade, Erika Hirsch, Stella Juergensen, Carsten Vitt, Hans Bongers, Sakhi Poya, Robert Wagner, and Timm Albes.

The faculty and staff at FSU inspire my daily engagement with dance scholarship and have generously cheered me on throughout this process. Thank you Jen Atkins, Josephine Garibaldi, Patty Phillips, Jawole Zollar, Ilana Glazer, Loren Davidson, Gwen Welliver, Doug Courbin, Rick McCullough, Tom Welsh, Tim Glenn, Dan Smith, Anthony Morgan, Russell Sandifer, Sally Sommer, Kehinde Ishangi, Carla Peterson, Ansje Burdick, Laura-Paige Kryber, Chris Cameron, Stephanie Mills, Anna Singleton, and Jasmine Johnson. Because of the generosity of the School of Dance, I have been fortunate to receive the help and camaraderie of research assistants and budding scholar-artists in their own right, Madeline Kurtz, Gianna Mercandetti, Jasmine Booker, and Sarah Rose, who have masterminded the endnotes, image permissions, and sensitive negotiations of working with a first-time author while managing their own sizable workloads as graduate students.

To my coven of girlfriends here in Tallahassee, who refuse to be called the Interdisciplinary University Women's Group as I first named us, and whose friendship I have come to cherish, I owe huge thanks. Ilana Goldman, Malia Bruker, Jeannine Murray-Román, Christine Nieves Rodriguez, and Loren Davidson: I thank you for holding me and each other as we grow up into ourselves and continue to indulge everyday joy. Tallahassee has been a wonderful home for the last two years of this book's coming to fruition, especially because of my colleagues across campus: Anais Nony, Raquel Albarran, Samer Al-Saber, and Warren Allen. Shout outs to my comrades Cal, Brad, Lisa, Lauren, Tenee, and James at 621 Art Gallery; Tyler, Robert, Noll, Adam, and Christine at Fermentation Lounge; Susie, Sari, Jamie, and David at Bread and Roses Kitchen; Len, Craig and Pastor Jim at Legion Hall, and Fajr, Sabrina, and Shala at the AfroCarribbean Dance Theater for extra love, food, prayer, and care during the heftiest phases of revision.

I also thank Christine and David Leapman as well as Mercedes and Donaldo Lopez, who have welcomed me into their families during these critical years as extra sets of parents and friends. If not for their love and that of so many others, but especially Alicia, Marika, Marilyn, Keenan, Jori, Lucas, Louis, Julia, Mom, Dad, and Cesar, this would not have been nearly as fun or feasible.

Finally, I am indebted to the women about whom I have written this book and the brilliant minds who presented them, cast them, came to see them, wrote for them, printed them, published them, and photographed them so finely in their element. Thank you Susannah Perlman, Minnie Tonka, Darlinda Just Darlinda, Little Brooklyn, Zoe Ziegfeld, Sandra Bernhard, Sarah Silverman, Abbi Jacobson, Ilana Glazer, Fanny Brice, Sophie Tucker, Betty Boop, Barbra Streisand, Madeline Kahn, Gilda Radner, Bette Midler, Natalie Portman, Winona Ryder, Barbara Hershey, Mila Kunis, and Joanna Angel. To funny girls everywhere, I dedicate this book. As Winona Ryder wisely reminds us, "The work is the reward."[1]

I am grateful to Oxford University Press and University Press of Florida for granting permission to use portions of previously published material. Excerpts of chapter 2 originally appeared in Hannah Schwadron, "Ballet Bawdies and Dancing Ducks: Jewish Swans of the Silver Screen," in *Oxford Handbooks Online* (Oxford University Press, 2017); permission granted by Oxford University Press. Excerpts of chapter 5 originally appeared in Hannah Schwadron, "(Post) Pious and Porn Spectacles: Frontier Choreographies of the US Jewess," in *Perspectives on American Dance*, Vol. II, ed. Jen Atkins, Sally Sommer, and Tricia Young (University Press of Florida, 2017); reprinted with permission from University Press of Florida. A significant portion of chapter 4 on Darren Aronofsky's *Black Swan* was previously published in Hannah Schwadron, "Black Swan, White Nose," in *The Oxford Handbook of Dance and Politics*, ed. Rebekah Kowal and Gerald Siegmund (Oxford University Press, 2017); permission granted by the publisher.

Introduction

THE CASE OF THE SEXY JEWESS

This book tells the story of the rise of an unorthodox figure in contemporary American Jewishness: the Sexy Jewess. She appears as the dancer or dunce in various guises in neoburlesque and cabaret, comedy television, mainstream movies, and progressive pornographic films, constructing the twenty-first-century Jewish American woman through embodied acts of self-display. She is known for her charisma and comic craft, her in-your-face antics and offensive charm. With a klutz joke here and an ethnic accent there, she recalls the cherished Jewish female comics of twentieth-century entertainment lore. And yet her act is not as lovably known, playing as it does with roles less familiar. She's a pinup or a porn star, a self-commenting plaything, or the passing face of horrible perfection. The aftermath of American assimilation and women's liberation, her funny, sexy power navigates aging territories with new scripts. Oscillating as she does between ethnic difference and race privilege, emboldened femininity and its failures, her antics embody positions that she remains forever in-between.

To be frank, the Sexy Jewess does not exist. Well, not in the sincere sense. She is an imaginative fiction, a telling construction, a twisty kind of joke, and often a funny one. She invokes the Jewish girl in America but is not quite that girl, claiming ties to tradition and change that she resists with equal force. Even when the performer delivers herself or some outrageous version of a self, the spectacle refracts its ego-inflated/ego-effacing creation, blurring all that the parodist stands for in the midst of identifications gone purposely awry. The Sexy Jewess, dancing and talking herself in circles, heads face-first into the representational abyss.

Categorization of the Sexy Jewess underscores her constructed nature, the performativity of her image, and the ruse of her symbolic authority. She is not, in other words, a she at all, but a possibility, a contemporary characterization, a conundrum. Her invocation takes physical form, however, in performances by any number of social actors with real legs. The "case" of the Sexy Jewess in this sense presents a study as if it were singular, when in fact her moves maneuver across a slew of celebrity and amateur scenes. Her case then is a range of embodiments that refuse the singular, even while reiterating the Jewish woman as punningly classifiable. In this sense, her case might be seen as psychosocial pathology, or deserving of legal review.[1] For the purposes of this book, however, she is a matter of history and culture, representational performance and identity play. As the female lead of this book and addressed differently in each chapter, the Sexy Jewess slips in and out of expectations with a trickster power she repeatedly trips over.

In reflexive plays with sexed-up self-display, today's Sexy Jewess updates long-standing stereotypes of the hag, the Jewish mother, and Jewish American princess that imagined the Jewish woman as overly demanding, inappropriate, and unattractive throughout the twentieth century, and even further back, to the late nineteenth-century literary figure of the belle Juive, or exotic Jewess. As opposed to derogative stereotypes that portrayed the Jewish woman as ugly, homely, and old worldly, the exotic Jewess was depicted as a desirable young woman with "ancient sufferings and alien custom" whose fatal negotiations of past and present were the fetish of gentile men.[2] Ultimately dying off in the high-art scene, she reappeared on the minstrel and vaudeville circuits as a bawdy act that made humor of the horrible tropes; she embraced her damned role as a failed femme, a social misfit, a funny girl in low-brow moves that comically undermined herself as much as the world around her. These are the sustained hi-low backdrops that still set her stage in both mainstream and amateur acts.

But why does "sexy" work to update old tropes of the Jewish woman, first an exoticized fetish and then the ugly duckling? And how does sex link to humor in order for this upgrade to work? There is not one answer, and the questions themselves aim to encourage more productive thought. This book underlines the ways in which gender, ethnicity, race, and sexuality intersect through performance of self-representation and parody. Chapters identify a cross-section of popular and subcultural performers who defend what funny sex appeal means for Jewish stage and screen women in their respective domains. More specifically, the selected bill of performances offers diverse responses to the question of Jewish and gender difference in an era after assimilation and second wave feminism. As performers navigate new race and class privileges through self-parody, they embody displays of funniness and sexiness that simultaneously rehearse and revise histories of contemporary American Jewry as well as feminist performance.

To watch the Sexy Jewess do her thing raises questions about what happens next, as the postassimilatory and postfeminist implications of Jewish female performance modalities perpetuate stereotypes in order to disrupt them. In the context of this book, postfeminism accounts for those mechanisms of performance that sometimes claim and at other times resist the banners of second wave feminism and its anthems of women's liberation. Sliding between such affirmative and resistive citations, performers go "bad" by way of a sex-positive girl power, and worse, by way of its ironic critique.[3] Pushing past concerns with objectification, performers play with the very terms of themselves as subjects and objects, manipulating displays of bodily command, control, and comic lack thereof. Postfeminist performances outlined in the book allow for these simultaneous possibilities. They toy with a sex appeal counterindicated by Jewishness, whose funniness is always already effeminately male in mainstream media, where it has etched itself as an American stock figure and the familiar material of unsexy self-ridicule. But more on that in a moment.

In addition to postfeminism, Postassimilation provides the book's parallel framework as a class- and race-based concept tied to the Jewish female body. Across contexts, I argue that postassimilationist performances return to categories of cultural and religious Jewish difference from secular positions of majoritarian sameness.[4] Performances return with nostalgia to earlier eras of American Jewishness defined by ethnic otherness. Doing so allows performers themselves to stake claim to new identities that break with the past, but in ways that are regularly contradictory, and left deliberately unresolved.

As postfeminists and postassimilationists, Sexy Jewess performers bite the hands that feed them only to then kiss them with a smile. They offend and apologize again and again, to a range effects. In some cases, patterns emerge. Select performances share what looks like utopic concerns, as in the liberation from hetero-patriarchal discourses in and out of Jewishness, a progressive ethos that exposes their own coming-into-whiteness through playing up privileges and blind spots. In other cases, performers opt for provocative techniques (e.g., pornography or ballet horror) that question the very premises of social progress while cashing in on the lucrative confusion. In all cases, performers appear to blur stances on the consequences of their actions, and the implications of their purposeful open-endedness. In theoretical relationship with one another throughout the book, and often through joke-work that shares the same pop-cultural citations, performers amass individual and collective responses to the question of Jewish female embodiment as both radical and conservative critique.

REPETITION WITH A DIFFERENCE AND THE JOKE BODY

As late twentieth-century and early twenty-first-century performers have ushered in a postassimilatory, postfeminist period, these paradigms have carried with them the very premises they appear to leave behind. More specifically, where the expected telos of assimilation and its afterlife might assume a long continuum of Jews becoming American, as if leading linearly from start (difference) to finish (sameness), this book underscores how performers offer an alternative assimilatory model through repetition and revision, a kind of reiteration that marks a simultaneous relationship with the past and politics of progressive movement forward. This reiterative effect is a primary play of the "post" framework, and one which foregrounds the cultural histories performers both extend and modify. Artists return to the verbal and embodied jokework of early performers, galvanizing its accumulative power in new contexts. The Sexy Jewess reiterates her own performance history to move beyond it.

And yet, as Jacques Derrida and other philosophers across disciplines have shown, any reiteration is a condition of its larger context that makes iteration possible in the first place.[5] That is to say that every iteration is a reiteration, and for it to be understood by others, it must be repeatable. Dance and performance studies have concerned themselves with the question of what this means for the individual agent on stage or anywhere else. What is her role in the repetition, and especially when she sets out to cite outright? In Judith Butler's seminal study on the performance of gender as a citational act, she argued that it is not the individual's own choice to perform these contexts or not.[6] Instead, the iteration-as-reiteration loop invoked by the individual, and in this case the Sexy Jewess, necessarily reflects larger structural forces at play that she must then dance on, in, among, amid, and against. How the artist then makes her reiterative, citational moves relates directly to parody, and humor especially. What is so culturally rich about joke-work is the way it plays with its own points of reference for audiences clued into shared ideals: rules understood collectively in order to be broken. When viewed in this light, reiteration, as an analytical tool, offers a conceptual frame that can attend to both the larger contexts and the minutiae of dancing punchlines, the macro and the micro registers, wherein the rituals of joking and laughing, whether out of glee or horror, frame the Sexy Jewess's techniques and their contexts as sustained and emergent citational plays.[7]

In this sense, invocations of the Sexy Jewess's image in contemporary Jewish female joke-work can offer a mode of understanding practices of assimilation and gender freedom as ongoing rehearsals of sameness and difference. Either idea acts as a Jewish and female point of creative and critical departure. A study of the Sexy Jewess reveals how assimilation—a core concern of secular Jewish American collective identity—is a performance of return and reimagination, as opposed to a linear track of becoming American or becoming white. Moreover, it is the gendered and racialized "in-betweeness" so ubiquitous in Jewish female performance that allows the repeated construction of whiteness and nonwhiteness to signal stances aligned with appropriate and inappropriate femininity for Jewish and non-Jewish audiences alike. Indeed, it is this gendered and racialized position in-between that makes the Jewish woman and representations of her so funny, because she is so "normal" and yet so far from normal. This insider-outsider frame has by now come to carry relatable connotations well beyond ethnic particularity, such that the Sexy Jewess can speak for queer causes and emancipatory clauses of all kinds, and by now often does.

For sexiness to be strategic—that is, to be a space of emancipatory negotiation for the performer and her audience—it has to ride this middle ground between expectation and resistance. In other words, it has to work this repetition, or redundancy of the familiar, and simultaneously propose or even proposition the next big idea. In the case of the Sexy Jewess, contemporary performers rehearse familiar ideas about sexiness, drawing on mostly masculinist, patriarchal traditions to signal new social meanings in intentionally queer contexts. For this, performers are either heralded or held culpably responsible for threatening their white male fan base (to the extent that they have one), or keeping it intact.

The "sexy" to which I refer accounts for an array of embodied aesthetics of Jewish female performers—aesthetics entangled in both postfeminist and postassimilatory discourses—wherein the potential of real and referenced sexuality lives at the intersection of live, filmic, and cyber genres. Beginning with the Sexy Jewess in person, and repeatedly, through ethnographic encounters in New York's nostalgic burlesque and cabaret circuit, I highlight neoburlesque's favorite Jewish acts: the Schlep Sisters, Little Brooklyn, Zoe Ziegfeld, and the Nice Jewish Girls Gone Bad (chapter 1). To offer a historical view of how we got here, I return to the comic iconography of early twentieth-century Jewish female performers, examining the legacy techniques of Jewish female dancing comedy. Early performances by Fanny Brice, Sophie Tucker, and Betty Boop act as protofeminist precursors to today's Sexy Jewess. That legacy extends across the stage careers of Barbra Streisand, Bette Midler, Gilda Radner, and Madeline Kahn a half century later to frame the funny girl body and how she becomes sexy or not through dancing joke-work (chapter 2). I then move through the end of the twentieth and beginning of the twenty-first centuries to articulate the social and self-critical ironies of a postfeminist, postassimilationist turn and what it has meant for Jewish comics Sandra Bernhard, Sarah Silverman, and *Broad City*'s writers and costars Abbi Jacobson and Ilana Glazer (chapter 3). Making links between humor and horror genres, I next discuss the terms of Jewish female representation in a mainstream ballet movie reserved for white looks: Natalie Portman in *Black Swan*, but also Mila Kunis and Winona Ryder in accompanying ballet roles (chapter 4). Here I argue that the swan sin of lesbian sex sells the film even as the sexual deviance dramatized throughout the film works to domesticate its featured Jewish female monsters. I then shift from mainstream film to the adult film industry to discuss the performance of sex outright as punk-porn princess and director Joanna Angel stars in the parody porn films she also directs (chapter 5). In the conclusion, I return to large frameworks of the postfeminist, postassimilatory contemporary period to synthesize the multisited study of the Sexy Jewess, while also underscoring the liberatory potential of dancing joke-work beyond the Jewish female "case." Drawing together multiple genres of performance executed by celebrity and lesser-known female players, the book aims for a wide reach of representational culture.

Throughout the book, an emphasis on the use of face in performance adds bodily specificity to the embodied maneuvers undertaken by performers. From burlesque stage to silver screen, these maneuvers start from the neck up. It is the face and its heightened expressivity that most notoriously identify the Jewish woman in America. Taking on this representational dilemma, my agenda goes straight for the nose. But in moving right toward her, my writerly punch doesn't mean to knock her out. Instead, by rendering more visible the very thing Jewish American women have aimed either to change or explain, I repair the nose's place in female performance history and its contributions to Jewish dance scholarship, as a kind of reverse rhinoplastic project and a recuperative social surgery.

Where these intentions mean to empower readers with a sense of their own misfit power, recentralization of the Jewish female nose is less than comfortable. In fact, it raises significant anxieties about the ways Jewish women see themselves and may wish to be seen. Even more, the Jewish nose lives at the center of a contemporary paradox, in which the funny face and the body that hosts it remain the uncertain subjects of Jewish female joke-work and identity performance. As the Sexy Jewess tropology takes shape across ensuing book chapters, I keep track of talk and dance that highlight the nose as core to ideas about Jewish female corporeality and its expressive confessions.

EXPRESSIVE CONFESSIONS OF A "FACE LIKE THAT"

My own face issues? I am eight years old at drama camp. We're all on stage, lined up to audition one by one. I'm anxious, short and sweating. I can feel my neck swell up. I get to the front and open my mouth, and the director, who is also our accompanist, starts to laugh. Uncontrollably. She can't stop and has to keep playing the opening chords over and over, apologizing. I had practiced that thing for days. "Look at me, I'm Sandra Dee / Lousy with virginity," I sang in my room, imagining the whiter world of the movie-musical, *Grease*, doubling as my fantasy high school. Downstage alone, I start to sing, and the director's laughing so hard, she's snorting. She's snorting through the nose she always said used to look just like mine. I was the exact image of her life before the nose job and the comic relief of the show, she told me then and over the next several years at drama camp.

And so I learned to be funny, queering all the parts like a good little Jewish girl should. I was cast instead as Jan, the "Pink Lady" who was too into her Twinkies and dessert wine to care about the Greaser Boys. The next summer, I was the Yiddish-inflected nun who was always a klutz in our majority-Jewish West LA revision of *The Sound of Music*. I got my big break at twelve in our production of *Damn Yankees* as Lola the vamp, but instead of playing it straight, I was coached in the ways of wayward Jewish stage women before me who couldn't dance without tripping over a mismanaged rose or fallen garter belt. By age thirteen I was butching up an Italian inflection of my typical Jewish caricature "isms" to play the caboose train in a staged version of *The Little Engine That Could*. Penning a heart-wrapped MOM on my arm with eyeliner borrowed from a friend's caboodle, the unfeminine was a practiced role in my repertoire, a public imperative of my funny face and the funnier ways it would make me move.

My forays into a funny face performance tradition are personal evidence of a contradictory corporeal scheme for Jewish female performers. Our excessively expressive faces, heralded as exceptionally good (hilarious, expressive) or bad (haggish, distracting), counteract bodies deemed otherwise appropriate, normal, and acceptably white. Such issues no doubt reflect those that caused early modern dance choreographers Doris Humphrey and Charles Weidman to celebrate an auditioning Jewish dancer's technical abilities and expressive emotional capacity but wonder "what to do with a face like that."[8]

My own recollections of unmet childhood aspirations to play serious roles and a slew of similar experiences in modern dance ever since personalize my academic interests in a broader funny face and its attending Jewish issues. "Face issues," as one colleague diagnosed them, offered a probing framework for thinking through representations of Jewish women as overly emotional, insatiably wanting, and famously inappropriate.[9] Like some kind of hysterical bodily condition that affects the body above and below the neck, the Jewish face raises questions of performer agency or lack thereof that thread throughout this book.

I thus introduce this conflation of face issues that collapses the space between deliberate and unintentional impact. Observing this phenomenon across a spectrum of Jewish female performances, I theorize the expressive, excessive Jewish female face and its funny dancing accompaniment: the body moving beneath it. To sever bodies at the neck is to catalog the character of a face as part of a Jewish female body in often self-parodied need of constant fixing. Such a face is both figural and figurative in this regard. It is of the body and also somehow detached from it. It mixes messages in serious and spoof roles, performing all the while as if on its own terms.

Foregrounding the face, I build on Sherill Dodds's concept of the "choreographic inter*face*," whereby a facial expression "acts as a site of meaning-construction."[10] The concept helps explain how the face enters into choreographic relationship with other dancing faces and also attends to the relationship between one's own face and body as a site of critical commentary. Finding that too little attention has been paid to the face in studies of contemporary dance, Dodds advocates for research on its coded aesthetic and social values across diverse dance practices, including neoburlesque striptease, hip-hop, and screendance.[11] Where my own face issues guide me to comic Jewish female performance traditions that inform it consciously and not, I take on Dodds's call for further thought on the contextualization of reflexive, dialogical facial plays as indicative of larger cultural cues.

As performers direct attention to their faces at key moments of larger bodily comments, they work to configure and reconfigure the whole body and its strategies of self-display. Along with the nose, they highlight other body parts in just as awkward a dissection of their physical figures. Presenting their appearances as a spectacle of excesses, performers display in different ways their boobs, butts, legs, lips, and self-described phallic necks, picking at their bodies as if to take them apart. Such dramatization of bodily fragments serves up the body's juiciest Jewess parts while enacting self-imposed horrors of gruesome disfigurement.[12] This is funny (chapters 1, 2, 3, and 5) or deliberately not (chapter 4), but reveals a certain representational deconstruction. In attending to the ways performers deconstruct the body through verbal and physical joke-work through directing audience attention to their noncohesive, slippery, in-between, inappropriate, impolite, contradictory, or otherwise offensive bodies, it becomes possible to magnify multiple social meanings and stereotypes. The aim of minding faces and other bodily fragments is finally to reassemble a bodily whole for Jewish women as more complex than any sum of their physical parts.

LOOKING TO MOVEMENT

The stigma of a Jewish face overlays a looks-based problem with a movement-based one. Historically speaking, as Jewish dancers became white through various bodily techniques of de-ethnicization, from plastic surgeries to ballet training, a "white nose" came to signify shifting allegiances to American standards of beauty. Such bodily concerns reflect gendered resonances of a long-standing racial culture of Jews in America. As pointed out by Jewish studies scholar Eric L. Goldstein, since the nineteenth century, feeling themselves to be an integral part of American society, Jews have adopted American ways with zeal. Since their immigrant beginnings, "they have changed their habits of dress, their language, their dietary and leisure practices, and even their mode of worship to conform to American styles" even in the face of discriminatory social practices by status-conscious non-Jews.[13] This malleability of American Jews marks its own history of marginalization, as American Jews have sought definitions of Jewishness that would not interfere with their whiteness.[14] It is Goldstein's central point that for an assimilatory century Jews have championed Americanization, even though it has come with the price of sustained anti-Jewish sentiment.

But how has the Jewish female body been a unique site of marginalization throughout a process of assimilation, and what does that mean for a study of performance? In my emphasis on these subjects, I build on a growing movement in scholarship concerned with race, gender, and Jewishness as they relate to dance and performance. Like dance studies at large, Jewish dance studies is a small and mighty field, growing from its roots in artist and company biographies as well as histories of cultural dance traditions to engage with revisionist histories and critical theory. Jewish participation in modern dance has received the most scholarly attention, clarifying the presence of Jewish identity within concert dance histories as well as opening space for the conversation to expand.[15] Of particular note among these studies is Rebecca Rossen's *Dancing Jewish: Jewish Identity in American Modern and Postmodern Dance*. Charting a history of Jewish concert dance choreographers across the twentieth and twenty-first centuries, Rossen introduces the unique potential of dance to tell the story of modern Jewish America. As Jews navigated coexisting poles of tradition and change that reflected shifting public desires for dance, Rossen writes that largely secular Jewish dancers have been "acrobats" of both particularity and assimilatory aesthetics, as if on a tightrope of contrasts.[16] The balancing act helps frame the relationship between dancers and their audiences, as well as the "dynamic positioning" that Rossen attributes to the American Jews who have negotiated changing race and class identities over time.[17]

Linking a study of Jewish American identity to concert dance practices, Rossen asks the provocative question, "Can dance act like plastic surgery?" In what ways can dance technique and performance transform bodies from marked to unmarked, ethnic to white?[18] The question itself exposes the ways Jewishness is able to read differently on the body, depending on what it is doing, when, where, and how, even as it would seem to still speak for dancers whose looks can pass as white. In this way Rossen's comparison of dance to aesthetic surgery reveals the key triangulation of Jewishness, femininity, and assimilation as it relates to the body. As Jewish dancers in the first half of the twentieth century became white folks through dancerly techniques of deethnicization, as implied by Rossen's rhetorical question, they reveled in being seen for the first time as acceptable women of the main stage.

While the body can be trained, however, the face cannot, or at least can only be less so. Competing cultural perceptions of concert dance and cosmetic alteration complicate the potential of dance as a transformative endeavor. One signifies the value assigned to training, while the other signals vanity or shame. Taking on Rossen's question, I extend the concept of dance as bodily alteration beyond the concert stage. Through analysis of performances that lean on impersonations of self and Other, this book aims to push the field of Jewish dance studies into diverse realms of embodied performance such as neoburlesque, stand-up, and pornography, where the social and ideological premises of participation often complicate a traditional relationship between audience and performer. My objective in this regard is to theorize how various experiments in performing identity morph differently across race and class lines through humor about sexiness, as expressed through a range of performance genres not generally theorized through Jewish lenses, if at all.

THE CORPOREAL TURN FOR NEW JEWISH STUDIES

This book's focus on Jewish American identity and the body extends from dance-centric texts such as Rossen's and from texts that participate in what Barbara Kirshenblatt-Gimblett has called the "Corporeal Turn" in new Jewish cultural studies. In her estimation, and in contrast to the reception in dance readership, the emergent discourse dealing with corporeality has provoked anxiety among those still heavily invested in Jews as a disembodied "People of the Book."[19] But as Kirshenblatt-Gimblett argues, "the Book" creates an empty space that dismisses the body and bodily processes, as outlined in much of the scripture. In *People of the Body: Jews and Judaism from an Embodied Perspective*, Howard Eilberg-Schwartz aims to deconstruct this doctrine of the bookish Jew as part of a modernizing strategy since the late eighteenth century that sought to transcend the body. As he explains, Jewish religious texts dealing with bodily emissions, circumcision, defecation, urination, and sexual intercourse have evoked shame for Jews ever since they joined European intellectual life. A self-conscious Jewish concern with enlightenment, whether religious or cultural, has perpetuated the idea of the Jew as weakly, "bookishly" male. Such images of the male Jew have effeminized him and also kept him at the center of Jewish studies discourse. By focusing on female bodies in performance as uniquely sexy about their funniness and vice versa, this book disentangles portrayals of the Jewish woman from even more ubiquitous portrayals of womanly Jewish men.

What has been criticized as a feminizing turn toward corporeality directly contends with this effeminate image of the bookish male Jew. A study of Jewish femininity in relation to the body necessarily extends this tension, even as it rarely mentions men.[20] As for any perceived departure of a study of the body from a study of text, I join Kirshenblatt-Gimblett who argues that readings of gender and sexuality strengthen textuality by including the body as text. This fundamental possibility of reading the body, she says, assists a critical turn toward the study of women too long left out of Jewish studies.[21]

In this sense, the book highlights female performers and the stereotypes they mock, modify, and mobilize. In shifting toward the corporeal and toward femininity, I lean on the work of those who have sought to underscore a refeminization of Jewish cultural studies and discussion of identity performance through performance. In this way, I continue in this book a significant thread of revisionist Jewish studies discourse that has worked to foreground discussions of gender. In doing so, I join a movement in scholarship to push back against the full discursive occupation with the womanly but male Jew, who has for too long stood in metonymically for the feminization of Judaism as a whole.[22] But even while foregrounding gender, critical theorization of Jewish effeminacy has still tended to displace the Jewish woman to such a degree that, as Ann Pellegrini so provocatively suggests, all Jews are womanly, but no women are Jews.[23] The collapse of Jewish masculinity into abject femininity has often erased women theoretically and actually.[24] Pellegrini's provocation guides the central premise of a study on women through the Sexy Jewess construction and guides my analysis of female performance practices in concrete and symbolic terms.

This is a book about representations that develop and evolve in collaboration with shifting discourses and formats. And yet it is a reiterative history, a way of looking at race and gender and expressions of sexuality that, while moving forward, always double back. To look at constructions and reconstructions of race, gender, and sexuality is to understand something about the performance of identity. While self-representation changes in relationship to the forces that contain it, there is more to say about the way it works and the way physical humor and dancing joke-work let certain distinct cultural tensions come boldly to the surface and face off audiences there.

The reiterative impulse of Jewish female joke-work allows women to perform themselves in light of a comic tradition that says she is always already funny, in ways both ha ha and uh oh. When the Jewish woman has appeared in popular culture, she has most often been stereotyped as having excessive desires of mythical proportions, whether for food, fashion, acceptance, or loyalty. Riv-Ellen Prell writes that Jewish male anxiety about assimilatory status scapegoated Jewish women for the bulk of the twentieth century as the reason for an as-yet-incomplete American assimilation. Prell writes that tropes of the ghetto girl, the wife, the mother, and the Jewish American princess appeared in television, film, and literature throughout the postwar period so frequently that, by the 1980s, Jewish female difference had become a widespread emblem of middle-class identity.[25] Jewish women became the ultimate symbol of significant economic and ethnoracial shifts for Jewish America. Karen Brodkin adds that as postwar suburbanization made space for middle- and upper-class Jews, new access to race and class assimilation complicated the relationship between Jewishness and femininity in a moment when the privileges of whiteness competed with the limitations of white womanhood.

Brodkin recalls more personally, "We all struggled with what it meant to be mainstream, 'normal' or white." She also reflects on what it meant to be a Jewish woman and what being any kind of woman meant in a time and place in which, according to the media, a woman wasn't a person.[26]

Scholarship such as Prell's and Brodkin's situates the image of the Jewish woman through the second half of the twentieth century and defends the need for yet more contemporary theorization. Their arguments ask us to consider how these questions of Jewishness and gender relate to twenty-first-century popular culture and discourse. While this book takes off from this premise, the prospect of articulating a female-led and expressly feminized "case" of the twenty-first-century Sexy Jewess inevitably approaches its own limits. A focus on bodily femininity risks foregrounding the associations of Jewish womanhood with cultural continuation as the task of its reproductive organs. In a moment when Jewish female performers regularly queer heteronormativity through progressive sexual politics in their respective domains—the increasing refusal of marriage, motherhood, marriage, and appropriateness altogether—they continue to bump up against a cultural logic bent on Jewish futurity. Underlying this Jewish heterosexual or heteronormative impulse is the most ancient of Jewish dicta: more Jews, not fewer. In such a scheme, the Jewish woman, it seems, is always inherently a Jewish mother and a *Bubbe* in training. In spite of these flaws of an all-female formulation—and more likely because of them—any effort to refeminize Jewish identity construction accompanies loaded questions for American Jews on the role women (refuse to) play in the preservation of culture and tradition.

IDENTITY ACTS AND IMPERSONATIONS

The Case of the Sexy Jewess returns to questions I have asked in performance as well. In *Love on Mars* (2009), I entered the stage with a song and dance to the Tin Pan Alley tune "Hard Hearted Hannah," whose lyrics tell of a "vamp of Savannah" and her dangerous ways, killing men by malicious plots she treats as mere accidents. In tap shoes, a tiny blue dress, and a matching umbrella hat, I apologized with arm gestures and facial expressions between each stanza's confessions of increasingly cruel crimes. Unpacking an armful of potatoes from my suitcase and a few choice pieces of lingerie, I tapped quick small steps in figure eights around my lot. At the instrumental break, I turbo-talked through my worries of late, oversharing my verbal confessions of enhanced autobiographic troubles. I shared my mother's advice to take a little time off and unfolded clippings of the studies she had sent me on the science of regular rest intervals. I reveled in a dress-up Jewishness that made fun of myself, my mom, and my cultural identity at large. Next, I revealed my delight at discovering the website loveonmars.com, a dating service aimed at "adventcha seekuhs" tired of the same old "tuhrestriality." I recited my fictive grant proposal to a make-believe Jewish organization run by lesbian philanthropists, the Dorothy and Pearl Rosenblatt Foundation of Interplanetary Women's Vision's Abroad. Convincing the committee of the artistic merit of the Sexy Jewess and her strategic embodiment, I win the grant; pack my luggage, flippers, and a mailbox; and head off on my exotic vacation by inflatable boat.

The Yiddish-inflected fantasy of love on Mars was my play on a familiar Jewish funny girl who is always full of hope for romance, but somehow doomed from the start. This piece was my initial answer to the range of sexy shows by Jewish women I was watching and writing about, and it became a precursor to several performances I staged as part of the research for this book, grouped together under the banner of "blueface" performance scores. To describe my addition to a long history of identity drag (i.e., Jewface, blackface, yellowface, redface), I used the term "blueface" as a reference to the Jewface impersonations I observed and responded to in performance. Performances allowed me to raise questions of the research in real time with an audience.

Over time, my blueface scores ditched the accent and the dress, trading tap shoes for blue high tops and adding plastic glasses that covered my face like a half mask to transition away from the female romantic and morph toward a less certain fate. The movement often became grotesque and robotic, repeating certain images until they amassed a kind of violence implied by their exaggeration. Morphing through comic personages and manipulating their possible effects, I experimented with shifting the bodily, gestural, and facial significances through their reference and hyperarticulation.[27] My point was to see how my own embodiment of Jewface performance tropes could get me closer to a bodily definition of what they are and how they move. I wanted to test how dancing "Jewishly," somehow impersonating Jewishness, was an act to be put on and taken off the body, and the face too. Such choreographic research complemented my historical and ethnographic investigation of contemporary Jewish American identity performance and its histories of race and gender parody. By the time I performed a version of blueface in 2016 for neoburlesquer Zoe Ziegfeld in the living room of my colleague's New York apartment for a class of my students, I was touched when Zoe commented that she saw all of her ancestors in my act. Blueface had become a way to access the past and comment on it at the same time.

This improvisatory performance practice helped uncover and enact a history of Jewish identity performance and race impersonation and track its American roots in turn-of-the-twentieth-century performance history. The scholarship on the subject tends to be most interested in the degree to which the practice is more sympathetic or exploitative. Jewish studies scholars such as Irving Howe and Michael Alexander defend the tradition of Jewish blackface as having provided foundational avenues through which Jews Americanized themselves in relation to blackness from the position of similar nonbelonging.[28] Other scholars such as Michael Rogin and Eric Lott align more closely with arguments in critical race and whiteness studies that insist upon cultures of identification predicated on a structure of exploitation.[29] While the first camp tends to find blackface a sympathetic position, a way of being in positive relation to blackness, the second argues that it enacted social dramas of distance and desire that further separated Jews from blackness. Both arguments may help explain assimilatory practices in the early part of the twentieth century. And yet the debate in the scholarship has largely focused on male performers and their representative ties to whiteness or blackness.

The critical addition of women to the discourse on Jewish blackface has opened up avenues for the intersection of race and gender at the turn of the century and its foundation for the joke-work of generations that followed. Joyce Antler argues that Sophie Tucker's early twentieth-century use of blackface functioned as gender drag, launching a career that centralized her large physique and not-a-pretty-girl shtick.[30] While Antler's synthesis rationalizes racial impersonation as gender drag, Lori Harrison-Kahan frames Tucker within a discussion of white and black women relating to one another, arguing that Tucker's use of blackface reflected two-way interactions, even if still "uneven."[31] Distinct as these paradigms are, both foreground gender performance in the discussion of Jewish assimilation and acculturation. These perspectives likewise provide modes of rethinking gender in a century-long Jewish imaginary of black-Jewish kinship. I return to these frameworks to ground the historical relationships among race, gender, and homosocial female desire that have been sustained across an assimilatory century and into the present day.

When it comes to the question of Jewish women and race impersonation, Susan Manning makes important contributions in her *Modern Dance, Negro Dance*, by analyzing performances that mimicked blackness without burned cork. Historicizing the mutually constitutive genres of early twentieth-century modern dance and Negro dance, Manning outlines the potential of a "metaphorical minstrelsy" on the concert dance stages of the 1930s as common practice reflective of hierarchical racial politics.[32] Jewish choreographers like Helen Tamaris danced to black spirituals with universalist claims, appropriating historical black struggle as a theme to which all could presumably relate. These choreographers, known for their affinities with the Jewish Left, shaped an American movement of modern dance heralded for its expressivity. Such practices of dancing spirituals fit well within the scope of a larger debate about Jewish reliance on black tropes and the asymmetrical effects of these appropriations.

As is indicated in such metaphorical performance of otherness, Jewish in-betweeness pivots around questions of sympathetic identification and a simultaneous racial privilege of uneven exchange. Contemporary Jewface performances extend out of this legacy of black appropriation, updating these paradigms to address or deny the problems of modern-day racism and what racial jokes can do. More than landing on answers, performers use race and gender parody to throw into question the fixity of identity categories as postmodern material for social comment. Such parody invokes an assimilatory black-white race logic with gendered implications, wherein the postassimilationist, postfeminist frame means to muck up identity altogether.

As they deploy comic alternatives against sustained histories of racial injustice, class inequities, sexual repression, and gendered marginality, however, such performances nevertheless fall back on the guilty pleasures of whiteness and the privileges such access brings. Addressing the Sexy Jewess as postfeminist, postassimilationist figure, I ask how her embodied performance schemes construct the female body as a site of transgression as well as appropriation. When she makes explicit fun of her Jewishness, the Sexy Jewess relies on the duplicitous performance of heterosexist aspirations and of sexual boredom, failure, or other frustrations with invisibility. When she employs conventions of race impersonation, the Sexy Jewess indicates a mocking tenor meant as an apologetic cover-up for the guilty pleasure of entry into whiteness. Lingering on the sting of these techniques, performers "Other" themselves through a deliberate autoexoticism that reappropriates and misappropriates identities.

My understanding of autoexoticism in a Jewish context borrows from tango scholar and personal mentor, Marta E. Savilgiano as she has defended it in *Tango and the Political Economy of Passion*.[33] In Savigliano's formulation, those identified as exotics refer to the categories that keep them bound and struggle to expand their identities through exotic reappropriations.[34] The Sexy Jewess performer in the US occupies an entirely different position than the exotic figure of Savigliano's tango analysis and its Argentine colonial context. What I am calling "Jewface" impersonations perform the Jewish female between positions of sameness and difference to standards of white womanhood, and in doing so, exoticize themselves through celebration and mockery of the delimiting categories that keep them bound.

By using the term Jewface, I make deliberate reference to the tradition of codified stage makeup techniques designed to accentuate stereotypical Jewish features, a common practice in the first decades of the twentieth century. Highlighting around the eyes and shadowing around the nose extended phenotypical markers of the Eastern European Semitic face, while also exposing the fiction of the very same appendages as natural or normal attributes of a single Jewish archetype.[35] My discussion of Jewface, however, extends beyond the use of makeup to address a bodily repertoire. By considering this corporeal aesthetic in addition to props, costumes, and humorous narrative devices, I redefine Jewface as an extension of the manipulations of the face.

As a self-Othering act performed by women, Jewface is comparable to other impersonations of race and gender that draw repressed identities out from under the lid of social etiquette and political appropriateness. How and when this is funny or offensive is a matter of address as much as reception. To whom and for what does it matter, and through what mechanisms does it materialize? If social and sexual discourse tied to structures of power shape thinking and feeling, as Judith Butler has so productively argued in *Bodies That Matter*,[36] it follows that humor of and between bodies also materializes structures of power. Jewface joke-work can be understood as critical matter and material both structured by and in defiance of dominant structures repressive enough to be recognized collectively. And yet a single framework for theorizing why it is funny or even why it succeeds in inducing laughter would struggle to find coherency. After all, the nuances of laughter's embodiment—its snickering judgments and confused uncertainties, its nervousness, its self-assuredness, its lack of control, and even its forced nature—expand well beyond a single set of conditions.

JEWISH JOKE-WORK AND THE DOUBLED FEMALE SUBJECT

In the context of Jewish humor, a rich comic legacy has been most commonly understood as the acceptable way to process the pain of diasporic displacement and an ongoing rhetoric of unlikely survival.[37] And when it comes to women, there is an important distinction to make between jokes by women and about women. But what happens when Jewish women joke about themselves? Two types of jokes discussed in Sigmund Freud's *The Joke and Its Relation to the Unconscious* relate well here: those of and about Jew and woman.[38] In the first case, the Jewish joker is a doubled subject that Freud understands as the mocker who participates in the defect being mocked. Freud writes: "A situation particularly favorable to the tendentious joke is set up when the intended criticism of protest is directed against one's self." He continues, explaining that the tendentious joke directed at oneself is reflective of a collective imagination. In Freud's terms, "put more circumspectively, against a person in whom that self has a share, a collective person, that it, one's own people, for example." Ascribing this shareholding self to Jewish cultural traditions, Freud proposes that "this determinant of self-criticism may explain to us how it is that a number of the most telling jokes . . . have grown from the soil of Jewish popular life. They are stories invented by Jews and aimed at Jewish character."[39]

The "tendentious" joke that Freud attributes to Jewish popular life accompanies lust, hostility, or both. When it is directed at the joker herself (note that Freud's jokers were always male) or the collective person in whom she has a share, Freud suggests that the sting of a tendentious joke is the self-criticism that is funny for the group of people it attacks as well as the group laughing at them from the outside. This framework of the characteristically self-critical tendentious joke and joker has been foundational for readings of minority humor, and Jewish humor especially.[40]

Distinct from this doubled self-critical subject, Freud discusses the second kind of joke, which he calls the dirty joke or smut, in which woman functions as the butt of the joke and is structurally excluded. The dirty joke necessitates that the female object of desire be absent and replaced by the one to whom the joke is addressed.[41] In such jokes about women, the exclusion of the objectified woman facilitates the forging of a homosocial relation between the teller and the listener, both constructed as male.[42] Postwar jokes about the Jewish American princess, or JAP, as sexually uninterested and overly materialistic do this work. A hostile tenor of such jokes reveals an aggressive avenue for the expression of ideas between men not otherwise so openly discussed.[43]

The more contemporary Sexy Jewess trope draws on the two joke genres of the self-critical joke and the dirty joke. From the neoburlesque song and dance strip to Joanna Angel's alternative films that are "not your daddy's" porn, Jewish women address crowds of other women from their performance platforms, making fun of themselves while "going bad" as comic femmes fatales. As if winking at their female accomplices in live and onscreen audiences, they invite laughter at a Semitic brand of self-effacing smut that blends a Jewess's nostalgia and naughtiness. Where men come in changes the terms of the joke-work, of course, as varying reliance on male patronage often mediates women's moves with more patronizing dynamics.

In Ruth Johnston's reading of Jewish joke-work in relation to American film, she writes that it is through this simultaneous position as self-critical joke and joker that Jews construct a postassimilatory status, producing and reproducing Jewish difference as postmodern identity.[44] Focusing on the ways Jewish women enter postmodern cinema by way of stepping into roles regularly reserved for men, Johnston revises Freud's doubled subject of the Jewish self-critical joke-joker as a gendered subject-object. Her emphasis on Jewish female joke-work in films like *Kissing Jessica Stein* (2001) and *Amy's Orgasm* (2001) turns the attention to the possibility of women leads who adopt the familiar neurosis of self-critical Jewish male humor as sexual schlemiel while foregrounding women's ambitions in love and life.

As Jewish women step into the comic limelight, their humor about sex and sexiness suspends rather than transcends gender roles and stereotypes. The poles of Jewish self-critical jokes and the displacing effect of smut highlights how tenuous the possibility of Jewish female joke-work really is, insofar as it would attempt to be transgressive, subversive, or liberatory. So long as the humor sustains women as sexy objects in a heterosexualist sense, the question is whether there is real room left for the woman's sexual wants, directions, and desires as agentive subject. Whereas the comics in this book play up their stilted desire and direction as part of their act, the mainstream and adult films discussed here revolve around the dramatization and sensationalization of sex and ambition as fleshed-out effects of social parody in their own right. Still, if we take on Freud's theory that men seek pleasure in the manipulation of restrictions, it may follow easily enough that women also do. Maybe all performers seek to utilize the very limits imposed upon them to get around designated restrictions. Maybe all performers take pleasure in the jokes that previously scapegoated them, enjoying that same cherished space of laughter and critique. If this alternative humor functions because and in spite of a repressive society, to what end can joke-work that messes with social order carry across contexts, when some of those contexts must cater to the mainstream more than others? How can the mechanisms of humor and laughter reveal the extent to which performances provide incisive social criticism while making and having fun?

Performers in this book ask themselves these questions, whether through their acts, in promotional materials, in posted comments, or in conversations with me. Core participants of the neoburlesque Hanukkah circuit, for example, contend that their annual performance material is meant to entertain more than anything else. And without a doubt, the fun had by audiences of punk porn princess Joanna Angel reveals a realm of entertainment that strategizes its layered engagements with progressive social discourses, likely relishing in its lucrative contradictions. In each of these cases, parody, more than humor outright, frames the politics of representation. Parody need not be reducible to humor. Rather, as Linda Hutcheon argues, parody construes a self-reflexivity and inter-art discourse.[45] As an avenue of social commentary that resists a single definition, or single discipline, parody forces a reassessment of artistic processes that depart from aesthetic and social norms. Even as the tropes of the Jewish female performer tend to harken back to humor, Hutcheon's theory makes room to divorce parody from laughter long enough to see it as social commentary that extends across performance contexts.

As a critical tool, parody can be sympathetic to status quo norms or subversive of it. In this sense, it can do its work in humor as it can in horror, creating monstrous depictions of women—whether they choose those roles themselves or not—that sympathize with social logics that contain them or refuse to. In Hutcheon's words, parody can wage conservative or revolutionary critique.[46] Whether through techniques of irony, imitation, pastiche, or quotation, Hutcheon reminds us that the political thrust of parody will depend on the intent of the artist and its reception. This idea is consistent with much of the writing on humor, which makes it the task of the audience to get it or opt not to.[47] And yet the terms of a performer's intent and her reception are difficult if not impossible to measure. When it comes to analyzing performer intentions, the use of individual interviews can help support the ethnographic case, but performers may freely tell the stories they wish to tell or think others may wish to hear. Regarding the issue of reception, audiences just as often forget what they found so funny in the first place or otherwise write off performances as entertainment unworthy of critical review. Still, the operating idea of humor in academic writing and popular discourse has been that audiences make choices about what they find funny or not, and that analysis of what makes people tick reveals underlying social values tethered to the perpetuation or disruption of mainstream logics.

While it is likely that the audience decides the fate of performance, particularly on a pop cultural scale, this book turns its focus to the performers themselves as agents. For this, I borrow from Teresa de Lauretis's discussion of address. As distinct from ideas of intention or reception, de Lauretis outlines the address itself in her description of women's cinema and aesthetic forms, as in "who is making films for whom, who is looking and speaking, how, where, and to whom."[48] Calling this "the production of a feminist social vision," de Lauretis ascribes importance to feminist doings, which though still vulnerable to the parameters of public thought highlight the work of social actors to direct the focus in distinct ways.[49]

This emphasis on address helps mobilize the vague positions of a performer's intention and her reception in order to recognize the ways she engages discourses and audiences. Framing the performer's feminist agency in this regard, the close reading of a performer's address still confronts the question of her transgressive capacity. To whom and for what do neoburlesquers, stand-up celebrity comics, award-winning actresses, and pornstars/directors address their identity acts and impersonations? Close observation of stage performances and inclusion of remarks on the subject by performers in the field help identify how conservative or revolutionary the rhetoric of transgression may be. The aim of this book is thus to investigate the transgressive terms of these self-Othering displays of funniness and sexiness as feminist/postfeminist addresses that move between assimilation and its reiterative rehearsals into an whiteness and its privileges. Physicalized parody is at the heart of this quest.

THE QUEER PLAY OF SELF-DISPLAY

In what ways does the Sexy Jewess trope "queer" Jewish femininities in relation to larger discourses of heteronormative power?[50] And how does it perform a distinct intersectionality of race and gender representations that sustains or changes across mainstream and subcultural performance venues through this queerness? Inclusive but not reducible to same-sex expressions of sexual identities, the queer potential of all of these social and sexual manipulations happens through the body and body talk.

"Queer" in its academic and colloquial usage covers a wide range of meanings. Scholars, artists, and audiences readily queer time, space, and technique across genres and disciplines and increasingly dislodge their definitions from sexual identities and preferences.[51] As a multivalent framework-in-progress, meanings of the term extend as readily to practices of foregrounding archival absences as to praxes that decolonize discourse in pursuit of fragmented hunches, intuitive interpretations, and revisionist histories.[52] Along a spectrum of queer imagining, utopic premises have envisioned the queer as a futurist imagination, and radical change that has not yet been fully achieved.[53] There is also growing momentum around the concepts of queer orientation and disorientation, as part of a spatial arrangement of social relations in which queerness disrupts and reorders these relations.[54] These theoretical moves have embraced subjects and their doings to include expansive notions of a political and social potentiality tied both to individual identities and to collective actions, subcultural scenes, and movements.

In the context of Jewishness and Jewish studies, an analysis of queerness takes on additional meaning. The editors of *Queer Theory and the Jewish Question*, Daniel Boyarin, Daniel Itzkovitz, and Ann Pellegrini, argue that modern Jewish and homosexual identities emerged as "traces of each other."[55] Discourses of anti-Semitism and homophobia relied on stereotypes of the Jew to underwrite pop cultural and scientific ideas of the homosexual (and vice versa). Both categories arose in the nineteenth century; both reflect socially constructed categories, not natural givens. These developments effectively secularized Jewish difference such that the race and effeminacy of male Jews became more important than their religious distinctions. When it came to Jewish women and sexuality, the nineteenth-century ideas of both the "Jewess" and the "sexual invert" shared the alleged defect of being "too active in their desires."[56] If the sexual invert, the term used for lesbian, was presumed to perform her gender somehow upside down, the Jewess's femininity was a cover for femininity's failure as simultaneously too much and not enough of a woman. The contradiction was germane to the stereotype itself. As with misogyny, anti-Semitism, and homophobia, the paradox animated the prejudice rather than incapacitated it.[57]

Both Jewish cultural studies and queer theory find an alternative impetus, less in the positivism of identities than in the shifting terrain of discourse.[58] As Boyarin, Itzkovitz, and Pellegrini deduce, if "queer" is to be more than a replacement for the homosexual, and if queer theory is to extend beyond mere questions of sexual preference, the thinking on the "Jewish-queer" intersection must thus work at the in-between spaces in which no one kind of difference is elevated above the rest. And yet as the authors warn, in the effort to make difference newly visible, the analogy of Jew to queer may flatten difference. In an essay included in the anthology, Janet R. Jakobson argues that a "logic of equivalence" has allowed recuperative moves that foreground aims to visibilize historically marginalized groups but has provided little basis for coalition between such movements.[59] Building on that premise, my analysis of physicalized performances and dancing joke-work looks at how performers stage the intersections of Jewishness, sexuality, and liberatory politics through various and sometimes conflicting techniques of the body, which may in effect erase important differences they mean to make visible.

In queering the Sexy Jewess, I consider how distinct performances bring to the surface a transgressive power and a liberatory potential. Doing so, however, not only accounts for performances that intentionally break standards of appropriate womanhood from platforms of race privilege, but also requires analysis of those performances that sustain normative standards in rehearsals of the status quo, whether by genre or effect. As sociosexual embodiments of broad cultural and political critique, I question what may be "queer" about Sexy Jewess performances that strategically blur expectations about sex, sexiness, and sexuality, and do so with gusto—something I refer to in chapter 3 as comic glory and guilt. This stems from a critical staging of familiar Jewish female in-betweeness and entails the simultaneity of appropriate and inappropriate doings and undoings, the staging of racialized and sexualized sameness and difference, and the movements toward and away from stereotypes through both new and nostalgic forms.

In contributing queer analyses to Jewish dance discourse, I pay deliberate attention to the ways performers link social and sexual politics in resistive ways and do so through the female body.[60] As that unfolds, my own queer presence pops up in sideline admissions of attraction and anxiety as noted biases of the research. Such efforts invite readers to also see and perceive in queer ways, identifying and disidentifying with the material from inside-outside points of view.[61] As topics slide between the personal and political, the reader may side with some artists and not others, complying with or resisting dominant logics at play.

METHODS AND MATERIALS

The range of scenes presented in the chapters that follow contributes to Jewish performance scholarship concerned with gender and the body by way of an interdisciplinary approach. The thinking reaches across dance and performance studies, Jewish and humor studies, and women's and gender studies. In this sense, the project reaches beyond the bounds of dance to talk about embodiment in the context of Jewishness, gender, race, and sexuality. Methods of choreographic analysis, performance ethnography, and archival research overlay race, ethnic, and gender frameworks to (1) introduce how Sexy Jewess performers complicate self-critical jokes of the inferior, excessive Jewish female body by playing up their Jewish *Otherness*; (2) document the techniques that Jewish female performers employ to mimic and master different ideas of *sexiness*; and (3) theorize how performances of Jewish female identity use the body to participate in and parody notions of *appropriate femininity* as they relate to assimilation into white womanhood.

The results of my research not so much contain a single definition of Jewish female identity as expose the multiple maneuvers of a performance spectrum predicated on the construction, deconstruction, and reconstruction of identity. As I have learned from feminist theory and from Jewish studies, the tensions raised by the irreconcilable, ambivalent, and even opposed performances of ideas and identities are powerful sites of social and cultural meaning. Furthermore, though this book considers Jewishness and gender as they relate to US pop culture, the performers under review are largely but not entirely based in the United States and largely but not entirely bound by avenues of popular culture. The enactments and embodiments selected for analysis are largely but not all of, by, and about stereotypes of Ashkenazi women, or those with Eastern European ethnic origins. And the jokes are not all funny.

Chapter 1, "Nice Girls Gone Blue: Neoburlesque Nostalgia and the Downwardly Mobile" foregrounds my performance ethnography among New York's Jewish burlesque and cabaret spoofs on the Hanukkah circuit from 2011 to 2016. By looking at what the body does to mock and modify stereotypes of the Jewish woman, I introduce the ways that performers utilize physical humor to critique harmful images of the unsexy hag, Jewish mother, and JAP, while posing new identity gags. And yet in performing Otherness from positions of race privilege, neo-Jewish burlesquers distance themselves from the very epochs they evoke, securing their status as white women who can presumably put on and take off Otherness at will. The chapter invites readers to wonder what kinds of self-Othering schemes the Sexy Jewess poses in this format that resemble or disassemble race and gender tropes of their mainstream comedy counterparts. In figuring out the theoretical implications of burlesque's nostalgic roots as part and parcel of its contemporary appeal, I ask what questions this return to "low" and "lowly" performance traditions raises in relation not only to gender and sexuality, but also to class. Finally, in contextualizing an art form that garners little to no pay, I argue for an evident downward mobility enacted though a do-it-yourself production aesthetic.

Chapter 2, "Hello, Gorgeous, and the Historical Lens: How Funny Girls Became Sexy" tracks back to a US performance history of Jewish female physical comedy that spans a nearly a century of gender and humor radicalism. It moves from early twentieth-century performances by Red Hot Mamas Sophie Tucker, Fanny Brice, and Betty Boop to touring acts, movie dance scenes, and comedy sketches of the late 1960s, 1970s, and 1980s, including spotlights on Barbra Streisand, Gilda Radner, Bette Midler, and Madeline Kahn. Specific performance examples showcase how these giants of comedy deployed various techniques of a Jewish bawdry body to stage critical responses to Jewish race and class assimilation and construct its roles for women through performance. Their embodiments help establish the book's foundational understanding of joke-work and sexy ruse in the context of Jewish femininity, as well as their influence on the twenty-first-century Sexy Jewess spectacle. In linking dance humor to the performance of gender and sexuality, the chapter foregrounds the significant addition of women to the overwhelmingly male-centric historical record on Jewish identity and comic performance.

Chapter 3, "Comic Glory (and Guilt): The Appropriative License of Jewish Female Comedy," continues the book's chronological treatment from where chapter 2 leaves off, moving from the early 1990s into the postfeminist, postassimilationist decades that followed. In tracing a contemporary period that extends to 2016, it asks what the last three decades of celebrity spotlight add to a theorization of gender, race, and the body in representations of Jewish female comic bodies. Discussing the new brands of Jewish female joke-work in a period of what has been called an American comedy zeitgeist, the argument draws on self-ironizing performances by Sandra Bernhard, Sarah Silverman, and *Broad City*'s Abbi Jacobson and Ilana Glazer. Discussion of implicit and explicit blackface and Jewface performances returns to scholarship on black racial impersonation by a history of Jewish performers and adds a contemporary focus as it relates to gender and sexuality. As artists playfully shock bourgeois sensibilities, they upturn TV precedents, foregrounding the normalcy of homosexuality, interracial relationships, job insecurity, class consciousness, and the humor of Jewish girls in regular recognition of white guilt. Mocking girls who try to be good against the brunt of an aggressive world, they make postfeminist, postassimilationist life look more livable through reimagining the lovingly embarrassing dance scenes of a Jewish female comic legacy, but with a variety of allegiances and effects.

Continuing this emphasis on Jewish female celebrity figures and their dis/figuration of racialized and sexualized bodies, chapter 4, "*Black Swan*, White Nose: Jewish Horror and Ballet Birds by Any Other Name," focuses on Jewish celebrity Natalie Portman as the female monster in Darren Aronofsky's Academy Award–winning psychological thriller and ballet movie *Black Swan* (2010). First I read *Black Swan* as an ambiguously Jewish film with horror appeal. In the context of an assimilatory century of Jewish American representation on stage and screen, the narrative of a New York mother pushing her willful, unyielding daughter to succeed illustrates the iconic stereotypes of Jewish mother and Jewish American princess taken to the extreme. More than even the ambiguous Jewish narrative content, the chapter considers the paratextual inflections of the film by attending to the white racial passing of all four costarring actresses. As a *Swan Lake* remake, *Black Swan* makes visible a site of racial and sexual containment for Jewish actresses in ballet roles. Against the damaging pressures of professional dance on the female psyche, the film recasts the White and Black Swan roles as monstrous representations of the ethnic Other, the woman, and the sexual deviant. My analysis challenges fatal disfigurements of the film's female characters, asking how *Black Swan* uses ballet to appropriate social and political identities with tenuous relationships to the mainstream. I argue that these appropriations amount to an ultimate domestication of the very identities the film puts forward for thrilling appeal. This linkage of dance and politics intersects critical race theory, queer theory, and horror film theory as revealing dimensions of classical dance in narrative cinema.

Chapter 5, "Punk Porn Princess Joanna Angel and the Rise of Jewess Raunch" then shifts the focus from mainstream film to the adult film industry, highlighting select performances by popular Jewish porn star and director Joanna Angel. As Angel leads an altporn phenomenon through punk and parody film, she exemplifies the successful salability of the Sexy Jewess who sells sex outright. Her brand of Jewish joke-work is neither the ironic suggestion of sex in the mainstream comedy realm nor the neoburlesque striptease and its employment of vintage nostalgia in the name of the new. The chapter foregrounds the physical humor in porn performances that signal Angel's Jewishness in relation to dance, corporeality, and face work, while framing the ways her films work to position her and her models as empowered postfeminists. I return to Ariel Levy's *Female Chauvinist Pigs: Women and the Rise of Raunch Culture* in order to investigate the ways Angel interrelates Jewishness and postfeminist raunch to navigate male-dominated markets in alternative porn. Angel's explicit references to Jewishness extend to other identity impersonations as well, including blackface. Angel's interracial foray configures Jewish female blackface as a site of desire and distance. The chapter thus asks what it may be about Jewish blackface impersonations that appeals to "punk-porn" audiences as a quintessential part of a Sexy Jewess routine. That is, compared to the performers in previous chapters or in dialogue with them, how does Angel's blackface allow her to galvanize mainstream markets?

The conclusion returns to the question of Jewish female representation through an embodied Jewface genre as reflected differently throughout the book. In some cases the Sexy Jewess embodies familiar versions of the comic personages made most familiar across an assimilatory twentieth century. In other cases, she performs Jewishly through sexier means, revamping iconic personifications of the pinup, porn star, and magazine minx in raunchier acts that throw back to vintage aesthetics with nostalgic appeal. In all cases, the performers appear to negotiate the guilty pleasures of whiteness within self-conscious reach.

This book brings together interdisciplinary performance and scholarly texts through an intersection of historical, ethnographic, and choreographic methods. Foregrounding the body and talk about the body as Jewish female sites of cultural meaning and production, chapter analyses focus on multiple embodied provocations to think through the potential of liberatory performance practices in a range of domains. What emerges in each chapter differently is the transgressive potential of Jewish female performance that subverts social boundaries by design and can as easily fall into the traps of a misunderstood girl power, warped by its commercial consumability. The very impulse to celebrate women on an all-Jewess bill, as competing Jewish swans, or through a progressive porn montage, may even pit women against other women as amusing varieties of femininities from which to choose.

In this sense, I worry about what kind of meanings slip beyond my control in a book that groups women going *bad* in ways that play with sex appeal. My analysis may appear as if it picks and chooses the most provocative ones for the reader's judging enjoyment in an academic take on the nudie magazine, which, if more fully or visually fleshed out, would likely sell more copies of the book. The stakes of a study like this risk reissuing the essentialized, objectified thing of bared female bodies, and Jewish ones at that, in new ways still vulnerable in the same old terms. For this, there is likely no complete fix, except to ask that that rub itself invites your close attention. Find in it what you can use, whether to build your case in fights still worth winning or to otherwise catch yourself generatively off guard. The aim can be to read the ethical, ethnic stakes of such a project and consider, at each turn, all the movements in-between.

CHAPTER 1

Nice Girls Gone Blue

Neoburlesque Nostalgia and the Downwardly Mobile

A New York neoburlesque act, the Schlep Sisters, regularly packs the house with the annual *Menorah Horah*, a Jewish-holiday-inspired performance extravaganza produced by the pair and Thirsty Girl Productions.[1] The Schlep Sisters, who have performed together since 2004 and have hosted the yearly Jewish pageant since 2007, are the comic collaboration of Minnie Tonka and Darlinda Just Darlinda. The two burlesquers are touted for bringing Jewish culture and humor to striptease, a nostalgic performance form with infinite potential and growing momentum for vintage vixen types across New York's five boroughs and beyond. To *schlep*, a widely used Yiddishism, means to haul or drag a heavy burden as if across a huge distance. It is this epic baggage that the "long-lost sisters" with native roots in Yiddish theater and vaudeville claim and revise as a love of culture that takes them all over the world.[2]

Following tradition, the sisters open with their signature piece, a life-sized menorah kick line. The *menorah* is the candleholder brought out each year in every Jewish home to celebrate the eight nights of Hanukkah, the winter holiday known as a celebration of light. The *horah* is a celebratory folk dance done in a circle of happy people holding hands. The novel pairing of menorah and horah is especially festive, as it introduces the evening of neoburlesque with rhyming ritual flare. In the Schlep Sisters' rendition, the human *shamash* ignites each dancer's headpiece flame by striking fabric fire off the tips of sequined pasties, effectively lighting up each glowing performer.[3] The crowd claps in rhythm as synchronized steps of an iconic kick line complete a slow rotation, abstracting the horah circle pattern and revealing the fleshy backsides of performers picked for the part. The contrast of the classic leggy trope and the equally iconic Hanukkah item perfects the Sexy Jewess joke at the start of the single performance evening, an anticipated yearly holiday spoof of Jewish female exotics and their mostly female friends.

With its demands of convincing poise and careful attention, the menorah number requires serious comportment as the ensemble turns while staying hooked together. And yet, costumed in strappy, flashy showgirl garb, performers laughably subvert the religious sanctity of the winter festival with a brand of Jewish chutzpah that celebrates with sex appeal. This chapter explores the funny sexiness of this holiday observance in Hanukkah-themed neoburlesque showcases that I saw between 2011 and 2016 in New York City. Scenes open in the Highline Ballroom on West 16th Street, then move to the Soho scene of a basement gallery venue. Culling comic material from notes, memory, and interviews, I zoom in on select live performances of bodily self-display to theorize neo-Jewish burlesque as a critical site of Jewish representation with queer collective power. Focusing on the affect of laughter and envy alongside dance moves and their analysis, I slide between my own impressions and those shared with me by performers and their audiences.

The findings of my ethnography frame how neoburlesque sexiness functions as a means through which female participants playfully objectify themselves in the name of fun, flirty girl power. Understanding neoburlesque as a site of homosocial identification, I observe how performers present versions of the exaggerated Jewish woman as a source of postfeminist agency; that open-ended, but yet unresolved thing inherited from the second wave feminism of their parents' generation. Likewise, as Jewish-themed acts stage their sexy ruse, they return to ethnic Otherness from positions of postassimilation. As white women performing Jewishly, they flesh out embodied techniques of a nostalgic "Jewface" genre as a celebration of cultural identity and the freedoms of an art form predicated on open embrace of difference, widely conceived.

The Jewface performances of neoburlesque both relate and depart from what is possible in mainstream formats. Neoburlesquers take on Jewish content, gesture, and vocal intonation in self-othering jokes, but adopt a definitively celebratory stance, permitted by their genre. From skilled strippers to klutzier clowns, Jewish-themed neoburlesquers draw on techniques familiar to the stand-up and sketch comic, while championing sexiness as nightly entertainment. As performers try on and disrobe Jewish joke-work through the neoburlesque striptease, they also address a range of audiences in a variety of venues. In both professional and amateur acts, Jewish-themed neoburlesque bills its most committed performers, with many of its members actively pursuing a niche revival taking new root since the mid-1990s in New York City.[4] The growing popularity of neoburlesque now spans the globe as a protected form of bawdiness that lets girls, and increasingly boys in boylesque, blend comic mayhem, striptease, and performance art to satirize a range of social discourses. The result is a queer art form that champions its own fabulousness, drawing on drag and vintage aesthetics to perform femininities largely for and by women. While major productions exist for neoburlesque, most prominently at the yearly Miss Exotic World Pageant, much of the performance form takes shape in low-budget, nightly showcases that exist outside of significant profit venues. The stakes of performing self-mockery in such scenes are necessarily distinct from more lucrative platforms that buy and sell ideas for the general public.

Cultivating an intimacy with audiences through proximity—not unlike the stand-up club comic before she goes big—neoburlesque performers are often only feet away from their first-row fans. But whereas success in small comedy clubs often means moving up in the industry ranks, neoburlesque performers stay loyal to the bar spaces and rental venues that top comics eventually surpass. In contrast to the big-name acts discussed in the following chapters, this chapter highlights the work of lesser-known stars of a smaller scale scene. Practiced self-promoters who tour with their acts, they opt for the freedoms of do-it-yourself productions, in which they can set the rules. The effect is downwardly mobile, as performers put out more cash than comes back in. The homosocial potential of the scene thus intersects with its downwardly mobile scheme as co-constitutive aspects of the art form. This fluidity of gender and class identities and aspirations is what finally coheres the queer comic sexiness of Jewish female performers as more a labor of love than a livelihood.

Moreover, in its social and sexually tinged subversions, the neoburlesque genre highlights a conspicuous component of ethnoracial impersonation: the ability of Jewishness to be actually, in addition to figuratively, put on and taken off. In concrete and symbolic ways, performers construct and deconstruct Sexy Jewess identities across the length of a song and dance. This is unique about the art form, while also unprecedented in the rest of this book's discussion of Jewish female joke-work on stage and screen. The swans, mermaids, bunnies and lounge acts covered in the rest of the chapters are costumes that either only reference their artificiality, such as Brice's bodice, which she tries to yank off between stanzas (chapter 2), or are removed in quick costume changes off camera, as in Silverman's cameo as a lounge singer in a long red dress (chapter 3). In different ways than their mainstream comedy counterparts, neoburlesquers expose the constructedness of identities as impersonations to don and then dismantle, stripping them off as core to their physical humor. Where Better Midler's mermaid tale invokes a comic chastity by binding her legs (chapter 2), the neoburlesque strip score presumably frees the body for sexier encounters. Teasing until the last moment of her act, neoburlesque's Sexy Jewess takes us on the ride of her own self-pleasure, equal parts seducing her audience and satirizing that very premise.

In addressing these observations of live performance, the stories I tell about the Jewish burlesque performance circuit may be just that—stories.

But together these bits of evidence amass years of live performance notes, conversations, conference papers, and my own self-reflexive provocations that make up this chapter's ethnographic analysis. As with any narration of events, there are inconsistencies, shifts in value, and changes in perspective or insight. This reflects a moving position in relation to the material, new relationships forged, and the changing roles for research they bring.

ROCKETTE FANTASIES AND *MENORAH HORAH*

I attended my first burlesque revue in 2011 at the seventh annual *Menorah Horah*, at which the opening kick line set the stage for that year's theme of the evening, a Rockette audition and the reclamation of Jewish identity. Briefly, "backstage" one of the Schlep Sisters got the chance of a lifetime to audition for the Rockettes at Radio City Music Hall, thirty-odd blocks uptown. We watched Minnie Tonka run through the live audience and out onto the street, where a prerecorded video of her showed her hailing a cab only to decide in her on-camera testimony that the fame of a Rockette fantasy pales in comparison to having a home in makeshift *Menorah Horah* productions. A feel-good return to roots and a videoplay portion of the evening, the intermission interlude restored a sense for all present of what the night was all about. The taped show within the show revealed the real terms of a race and gender play characteristic of today's Jewish burlesque scene. The Rockette dream—newly and enthusiastically within reach was still morally outside the bounds of a Jewish self-identity. A role in the Rockettes signified the ultimately unwanted, ultimate stage (proscenium and sociopolitical stage alike) of an all-American assimilation into white womanhood, and into *sameness*.

The promotional photo shoot for that year's *Menorah Horah* envisioned the headlining Jewish burlesque duo as busty blondes in signature mockery of religious modesty.[5] Back to back against a blank backdrop as if plucked from another world, the Schlep Sisters sit in poised profile with downstage legs folding in to cover revealing parts. Leaning into a mirrorlike center, they each hold an oversized Star of David. Bare from their matching golden locks down to glitter-coated dance heels, the sisters freeze frame in visual parody of the treasonous shiksa fantasy (see figure 1.1).

Embodying this gentile threat to all promise of Jewish continuity, they manifest in mannequin form the minx-like menace of goyish sex appeal[6]—a white girlfriend (or two!) and not a Jewish wife. But as these Brooklyn-based burlesquers usurp the promise of an American wet dream through personifying it, they return to vintage burlesque nostalgia with postfeminist, postassimilationist charm. Revising the familiar Jewish female shtick of a funny unsexiness, funny because of its failures, the Schlep Sisters perfect a pinup

Figure 1.1: The Schlep Sisters in *Menorah Horah*. Photographed by Clint Hild.

play that doubly objectifies and reconstructs a Jewish femininity as white women with defendable sex appeal.

The photograph is an evident departure from earlier years. Gone is the garishness of previous Horah photo shoots, in which one Schlep Sister might smack the ass of the other amid bottles of Manishewitz wine or other drunken Jewish paraphernalia. Instead, the two wear classier, sexpot expressions with deep red lipstick and withheld smiles. Their bleached wigs are better kempt than in previous images of the sisters and are convincingly real, and the effect is of polished, playmate impersonators. At the funny crux of their burlesque schlepping feat is the implausibility of a Jewish sexiness, yet the updated photo-play does a certain kind of assimilatory work to manifest a normative femininity. It poses Jewish Otherness as at least as much a part of the white mainstream as different from it. In similar ways, the photo returns to pinup perfection while continuing to perform Jewishly, through the use of props as well as the comic incongruity of the face and body. Playing in the middle ground, the poster image promises an evening of sexy ruse that blurs the lines between what may be funny (meaning unsexy) about Jews and what may be sexy (as in unfunny) about women.

Whereas the reverse rejection of the Rockettes audition ultimately refused a white embrace-within-reach, it also seemed to justify the ethnoracial, in-between position the Schlep Sisters occupied. The fact that they failed to win the title at the Las Vegas 2009 Miss Exotic World Pageant seems nearly intentional in this light. In matching pink umbrellas and polka dot dresses, they strutted in sync with a vintage recording of Yiddish-English song sisters the Barry Sisters. They outed themselves and their fans as farces of real-life Jewish women who choose either to renounce Otherness or bask in a nostalgic Yiddish niche.[7] Still, neither Othered enough for the Miss Exotic World title or (wanting to be) white enough to attempt a Rockette reality, the humor of their act appears to have consciously rendered them unfit for either crown.

Regularly appearing on the same bill as bona fide exotics like Tomahawk Tassels and Shanghai Pearl, whose fanciful names match their respectively feathered acts, the Schlep Sisters pale—literally—in sexy comparison. But it is their jab at Jewish tradition, or at least the public illusion of it, that renders them funny enough for the comic stripping feat. It is just for this reason, this tension tied to ethnic whiteness, that the Yiddish-inflected twins and other Jewish burlesque groups like them are finding their comic niche in sexy line-ups everywhere. A specialty act with in-crowd appeal for female spectators, fellow burlesquers, Jewish audiences, and their allies, the Jewish burlesque number always already exceeds even the most outlandish variety bill of queer, freak, and fetish burlesque coquettes. Among a burlesque revival community, whose array of costumes and caricatures ranges from the anthropomorphic to risqué acrobatic, the Jewish burlesque dancer reclaims her in-betweenness, consistently and comically resolved with her own Jewish female unresolvedness. It is this compounded Jewish burlesque solo position in-between white sameness and ethnic Otherness that can stage its nostalgic return to a vintage feminine aesthetic and count on its comic charm.

Back to *Menorah Horah*: about halfway down the lineup and anything but little, Little Brooklyn entered at least twice as tall as the rest, with a weathered smoker's charm and a Mandarin-collared polyester dress cut on a severe diagonal bias. She wore a black beehive, fashioned to mimic a mythic Far East–inspired suburban housewife from a McCarthy-era dream that never really was. "Does anyone else feel like a little Chinese?" the voice recording asked as the pear-shaped thirty-something traipsed heavily across the front of the stage. The orientalist fantasy read legibly to the in-crowd cackles of an audience familiar with the Jewish Christmas Eve takeout tradition. Updating a hundred-year legacy of vaudeville's yellowface minstrel acts, this Jewish rendition commented on itself with conspicuous reference to a history of race impersonation not acceptable outside of comedy, if at all.

Even as big Little Brooklyn stripped, her canned voiceover took the spotlight, stealing comedic timing from a weight shift gone intentionally wrong. When her body took center, it sauntered instead of strutting, a visceral and weighted gait instead of a grapevine. She played to the crowd with the comic fling of her arm flab to convey an iconic matriarchal inheritance: her grandmother's great feat of aerating a living room with the swing of the same fleshy parts. As if Jewishness itself stood in for the signs of inevitable aging, the professedly un-dame diva embodied the portrait of fading beauty and a gimmicky grasp at a Jewish MILF revisited. The "Oy Veys" of her prerecorded raspy vocals punctuated each efforted kink and kick, and the audience squealed with delight when "the floor work" on hands and knees was much too much for the professed sciatica the performer may or may not actually have had. But by the time Brooklyn loosened her bodice to spill out a Rolodex of her children's photographs, the anticipation of a sexy reveal was spoiled in the most Jewish way possible: a reprioritization of what really mattered. Not you, not me, but my *kids*, god bless them.

Little Brooklyn embodied the self-derogatory stereotype of unsexy Jewish women head on, made extra funny by its juxtaposition against the new-tech possibilities of the screen behind her and digital photo sharing that by now has done away with hard-copy family photos. Personifying the return to a simpler predigital age through this time-warped refusal of the now, Little Brooklyn's persistent antidigitalism won my personal title for best in show. It seemed to render all "postness" of the Sexy Jewess moot by the inevitability that just under the bustier, we were all just Jewish Mothers with Old World concerns about children and their successes.

Giving up a fantasy of sexiness altogether, Little Brooklyn mocked the very conditions of the self-display format. Her printed photographs spilled out like an accordion wallet. They fell like flab as her heavy (hearted) steps affected a physical effort for her noticeably aging female body across the stage. The effect was one that invited easy laughter at the beloved Jewish grandmother stereotype which audiences may forever hold dear. In doing so, she also implicated herself as somehow predetermined for early aging, excess attachments, and eager oversharing associated with unassimilable Jewish women. In this context, Little Brooklyn complicated the bodily reveal of self-display with another kind of confession; that of the Jewish woman ascribing to her own continuance as such. Claiming its worst parts for herself, Little Brooklyn offered an important counterpoint to the shiksa fantasy which the Schlep Sisters entertained as the theme of the evening.

NICE JEWISH GIRLS GONE BAD AND ORDERING CHINESE ON CHRISTMAS EVE

The Jewish adoption of Chinese culture fed the comic holiday appetite the following year as well, when the Nice Jewish Girls Gone Bad featured the secular cultural tradition of eating Chinese take out on Christmas Eve.[8] The evening of burlesque, stand-up, and cabaret-styled comic mayhem began by serving food to audiences who paid in advance for the dinner theater package, and I was the one to get it for them. It was the winter of 2012, and I had offered to usher for the New York–based comedy and burlesque group, the Nice Jewish Girls Gone Bad, in exchange for seeing their annual Christmas Eve show. I had not anticipated the preshow craze of ordering takeout to be served hot at curtain up. Mining the emails of Gold Star members who had paid for the gimmick meant making sure I was accounting for every request and dietary note. My own Jewish family never felt so clichéd, but I appreciated the work invested in this Jewish Christmas Eve joke and my role in pulling it off. I scrambled to complete my task while the crowd piled up outside. Emcee-director-producer Goddess Perlman's credit card in hand, I price-checked the local varieties of General Tso's chicken that would be delivered in the next ten minutes.

"They'll have the address on file," she assured me, "just give them my name." Perlman hollered the next set of Jewish tasks from the bathroom, and any pretense of professionalism between us was traded in for the familiarity of the preperformance get-it-done demeanor. She trotted back into the room in a drag queen's blue ball gown as Cinderella's evil stepsister in high camp. She asked suspiciously, was I from New York or not?

"Not," I replied, sensing it would be best not to explain that I had moved there with my family in the late 1990s, but was living again in California at that point.

I was visiting for the holidays and hustling to fund this research trip so that I could usher for her show. Would my non–New Yorker status endear me to her or make her question my ability to get the takeout order right?

"How did you say you heard about us again?" Perlman asked, with my older sister's suspicious tone.

She was already gone, chiffon train in hand, to set up the dessert table, managing the plastic Trader Joe's packages like a practiced host. I softened, appreciating the pressure on her as event ringleader, producer, and featured performer, whose Jewish charge was to feed everyone.

Downstairs, I sat in my reserved side seat in the front row and lit up when Perlman gave me a shout out early in her set. "There's actually someone here studying this stuff," she said, shielding her eyes from the harsh stage light and searching for me in the crowd.

My hand answered with an immediate pageant wave, as my thigh muscles tightened and I lifted awkwardly off the chair. As fast as I responded physically, my thoughts worked to catch up. I had ushered my way into her line of thought and for a split second, into the show. Aware that this was the best blessing I could receive from Perlman's comic pulpit, I swelled with equal parts pride and embarrassment. I was the near-mythic dance anthropologist and now butt of the joke, flattered by her attention and somehow ashamed not to be in the show. I laughed along with the crowd, agreeing to poke fun at the formality of scholarly research.

No doubt my usher-ethnographer persona set me up for this interplay, and yet it was her unbarred openness to my being there, as aide upstairs and critical spectator downstairs, that confirmed a kind of "in-betweeness" of my position. Sitting there in the front row, I knew Perlman could see me at any point, and in stand-up fashion, bite back with anything that might come to mind. I was eager to be on that edge with her and in such close proximity to the stage space. She had set the seat aside for me, and I had taken it. This spatial relationship offered a choreographic closeness for watching and being watched from vantage points on and off stage. It also offered a gesture toward inclusion, which I recognized as Jewish generosity. With a shout out that both celebrated and discredited what either of us was there to do, she seemed to say that so long as I was there to see her, she would see me back, and be sure everybody else did too.

A small handful of other stand-ups took a shot at the holiday-tinged humor, some more Jewish in content than the others, and I found myself biding my time until Perlman returned to the stage. When she did, she rushed the tiny cabaret stage in a spandex onesie, limbs flailing in all directions against the heavy drum and bass beat. For the length of the song, she splatted across the stage in smurfy blue apparel that hid her hands, feet, and face. The crowd shrieked with laughter, undoubtedly impressed with the bigness of Perlman's movements and the badness of her dancing.

I was tickled by the delight of my twin-like reflection, but wished that she would slow down to move with more clarity or perhaps do more with less. In this way, I judged her as I would myself in my own performances of a similar Jewess drag, dancing badly to warm up a crowd. Relating too closely to this comic doppelganger, I tried to create some distance by embracing my usher-ethnographer role: Who was this obscure female form emceeing the Hanukkah ceremony with an unpracticed solo improvisation, worse than bad and intentionally so? What was served up by Perlman's dance joke and its cartoonish exaggeration of the excessive Jewish woman?

I knew the question well, having asked it of myself in performance since I was a kid, typecast in dance and theater parts as the Jewish klutz role, and still sourcing that gender and ethnic content in solo performance. But never before had I so deliberately ushered the line between identification and distance with a fellow Jewish female performer. These were women whose identity dilemmas I knew best in the world, after all, and as much as they didn't need my saving, or my opinion of their work, the process of more deeply understanding the transgressive potential of what they opted to present on stage could render them visible to me in new ways. The act of defending them and translating their cultural work for readers would mean recommitting myself to a method of seeing and writing that could celebrate the kinds of shtick I also questioned.

Measuring Perlman and her dancing shtick against my own experience was a made-up ethnographic method, if also a misguided one. I knew full well that this impulse to vet performance against familiar versions of self was too much of a mirror game. Still, I found myself muted in the amplified laughter surrounding me. How could I join in the fun of the Jewish female body's laughability, when I took the humor to heart? I faulted us both for rendering the Jewish woman so legibly wrong, and chose instead to imagine how well Perlman probably dances in real life.

Perlman's next act featured a stand-up set in adult footsie pajamas. The punchline came early on as Perlman turned upstage, exposing her rear end from an opened back flap. Her bottom bared a cabinet of crass curiosity for all to see, and the crowd squealed at this play on the quintessential burlesque reveal. Word-stickers spelling out "divine" and "goddess" teetered on the edges of Perlman's fuzzy breast and belly before falling off completely. My friend and co-conspirator sitting next to me had cut and spray-painted the letters in a crunched preshow frenzy.

"I knew that wasn't going to work," my friend grumbled, interrupting my researcher's reverence.

The fallen lettering got a big laugh, which Perlman played up as if it were part of the show. Ah, I nodded in recognition, the tricky homemade prop that plays its own joke. No doubt others in the audience could also appreciate this conspicuous display of Perlman's having made the costume herself, finding it funny that it failed in the moment she and we needed it most for the dance joke. Though a ripe example of this do-it-yourself scene, it reflects on the laughter Perlman invites, intentionally and not. Bloopers make people alternately happy and relieved. They laugh at someone else's expense with evil innocence. Someone slips on a banana, and we laugh because it is thankfully not we who slip. In the performance context, bloopers also reveal the effort that was meant to go unnoticed. As the labor of the performer is suddenly visible, the clown comes momentarily undone, revealing herself as an act, as a construction. The humor of the mistake is somehow as funny as the performer's best joke, and the crowd laughs through it all.

Checking for a reaction, I flashed a look at Schlep Sister Minnie Tonka, a soloist on tonight's lineup and perched now just above the crowd on the stairwell. She met my eyes with a glance, not laughing at Pearlman's peek-a-boo behind the way others were. As the most practiced dance artist of the evening, Minnie Tonka carried a certain Jewess mystique, a more dancerly confidence less familiar among jokier Jewish acts. Prolific in her own act, she performs regularly throughout the calendar year, with an impressive repertoire of burlesque routines. Even seated on the stairs, her perfected burlesque "awarishness" seemed to exude self-pleasuring star power.[9] I wondered if Minnie Tonka recognized me from the previous week's show at the Highline. I'd made a fool of myself then, going on with compliments at the merchandise table, she glistening with sweat and I in a blue turtleneck sweater that seemed right for Jewish dance studies.

While Perlman carried on with her set, I watched Minnie Tonka rise from her seat at the top of the stairs to prep for her entrance. I saw for the first time her short sateen blue robe with a hand-stitched Jewish star on the back. Ooh. I ogled. She was so regal in the dark. I studied the svelte starlet ascending all the way up and out of view, hunting down some evidence of a step out of character, some shift of weight or gait that would uncover the girl beneath the gimmick. I convinced myself that these few seconds were a private show just for me, an invitation to follow. I recognized a wish to be like her and with her at the same time. Surely this doubled desire was a made-up method too, but what would I call it? Qualitative googly eyes?[10]

If my gawking was as much about envy, or momentary lust, as it was the candid scopic tactics of my ethnographer's gaze, it also had to do with Minnie Tonka's strange mastery of the hyperfemme Jewess spectacle I both desired and suspected. When she finally took the stage in the second half of the show, she began in a shimmering purple-silver gown and long gloves. Moving with smoothness of step, she shifted her weight with quick small kicks and tight crossbacks that sent her hips side to side. She stylized her walking pathway up and down the stage diagonals, rarely letting us see her straight on. Instead, frequent twists of her torso created spiraling lines down her legs. She worked the pointed flicks of her toes like counterpoints to the shifting angles of her nose.

A curiosity indeed; Minnie's was the perfected burlesque number that balanced beige character shoes and the phenotypically distinguished Jewish face. She could tease the audience with trained dancer legs and fully controlled carriage, while facing us off with a near-classic version of the infamous Jewish nose. And all the while, there was no Jewish mother reference. No mention of food, or her boredom with men, or views on family. No talking over what she was doing as she was doing it. No undermining her own act, or anyone else's, with irony. And yet, in the context of the cabaret evening, her sincerity still read as a funny bit, even as she pulled off the dance stunts without the need to self-criticize or sabotage. For the Sexy Jewess construction, this begs more questions. What does it mean that Minnie Tonka achieved the mythical Jewish female sex appeal she didn't really even mean to make fun of, and the crowd laughed anyway?

Against the adoring catcalls of the majority female audience, Minnie Tonka pleased the crowd with techniques opposite to Perlman's can't-dance routine. Both "went bad" through techniques of self-display and the reveal and conceal games of neo-Jewish burlesque. Both bore the Jewish female body as the brunt of the Jewess joke. Minnie's pastel pasties offered an glamorous juxtaposition to the harder humor of Perlman's self-abasing Jewish jester role. Inversions of one another in this sense, these kitschy broads embodied the possibility of a two-part Jewish female performance paradigm: Minnie through practiced dance perfection and Perlman's divine goddess through its dunce-styled disregard.

As two-part configurations of the postfeminist, postassimilatory Jewish woman, strategies of dancing or duncing cannot be reduced to a simple binary, even though I have just posed them as opposites. Rather, the order in which the acts unfold can help us understand them in relation to one another. Perlman's physical humor hosts the show, sandwiching Minnie's vintage elegance between deliberately unsexy acts. Minnie's calm and collected aesthetic comes across like a risqué accent among the evening's lineup, while Perlman's comic badness at dancing and at sexiness repeats the silly tenor of the evening that sticks closer to the stereotypes.

In this lineup versions of the Jewish female accumulate bit by bit, act by act, until they amount to an evening of shared joke-work. In contrast to the pageant-styled contest of *Menorah Horah*, however mocking its tenor, the Nice Jewish Girls Gone Bad are better seen as a collective force rather than individual acts or competitors (see figure 1.2). With more than thirty members, the cast of NJGGB has performed in various combinations since 2002. On any given night, the cast includes between five and eight female comediennes who sing, dance, and tell jokes.[11] Rather than rate single acts against each other, audiences indulge the collective ethos of their name and organizing principle. Perlman and her entourage make a deliberate claim to collective "badness." Their badness upsets the goodness of appropriate, acceptable femininity, jokingly counterpoised against prudish Jewishness but standing in for the recuperative take-back of all repressed identities.

As Perlman's Nice Jewish Girls staked a claim to badness as X-rated fun, they bolstered an underground contemporary performance genre in more than one way. With sold-out seats too squished together, the showcase stood in for the sexy shtick of a homegrown Jewish Christmas Eve tradition. A fitting venue for all things illicit, the basement venue helped make tactile the atmospheric implications of a dark-humored holiday and its dinge appeal. Inviting audiences to step and stoop down to a dimly lit performance dugout, the show boasted its low ceilings, low halves of the body, and basement dens of lowly ethnic humor as pathways of going bad. In contrast to the higher brow elegance of the Highline Ballroom, this was the literal and figurative embodiment of the downwardly mobile do-it-yourself model.

If *Menorah Horah* plays up an upscale pageant theme to celebrate women more than measure them against each other, the Nice Jewish Girls Gone Bad address this paradox too, as a movement of Jewish women misbehaving, more powerful en masse than in crowns of their own. Although that is the ultimate effect of *Menorah Horah*, too, the Nice Jewish Girls bring this agenda front and center. Their all-Jewish bill stages an earnest investment in feminist community in line with the burlesque revival more broadly.

"POLYESTER FEMINISM" AND THE STAKES OF SELF-DISPLAY

In her "Feminist Neo-Burlesque Speech," posted on her website and delivered to students at the University of London, Schlep Sister Darlinda Just Darlinda provides an insider account of what she calls a feminist neoburlesque

Figure 1.2: Nice Jewish Girls Gone Bad poster. Susannah Pearlman and Joanna Levey, copyright 2008.

movement with political implications.[12] She outlines a "polyester performance" style that borrows from classic burlesque striptease, performance art, various forms of dance, and comedy sketches with a feminist agenda that addresses the equal rights of all genders. Drawing important connections between generations of feminism that develop a burlesque revival, she stated:

To be a feminist is to be aware of those rights, understand that we have choices in life, and work toward implementing them in our society in daily life or political, performance based action. My mother was part of the feminist movement at UC Berkeley in the 1960's; she raised me to believe that I do whatever it is that I choose to do in life regardless of my gender. She even told me NOT to shave my legs. Well how do I live my life as a feminist? I wear a bright orange spandex outfit to a speech at the University of London, not all feminists wear Birkenstocks. I wear Birkenstocks AND high heels! I have a day job at a women owned and operated education sex toy store. I am an active member of the New York City Burlesque community. I have made a choice to live the life that I live.[13]

Pointing toward unshaven legs and sex-positive femininity as the bodily legacies of her mother's second wave feminism, Darlinda centralizes the reconstruction of normative gender expectations as key to the "polyester performances" of neoburlesque. She notes the agency inherent in how she pursues a "life as a feminist", and in doing so, links burlesque community membership and leadership with the liberatory sexual politics of women-run spaces. Wearing both "Birkenstocks AND High Heels," Darlinda politicizes life in her own shoes as she refashions the sandaled freedoms of her mother's generation with the spandex dress-up garb of a postfeminist life style.

If there is something that is especially *neo* about this "both/and" rather than "either/or" philosophy, it is the revealing way it interrelates race, gender, and Jewishness as overlapping discourses of the burlesque dancing body. In defense of a performance form that celebrates female bodies that do not fit the cookie-cutter images found on runways and in magazines, Darlinda announces: "I am by no means a supermodel, but according to the US Department of Health and Human Services, the average U.S woman is 5'3. 7" (162 centimeters) tall and weighs 152 pounds (69 Kilograms), so I'm almost average!"[14] The remark reaffirms the spaces burlesque makes for alternative notions of sexy femininity through the acceptance of real-looking female bodies.

In burlesque's open embrace of the "almost average," there are significant perks for Jewish women. Stereotypes have most frequently depicted the Jewish American woman as excessive in her material and emotional wants, as well as in her body (boobs, nose, butt, voice, volume, laughter), such that she has been seen as entirely unsexy in countless depictions in popular culture (Think *The Nanny*, CBS). A neoburlesque sexiness that celebrates the near-averageness is ethnically and racially significant. For Jewish women, "almost average" takes a positive spin on the familiar "not quite white" and thus not-quite-right status that sustains Jewish cultural imagination even in the postassimilatory contemporary period. Where Darlinda's enthusiastic proclamation celebrates a dance form that honors curves in contrast to other dance forms that may disregard them, there is also space allotted for the excessive dimensions of Jewish bodies.

As Darlinda's polyester performances build on the liberatory premises of second wave feminism and its sexual revolution, they also appear to slide in and out of "prefeminist" temporalities that date back to early twentieth-century burlesque and vaudeville circuits. In doing so, the bounds of neoburlesque overlap distinct traditions of performance known best for gender and sexual transgression. This composite performance of feminist histories is core to neoburlesque's postfeminist construction. Rather than a deliberate move to eschew these feminist histories, neoburlesque's postfeminism is both polyester and still in pin curls. In this sense, what is postfeminist in this case evidences a nostalgic continuance of the multiple forms that paved its way. Rather than expressing a break from feminism, Darlinda outlines neoburlesque's postfeminism as an extension of it.[15]

In addition to constructing a postfeminist performance agenda with various implications, Jewish-themed neoburlesque adds an ethnoracial dimension that shapes a postassimilationist ethos of the body. Performances of prefeminist sex appeal and a polyester liberation parallel return to racially stigmatized Jewish pasts when Jews were not yet white folks. In this sense, neoburlesque configurations of postassimilation also consist of movements in response to, but not beyond, the periods they reference. In this regard, the bodily attitudes, actions, and affects that construct the funny and sexy Jewish burlesquer reflect the most recent innovations of a long-standing Jewface performance tradition.

Jewish dance historian Rebecca Rossen historicizes the use of Jewface makeup in early twentieth-century modern dance to exaggerate stereotypically Jewish features.[16] Where her work largely focuses on male choreographers "Jewing up" to read as ethnic in concert modern dance works on Jewish themes, my usage of the term extends that reference to the reappropriative masquerade of today's Jewish female burlesque performers. In the small theaters of the showcases I describe here, stereotypical Jewish features like the nose are more legible than in the concert halls of modern dance venues. But more significantly, contemporary performers construct and deploy burlesque costumes, contexts, and gestures that function in new ways to mark Jewishness.

As they arguably always have, embodied Jewface tropes provide access to a range of race and gender impersonations in which the act of "Jewing up" extends to the performance of identities outside Jewishness. It does this through a Jewish filter, as a comment on itself. Little Brooklyn's forays into yellowface, for example, engage a Jewface repertoire as it performs a period-specific parody of Jewish orientalist fantasies in the 1950s. Reaching back to a period of conspicuous cultural appropriation, Little Brooklyn comments on the secular traditions of Jewish America that have constituted its imagination of itself as worldly, as embracing, as insiders-outsiders aligned with other Others, but not too much. She reiterates a century-long Jewish American anxiety about race in relation to other minorities that has paralleled its equally anxious appropriations. The humor for contemporary audiences is as reflexive as it is critical. It layers what may be funny ha ha and uh-oh as simultaneous reminders of appropriative Jewish life in America, where class and race assimilation has meant countless modes of copying. From the postassimilatory context of the present, Little Brooklyn's crude faux-Asian copy choreographs a self-conscious comment for Jews. As today's Jewishness can look back on this appropriative past, Little Brooklyn's act raises questions about the postassimilatory Jew in America and the extent to which the Sexy Jewess is still a ruthless copycat.

To link practices of race impersonation and appropriation as constitutive of the Jewish woman past and present raises questions about the stakes of performance that persist across shifting time periods, albeit in different ways. As discussed in the introduction of this book, a central debate within the scholarly discourse on race impersonations in the United States has largely focused on the degree to which such performances are sympathetic or not in this same vein. Most provocatively, Michael Rogin asked of Jews in turn-of-the-century blackface, "What does it mean that a structure of exploitation produced a culture of identification?"[17] In other words, what happens when exploitative structures—like racism—are invoked as part of performing alliance with other people's Otherness? Rogin answers his central question with the dangers of cultural appropriation. His pushback is against the belief that practices of skewed impersonation, in his case blackface, are undertaken by Jews with good intentions. Little Brooklyn's jab at the orientalist wives of the upwardly mobile carries a similar critique. She invites laughter at the very premise of appropriation by which mid-century Jews became white folks through cultures of identification that were likely also exploitative. Rendering these histories as Jewish joke-work in a burlesque context, Little Brooklyn thus enacts a kind of postmodern parodic comment. She looks back in time while peering right at her audience, daring them to laugh at the damage they have done. If there is a sympathetic aspect of such impersonations of the mah-jongg-playing Jewish mother, it is the idea of looking at one's own culture and rendering its bad behavior worthy of ridicule.

At the same time that Little Brooklyn can look back at appropriative and even exploitative cultural practices with the corrective lens of the present, I observe a way in which Jewish-themed neoburlesque invokes and provokes something that is not yet resolved or finished. Even in Jews' twenty-first-century position, arguably after Jews in America have become white folks, neoburlesque points to its uncertain incompletion and the impossibility or implausibility of a completed Jewish assimilation. Indeed, many American Jews continue to think of themselves as ethnic Others, outside the white majority, delinking class assimilation with ethnic or racial identities that remain in positions of alterity to the mainstream. Arguably, the Hanukkah showcases play up this self-Othering scheme, celebrating what's different about Jews as a source of pride.

The producers of *Menorah Horah* sells tickets with this range of allegiances in mind, appealing to a myriad of assimilatory perspectives that come together perhaps only for the holidays. "Whether you're a *yeshiva bocher*, an honorary Jew, or a bacon-loving while heeb," the Schlep Sisters post in their annual press release, "MENORAH HORAH will titillate and inspire your holiday spirit."[18] A *yeshiva bocher* is a student who learns in an orthodox school, an honorary Jew is any willing friend, and a "bacon-loving while heeb" refers to those secular Jews who betray kosher dietary law by eating pork. Jewish neo-burlesque will take all kinds, the invitation reminds. Indeed, this is a keystone of the genre that practitioners of the form say they like so much.

The newest member of *Menorah Horah*, Zoe Ziegfeld (see figure 1.4), explained to me on the phone, "Burlesque was this middle ground where you can be sexy or sexual, and you can also be intellectual, and also be in touch with your cultural heritage."[19] She added, "There's room for all of it. There's room for all facets of your identity, whatever that happens to be." Continuing with this theme of burlesque's openness, she described burlesque as a place where her Jewishness made sense too. Working as a synagogue preschool teacher by day and a strip club stripper by night when she started performing burlesque, the artist explained that burlesque was the place these disparate

Figure 1.3: Minnie Tonka with a menorah and potato pancake mix. Photographed by Peter Svarzbein, copyright 2007.

Figure 1.4: Zoe Ziegfeld in *Menorah Horah* at the Highline Ballroom, New York City (2014). Photographed by Mark Shelby Perry.

lives came together. "Burlesque ended up being the place where it was all OK," she said. It was "the place where people could conceptualize for themselves how a person could be a preschool teacher by day and a strip club stripper by night and be able to assimilate that information." There were not many at the synagogue where she taught who were necessarily open to the idea of her strip club life, and when she shared her preschool teaching with her strip club crowd, she found that people quickly became "hot-for-teacher" or otherwise didn't believe her.

Zoe Ziegfeld's conceptualization of neoburlesque as a "middle ground" where all was "OK" resonates with Darlinda Just Darlinda's appreciation of the form and its embrace of the almost average. The middle ground framework also suggests an in-betweeness of the form's expression of postfeminist, postassimilationist Jewish femininity, where it functions as a place to both experiment with identities and bring together seemingly opposed ones. Such a middle ground also speaks to the performance of liberatory or even liberated femininity, in which there may be a potential for objectification of female bodies by onlookers with less progressive views on women.

In this sense, neoburlesque also raises questions about gender exploitation. The striptease effect, if also a site of parody and social comment, renders performers vulnerable to the gazing of its audience, which, though largely on board with the progressive celebration of female bodies, does not screen its coed spectators for meathead sensibilities. Significantly, however, Darlinda assigns this power back to the performers themselves and their production teams, arguing that "the resurgence of Burlesque is not exploitative when the producers, performers and promoters are willing and inspired to participate."[20] Her utopic sensibility of producers, performers, and promoters imagines burlesque as a safe space, where all choose to be. Tellingly, she adds, "Shows can be exploitative if performers don't understand their choice to be in the show, if they are the brunt of the joke, if they are continuing a stereotype."[21] Darlinda designates the power of choice as what puts the shows on performers' own terms. But folded in is an intriguing requirement not to continue stereotypes, a point that my observations of Jewish burlesque would seem to refute. But when taken as an opportunity to ponder the meaning of stereotypes in performance and the potential to alter them through exaggeration, it is possible to understand Darlinda's comment as a reminder that the performance of stereotypes necessarily involves what a performer chooses to do with them. Performers I have observed make deliberate display of taking pleasure in being the brunt of their own jokes, and by way of rote stereotypes. Indeed, the Jewish joke-work of neoburlesque appears to rely on the very categories of stereotypes that bind performers—like klutzy, overbearing, or otherwise unassimilable Jewishness—to recuperate identities in-between acceptable feminine subject and objectifiable Other. This is neoburlesque's reappropriative power, wherein the exaggeration of stereotypes (already exaggerations themselves) reveal their cartoonish absurdity. In ways that follow what Sigmund Freud and Homi Bhabha suggest such jokes can utilize the very limits imposed upon them to get around designated restrictions.[22] Performers can take pleasure in the jokes that previously scapegoated them to open up a cherished space of laughter and critique.

In my observation, neoburlesque allows women to return to the categories that otherwise contain them in order to push boundaries tied to ethnic and gender identities and confined by social standards and status quo norms. The transgressive potential of neo-Jewish burlesque pivots around this act of perverting social norms in the name of liberatory progress, and it does so through the embodiment of stereotypes. As performers reappropriate delimiting ideas about the Jewish woman and what is so socially funny about her, they relish their choice to be in the show, as Darlinda just Darlinda says.

Playing out the central premise of their genre, neoburlesquers exaggerate their pleasure as an expression of this choice, calling on the bodily effects of the vintage burlesque "awarishness" that has upset patriarchal controls since the late nineteenth century. In donning personas that would otherwise delimit them, performers enact this pleasurable aspect of self-display that thus plays with its own exploitative sting.

However self-exploiting the personification of the Sexy Jewess may be, her iteration in neoburlesque raises different stakes than in more lucrative genres because of the question of money. As she borrows from striptease, but gets no tips, the Sexy Jewess of neoburlesque makes her message clear. She is in it for the love, and not the livelihood, and out of her own desire, which, her audiences understand, takes priority over our own.[23] For this, majority women audiences and coed crowds alike holler in celebration of the performer's own empowered pleasure, where no dollar bills are tucked under straps and no sex is bought or sold. In this scenario, it's good to go bad and healthier to happily strip than not to. There is finally no doubt that the rejection of patriarchal constraints comes with an independent ethos that is richer in spirit than in cash flow.

SEXY SPIRIT AND THE DO-IT-YOURSELF SCHEME

The high value placed on glamour by each year's *Menorah Horah* is evidence of a mocking celebration of this downwardly mobile reality. Even as it barely covers its own costs, the annual event grows bigger and bigger. While standing in line for the 2014 *Menorah Horah*, my friend commented on the upscale atmosphere of the Highline Ballroom. "Wow, fancy," she remarked, adding that the venue was much nicer than she had imagined.

The event had achieved the intended illusory extravagance and *Menorah Horah*'s pretense of glitz and fame, and this surprised my friend, who had discussed ideas with me about this chapter for some time. Knowing my claim of do-it-yourself aesthetics, she had expected something much less polished than the velvet red ropes and the multiple bouncers at the door.

The one-night-only extravaganza was an expensive display of resources, and the classy joint inspired holiday spending. I opted to join in the mood. My days of researching these scenes alone from a dark balcony corner were decidedly over, and I was proud of my effort to gather an ad hoc focus group and finance the evening's festivities with personal funds. I would not be held back by the amount of cash that this whole thing cost; I was buzzing on the palpable sense of nostalgia, and the night had just begun.

My team had successfully achieved our first task, arriving early enough to get a booth front and center. Centrally positioned as we were, ordering dinner was more difficult. The main floor and mezzanine filled up to capacity, and by the time the waitress took our order, the venue had sold out of the latke special. The only potato pancakes left in the place would appear on the headpiece of an evening's featured act, when Darlinda Just Darlinda would don them in a Jewish take on Carmen Miranda as cooking show host, while feeding us X-rated tips from her onstage kitchen.

We took in the table spreads of other groups, sizing up the crowd with scholarly interest. Check out 10 o'clock, one would say, and we'd make up stories about the nondescript couples edging into their seats up to the left. We stared in all directions, having to shout over clamoring voices and holiday cheer. Behind and above us. Not young, not old. Not too dressy. Middle ground. Tourists. Another dance researcher over by the bar? Maybe. And a scattered few more obvious New Yorkers, most likely friends of the performers. One such friend took the sixth seat at our table, amicably accepting our invitation to join in communal rounds of potstickers and observation.

A crowd warmer with an hourglass figure, long red curls, fringed panties, a crocheted yarmulke, and raffle tickets wound her way to our table. I bought five tickets and passed them out. I leaned in close to tell the artist I was writing about the show, and she agreed it was a good idea. I relayed how I had interned for Perlman as the usher-ethnographer, a title she said she liked. This usher, however, was working her way up the ranks, and her preshow schmooze-work was a steppingstone to future years onstage. This fact impressed me. Not only was she a committed apprentice, but she signaled growing interest in the genre. A figurative organizational chart now established for my ethnography an infrastructure for the event's continuance that supported development of the next generation of performers.

As our table's host for the evening, she was more than generous. She expressed outrage at the sold-out potato pancakes, and encouraged me to talk to the performers, something I had been too embarrassed to do. In previous years I had sat high and away from the action behind an obstructing pole. While others cavorted in herds before house lights lowered, I would take in the aerial view of the dinner theater. I would worry when to make my move from more comfortable web contact with artists to actual face-to-face conversation. Too nosy a practice, I would decide again and again, and figure myself as a muppet-styled Jewish gonzo journalist with a big nose, reporting from the inside but more willing to blast out of a cannon than talk to anybody.

But this time I was admittedly more comfortable in this scene, if as aware as ever of my own role not in the show but not quite simply a spectator, either.[24] I had softened, grown more appreciative of the fun of it all, less defensive about jokes I had once found offensive or derivative. I could let go of getting the ethnography right, or even of needing others to agree with me, committing to the probability of holes in analysis as necessary failures and even productive aspects of any singular ethnographic account.

The tension had been that the gap between what really happens, and for whom, exposes the work of storytelling implicit in representing the live dance scene and the embodied experience of it. While any ethnographer might confess as much, this might be especially true of projects taken on by those entangled in the identity politics of their research areas. A different study might present field findings devoid of the personal, but this would defy the intentions and preoccupations of my own, which remains self-conscious, self-reflexive, awkwardly enamored of my subjects, bothered, or otherwise wrapped up. Rather than turn away from these tensions or cover them up in the writing, I confess those paranoid bits that have come to shape my approach and change it over time. Paranoid because, well, the last thing I have wanted is to write these women into theoretical corners when they have so much more fun, front and center, on their own terms. In this sense, I have found myself joining in the fun of this scene, able to notice my original reluctance as the skepticism of someone too close to the subject matter and yet not close enough to avoid problems of interpretation.

When I met with Minnie Tonka in the summer of 2016, this was more evident than ever. We sat over drinks at the Beauty Bar before the first of her three shows that week, and Minnie was clear when she heard the title of this book that she doesn't even think of what she does as sexy.[25] Yes, she was taking her clothes off in front of people on a regular basis, and to music, but she said that she thought of what she was doing as "entertainment," not as being sexy. Huh. Suddenly the world was spinning as my muse and I met our first impasse face to face. OK, tell me more, I said.

Sexy is personal, Minnie said. "Who am I to say what people find sexy?" she asked with Jewish emphasis, throwing her weight back in her chair with her hands out and shoulders up. Her body language lunged back instead of inching forward as she did on stage, as she stressed the issue of individuality of preferences for performer and audience alike in neoburlesque. For baring the body to work as a source of postfeminist power, this personalization of sexiness without bounds and without definitions is crucial. Minnie's open-ended concept of the burlesque striptease revealed how it can comment on itself as a construction worthy of undressing. The entertainment Minnie laid claim to helps contextualize her play with the very subject of sexiness, whose effects, like humor, reveal a range of opinions based on any number of factors, while operating to do and undo a host of social premises. Not only does the range of what people may find sexy work in the same way that the different ways people take a joke does, but in the case of the Sexy Jewess, one is predicated on the other. This funny thing about sexiness and vice versa helps frame what is so entertaining about neoburlesque's awarish self-display and the play with identities put on and taken off during the length of a song and dance.

CONCLUSION

In nostalgic reference to twentieth-century vaudeville and minstrelsy circuits, neo-Jewish burlesque and the comedy basements that house it update bodily discourses of a twofold identification and self-mockery. Today's performers in

Jewish-themed acts thus enter into a middle ground between efforts to subvert hegemonic structures of race privilege on the one hand, and on the other, a Jewface autoexoticization, wherein self-Othering provides a self-conscious performance tool of a postassimilatory Jewish whiteness.

The transgressive potential of these reappropriations lives in the question of their ability to subvert heteronormative structures of power, Jewishly. In rejecting the upward mobility of their parents' and grandparents' generations, performers turn to low-budget shows that barely bring in enough to cover overhead costs to stage their break with race and class assimilation on the one hand, and the humor of its inevitability on the other. In choosing to rehearse ethnic difference and empowered femininity, performers-producers turn to grimmer spaces as part of the process of "going bad." Opting for the freedoms of a do-it-yourself ethos is both the creative impetus for an underground aesthetic and the practical challenge of its downward mobility.

Contradictions abound, but productively so. Neo-Jewish burlesque gestures to reclaim exoticism while performers move to distance themselves from the whiteness they ultimately enact. Aware of its time after anxious assimilation and second wave feminism, performers appear to go "bad" via Jewishness as if in recognition that it is finally not so "good"—meaning pleasurable, or necessarily profitable —to be same, white, and mainstream. Even if burlesque promises only downwardly mobile prospects, its popularity in a growing revival offers new visibility for recuperations and reappropriations of difference, however "almost average" it is.

After watching these women on stage for years, I realize that these performers are more my small heroes than my onstage representatives. For their sheer hold on my attention, I admire them as artists and provocateurs. Additionally, by undisciplining the ethnographic encounter to reflect my affective experiences as the one who writes these women into dance studies hopes to both explode and exploit the one-directional business of field notes that construct the other without mention of why or how. Indeed, if there is something capturable about the ephemera of live performance, it may be this recognition of the hyperconscious interplay of one's own recollected imaginations sparked during and surrounding the show. The ethnographic page can thus breathe space around the personal, laughing and unlaughing with its impulses to challenge the relationship between self and site. This approach deliberately joins a movement of dance ethnographers pushing against a range of disciplinary codes that demand objectivity, suspect the feeling body, and sustain the separate spheres for researcher and research subject. My ultimate hope is to open space for readers engaged in their own research processes to relate to these confessions in the name of transparent, reflexive scholarship, as always enmeshed in the "it" of one's findings and the questions that linger as a result.

As we move to the next chapter and its focus on a comic tradition of the twentieth century, it is helpful to think through this contemporary lens, in

which the exaggeration of ethnic and gender themes through various techniques of physical comedy reiterates again and again the Jewish female body
as always funny about sexiness and nostalgic about her Jewishness. A historical frame reveals the popularization of these themes over the course of a century and their reiteration of what is so strange, Other, and self-referentially
perverse about the Jewish woman in performance. By going back to the
joke-work of earlier Jewish female generations, it becomes possible to track
the continuation of embodied content, comic timing, and Yiddish-inflected
tropes. What accrues is a collective claim to cultural identity in which the
beloved tropes of a "funny girl" body become sexy ones in the celebrity spotlight, as money brings a new kind of power.

CHAPTER 2

Hello, Gorgeous, and the Historical Lens

How Funny Girls Became Sexy

"Hello, Gorgeous" a friend and mentor says to me when she calls. In an instant and every time, I blush. The flattery of the greeting hails me as a Streisand-esque funny girl, and I happily indebt myself to a long legacy of Jewish female comics, as well as the drag performers who play them.[1] The two words are the first ones Barbra Streisand says in the iconic American musical, *Funny Girl* (1968), a biopic of Fanny Brice's life in vaudeville and her broken marriage to Nicky Arnstein. When Streisand greets herself in the mirror at the start of the film, she pauses for a reflective moment alone before stepping into the empty New Amsterdam Theater several hours before taking the stage. "Hello, Gorgeous," she says with resolve. Having taken herself from ethnic immigrant roots to public stardom, Streisand-as-Brice is broken down by doomed love but stronger because of it. The mantra thus moves the quintessential funny girl forward.

The line reflects back too, as late 1960s America and its anthems of women's independence could gain traction by remembering Brice and other comic Jewish women of her era as models of emboldened femininity. In roles marked by their distance from the white mainstream, and beloved for that reason, Streisand and her Brice spoke for all things liminal but not stuck, in ways that resonated for Jewish and non-Jewish audiences. In a period when Jews were leaving the ethnic enclaves of city life, entering college en masse, and experiencing new wealth in upwardly mobile positions of all kinds, a charmed reminder of the "funny girl"—always unassimilable to love, marriage, and normalcy—would offer a queer social slant on Jewish femininity that could reflect back in the mirror a broad range of personal and political dreams.

A book about the Sexy Jewess as an updated construction of embodied Jewish joke-work begs that we go back to Streisand as Brice, not only for the quintessential reflective/reflexive lens of the mirror as object and metaphor, but also because their names and looks are synonymous with Jewish funny girls, and their dance humor is the best of female physical comedy, displaying its Jewish roots in Yiddish theater. To foreground *Funny Girl* is to highlight the recognition of beloved women who have established a critical legacy of funny Jewish femininity and its influence on the US stage and screen. The focus on these women and a host of others fills in significant gaps in the scholarship on Jewish humor in the United States. This chapter thus provides an embodied performance archive that is decidedly female driven and feminist. The tradition of gendered joke-work it outlines precedes and informs the book's focus on twenty-first-century celebrity and lesser-known social actors.

Spanning the majority of the twentieth century, funny bodily acts by comic stars Fanny Brice and Barbra Streisand as well as Sophie Tucker, Betty Boop, Gilda Radner, Bette Midler, and Madeline Kahn highlight Jewish female humor through comic dance sequences as well as faces, looks, poses, words, and lyrics. While a single chapter cannot cover the entirety of twentieth-century Jewish female comedy, the selected material reveals important ways in which distinct performance women straddled expectations and aspirations of the modernizing American woman on the one hand and the forever-racialized, always unassimilable social misfit on the other.

Performing in this provocative middle ground between insider and outsider came to constitute again and again what it meant to be Jewish and woman in the United States. As Jewish women made fun of upwardly mobile modern dance and bourgeois ballet, they stylized their routines with classed affects of hyper-Yiddish personas. Throughout the twentieth century they perfected techniques of the female misfit, laying queer comic groundwork for modern women and their friends. Their range of forward-thinking and faux pas femininities patterned a realm of danced, spoken, sung, or shrugged social parody that through its repetition has sustained a critical power into the twenty-first century in performances by Jews and non-Jews alike. Reconfiguring the "funny girl" body, always humorous about her abject physicality, they also build the backdrop against which today's Sexy Jewess takes the contemporary spotlight as a broad force of comic femininity that is by now so acculturated into US popular culture that it may not be known as such.

When we look to Streisand at the outset, we can take cues from the transformation of her own image. As the first celebrity to grace the cover of *Playboy* nearly a decade after *Funny Girl* came out, Streisand and her career arc help map the moves from what's so funny about Jewish girls to what may be seen as newly "sexy" about them well into the post–World War II period. Taking on this shift from funny girl to celebrity bunny, we can join Streisand in wondering, as she does in the front page image caption, "What is a good Jewish girl like me doing on the cover of *Playboy*?"[2] What follows here offers a partial answer, celebrating the performance prowess of this good Jewish girl and a slew of others in light of the social, economic, and historical conditions that got them there.

Hello, Gorgeous. This chapter thus hails its reader, greeting you with questions of the past. How did we get to the Sexy Jewess construction as a product and producer of postfeminist, postassimilationist cultural identity in the twenty-first century? And what does looking back at reiterative techniques of the "funny girl" Jewish body add to a study on what the Sexy Jewess is doing now, how she circulates, on what circuits, and with what creative and political power? More questions lead this chapter's historical frame: In what ways does a legacy of Jewish female comedy carry radical or resistive connotations, and what does it tend to rebel against? Why? And aligned with what cultural projects? Tracking back to outline this long stretch of twentieth-century Jewish female performance offers the reader an introduction into the ribald ways in which key entertainment women have negotiated complex cultural identity politics at the intersections of race, class, ethnicity, gender, and sexuality. At these intersections, humor erupts, bubbling up to the surface of social thinking with breakthrough displays of funny girl bodies and intrepid body talk.

FANNY BRICE, BARBRA STREISAND, AND THE JOKE OF THE JEWISH SWAN

A featured lead in the Ziegfeld Follies and the first female star of early talkie film, Fanny Brice was heralded for her versatility as a comic performer who sang, danced, and acted with the Yiddish flare that she learned on the streets of the Lower East Side. Most famous for her funny dancing, Brice's iconic performance of "Sadie Salome: Go Home!" combined physical farce and a strong Yiddish accent learned just for the part. Brice worked her facial expressions with what she called "oblique, grotesque gestures" to parody popular conceptions of the current show business cult of exotic dancing.[3] During a sketch called "Modernistic Moe," she made fun of modern dance and its biggest celebrity, Martha Graham, drawing out the modern dance expressive mode of addressing social issues of the downtrodden. According to Brice's biographer, Herbert Goldman, the star performed the scene with her hair down. She stuck out her thighs and twisted her thin body and "mobile face" in an outrageous parody of Graham's theories and performance. The loudest laughs came from the leftists, who had inspired the act while staying with Brice as summer guests on Fire Island.[4]

Well known for her childlike antics, Brice continued to grow younger with her nasal whine in the role of Babykins and then Baby Snooks, a radio-cum-TV role from the early 1930s through the early 1950s. Over forty years old by the time she became the perfect kid, Brice's bratty toddler could make use of comic material deemed too risqué for an adult. The part was a testament to Brice's youthful style, which Joyce Antler writes was "as bad . . . as [Shirley] Temple was good."[5] But Baby Snooks was not her first infantilizing impersonation nor the only one that would come to influence the future of Jewish female physical comedy with such force. One of Brice's early successes, and the act that Streisand later repeated in *Funny Girl*, is a sketch called "Becky Is Back in the Ballet," which Brice performed as part of the *Ziegfeld Follies of 1916* (see figure 2.1).

The song, written for Brice by Blanche Merrill and Leo Edwards, layers the comedienne's thick Yiddish accent with notes that flatten vibrato or vocal

Figure 2.1: Autographed photograph of Fanny Brice in *Ziegfeld Follies of 1916*.

decoration. Grainy recordings of the song summon images of the performer squeezing notes through sealed upper and lower teeth, like a child talking through a too-widespread smile, cheek muscles drawn all the way back. Brice's performance of the song likely depicted Becky's delusions of going anywhere near the ballet. While video footage of the piece does not exist, music scholar Ann van de Merwe confirms that Brice added a physicalized parody of prima ballerina Anna Pavlova dancing *The Dying Swan*.[6] Reviewing the performance, critic Sime Silverman referred to the number not as "Becky Is Back in the Ballet" but as "the Dying Swan."[7] The dramatic intensity of Mikhail Fokine's ballet, as well as its ubiquity in the dance canon throughout the early decades of the twentieth century, made it ideal material for Brice's parody. As is made clear by much of the writing on Brice's life and career, the performer was at her best spoofing the grand pretensions of high-brow art. Pavlova's notorious melodrama was perfect material for Brice's plain-talk delivery of forthright and funny lines, and the ballerina's famous expressivity opened the door for Brice and her Becky to be as boldly unballetic as possible.

The first stanza of "Becky" reveals her clumsiness: "Becky was a dancer, look how she danced / Night-time and day she triptoed away / She got a job in the ballet, but one night her foot made a slip / She fell on her back with, Oi! such a crack, she almost located her hip / They thought she was dead from the bump on her head / She should be in bed but instead. . . . Becky is back in the ballet."[8] The "triptoeing" Becky appears destined to fail. When she dances, she falls. And when she falls, she almost locates rather than dislocates her hip. The humor marks the funny language mistranslations of Eastern European immigrants learning English who misunderstand their own body parts. That Becky returns to the ballet by sheer willpower brings to mind a young girl's immigrant work ethic and outsider idealism that keep her happily dancing despite her injuries. Like Becky's bump on her head that didn't stop her from dancing, the funny girl body was a symbol of the unyielding immigrant drive to make it no matter the price. Such resilience would have also offered a deliberate contrast to white women's famous fragility, something idealized and aestheticized in the classical ballet. The funny girl body thus signaled the impossibility of assimilation to the elite ranks of society as part of its comic charm.

By the time the film *Be Yourself* came out in 1930, Brice's Yiddish swan was a popular entertainment phenomenon. Written and directed by Thornton Freeland, *Be Yourself* was one of the earliest films with synchronous sound and the first talkie to feature a female lead. As was common for celebrities in Brice's day, the goal for most studios was to find stars and then to create films that showcased the special talents of those stars. Protagonist Fanny Field is given Brice's own first name and, like Brice off camera, plays the part of an esteemed club performer whose swan bit is but one of her many acts. The role follows Brice as she sustains her performing career while becoming a boxing manager and falling in love with a prizefighter whom she trains with life smarts and business savvy. But as a man's boss and not his beauty girl, Brice's role picks up on the pain of the Jewish female, entirely too independent for men, and as reviews of the film imply, too funny to play the female ingenue. This barrier in love brings added life into the Jewish swan number, as Brice's ugly duck swan contends with this frustrated fate, fighting for male attention against the film's antagonist, the blonde foil, Lillian (Gertrude Astor).

In place of "Becky," Brice sings "Gorgeous to Be Graceful," whose lyrics provide a perfect counterpart to everything her body does. In the put-on Yiddish dialect that made her famous, Fanny sings, "The one consuming passion of my life / Is not to play a fiddle or a pipe / I want to be a dancer / my spirit sets me free / I long to be so slender and so sleek." She sings of the classic swan image. "To show my limb to him and him and him," she continues, pointing with her index finger adoringly at the crowd as if all are prospective lovers she not so innocently wishes to seduce. The next lines continue the caricature of a girl who dreams of ballet, but is not fit for the part or the costume: "My dress is a cocoon / If I don't breathe I'll swoon." She draws her flexed fingers down her bodice: "Oh I can get to dancing awful soon." In the comic moments before the next phrase starts, she futzes with the back clasps of the costume as if to loosen it. In the split seconds before the melody picks up, she blurts out, "Now let's take it off!" When the song picks up again, so does she, with a smiling set of hops skipping across the stage. "Oh it's gorgeous to be graceful / To fleek and fluck and fly / To make like dis and make like dat," she sings as she lifts her knees in an overly literal display of turnout, "and let the evening breeze go by." At this, Brice stands with legs spread and squats too widely in an overstated second position. She lifts up her tutu on the timing of the slide. With a childish self-satisfaction reminiscent of Brice's Baby Snooks, she continues through the next stanza knock-kneed, wide-eyed, and grinning.

The tone shifts to the Fokine ballet original. Camille Saint-Saens's *Le Cygne* begins, and Brice becomes the dying swan. She has traded out the traditional ballet's entrance of bourrées with a turning circle of soft steps in demi pointe and a slight plié. The bend in her knees pushes her pelvis forward as her upper body leans back. The weighted bobbing of her chin accentuates the rhythmic plucking of the strings rather than the melody. Circling in classical bliss, Fanny crosses her arms at her chest and casts her eyes coyly aside. Effectively romancing herself as well as the onscreen audience, she appears entranced in her own dancing jouissance. The performer's pleasure is so consuming that she fails to notice an elf-like creature pop up from behind the stage set. His pointy hat and impish steps are as spindly as his gaze, and he shoots an arrow that pierces Fanny's back. She reacts with a sudden pinch of her shoulders, and a muted trumpet cries out in cartoonish punctuation. Her eyes bulge and her hands flick at her nose as if wicking away a water splash.

The performance is a clear precursor to Barbra Streisand's swan parody in *Funny Girl*, which recounts Brice's story as an overnight stage success and a devastated romantic.[9] Rather than the *Dying Swan*, Streisand's is a full-scale ensemble remake of *Swan Lake* act 2, complete with a corps de ballet.[10] As classically pretty swans unfurl from the wings in perfect unison, sweeping camera angles do their part to match the amorous gaze of hunter-lover Prince Siegfried (danced by Tommy Rall). Enter Streisand, queen of the corps, arms in fifth high, and for an instant, regally convincing. As Siegfried gestures to shoot, she flaps her arms and runs without haste in a flatfooted circle, interrupting him and the Tchaikovsky overture. "What are you gonna do, shoot da swans? Dese lovelies? My svans girls?! What are you, dumb?" she asks in a Yiddish accent, and begins to sing over a string-heavy score more familiar to musical theater than classical ballet. Her exaggerated turnout highlights her long, lean limbs exposed under a high-cut tutu, as both her looks and her limericks mock the pretentions of white swan perfection. Streisand sings à la Brice, "Can't you see when you look at me what a lovely creature is a swan," on which she turns to her Prince, now perched on one knee. Lifting her too-perky skirt to make sure he's paying attention, she teases him with a flirty birdcall: "Yoo-hoo!"

A bird by any other name than a swan princess, Streisand sings that her imperfections are "only fit for consommé" and drives home the play on schmaltzy through the ballet's traditional sentimentality and the double entendre of a kosher chicken's cooking fat. In a temptress's voice, she then calls out: "Prince!?" He responds with a heroic leap across the proscenium. Undermining his zeal with a stock Jewish female lack of surprise, she condescends, "Vas that necessary?" Hands on her hips, she is a *Yiddishe Momme* who contrasts with all charm or grace (see figure 2.2). "You coidn't valk ova here like a poisson?" The chicken-like swan is thus revised as a heterosexual misfit. Too demanding and too prudish, she orders men around only to undermine them or then fly away too soon. A chicken from the Jewish ghetto, Streisand's swan is utterly unfit for marriage—and to a Prince, no less.

In one of the most, if not the only, dance-heavy roles Streisand has ever played on film, it is impressive that the singer-actress needs no stunt double for the several sequences that follow in this scene. Brilliantly, she does them all herself. Even in her pushy Jewish play with dancing badly, she commits herself in ensemble sections, leading the corps in simple but completed unison *emboîté* jumps from one leg in front attitude to another. That the step translates from French as "fitted together" bodes well for Streisand's full-fledged moment of blending in. And yet it is her dizziness after turning that the camera features in its swelling, circling movement, as if mirroring her essential bodily disorientation and impossible steadiness in the role. No matter how well she dances, the film role and camera work portray her as the classic klutz. In this sense, it is her Jewishness—her funniness, her unsexiness, the Jewish

Figure 2.2: Screen shot, Barbra Streisand in *Funny Girl* (1968). Directed by William Wyler.

nose that Streisand never fixed despite industry pressures—that throws her and her camera off balance.[11]

By the time Streisand's swan conjoins again with the Prince for the final pas of this scene, she lets him lift her up, only to then keep going up, like a set piece pulled up into the rafters to be moved mechanically offstage. The humor of bodies acting like machines is a classic comic trope.[12] Moreover, in the context of ballet, a pas de deux gone wrong mechanizes the male-female love duet as a manufactured trope to be taken comically apart. Its joke-work denaturalizes the heterosexual relationship that is so foundationally at play in balletic and social imagination. Even more, this failed love lift comments on the sociopolitical conversations of its day. When considered in light of the feminist liberation movement of the late 1960s, the humor of a princely mishap made fun of social pressures on male-female relationships by way of balletic partnering that in its codification and conventions is always mechanistic.

Streisand's self-sufficient swan foreshadows the film plot as the funny girl protagonist meets Brice's romantically unfulfilled fate. She ends the film singing Brice's hit ballad, "My Man" to the gambling husband, who leaves on account of her public fame that he could never match or manage. A funny girl's success is too much for a man to bear, the plot makes clear. For audiences of the late 1960s, the ending surely sang of their times too, as women pushed past glass ceilings at work only to fight similar battles at home. For the generation of Jewish women who idolized Streisand, her performance in the role expressed what it was to straddle models of emboldened femininity, in Brice's times and again in the 1960s, with the potential to end in similar isolation from family and marriage.

Ballet defenders might remember that the traditional white swan isn't particularly lucky in love, either. The many interpretations of *Swan Lake*'s ending focus largely on tragic separations of the swan princess and her prince.[13] And yet despite doom and gloom, the romantic ballet focused on love, naturalizing its assumed possibility. The *Swan Lake* fairy tale is one of magic sorcery, but Jewish swans only suffer the spell of their sustained stereotypes as inferior women. The classic swan's failed dreams of love are ones that Brice and Streisand say a Jewish swan could not have in the first place, let alone lose. In both films, financial authority figured by stage success partners an outspoken Jewish femininity that can only elude grace. And yet the female joke soloist, in loving audiences and receiving love back, finds herself otherwise alone. The head of her own flock, she remains a soloist both on- and offstage. Her dancing humor thus spotlights the loss of much bigger dreams than fame, as her man can only come and go.

While the Jewish swan's love fantasies fall apart, they indicate a queer comic potential that finally emboldens Brice and Streisand as independent women. For musical theater and film scholar Stacy Wolf, Streisand's performance of Brice in *Funny Girl* conceives of a queer Jewish womanhood through body, gesture, voice, and character.[14] Wolf argues that while no "homofolk" appear in the film, Streisand's performance queers representations of Jewish women in a number of ways, including most significantly the dissolution of Fanny's marriage to Nicky Arnstein (Omar Shariff). Like the film's swan parody, the plot line undermines heteronormative musical theater narratives, disappointing expectations of the musical theater happy marriage.[15] The pain of a relationship ruined through the corruption and emasculation of the male protagonist is both the queer cause and the consequence of Fanny's ultimate independence.[16]

The queerness of Brice and Streisand's physical comedy threads through these film plots on the Jewish woman and her funny girl body. As duckish swans and female clowns, their unmatched labors of love do and undo a significant Jewish female excess. What becomes visible through this excess is a defunct femininity made funny because of its exaggerated effort. Accompanying the physical humor are the assimilatory stories of success beyond what men can manage. As bosses of their own domain, the women remain unfettered and unstopped by love's arrows and leaps, proscribed as they may be. As modern American women, celebrities no less, these swans subvert the age old dictums with their hearts on their sleeves: they remain expressive, extroverted, and earthbound with an exceptional power to push on.

This resilience in the face of love's disappointments reinvests in independence and adds a tenor of queer resolve to the "Hello, Gorgeous" line and its feminist politics of personal affirmation. Said to herself in the mirror, and in that same moment to all who have ever felt left behind, Streisand's Brice speaks to herself and us all with knowing salve, a Jewish woman's guide to getting by on one's own terms. Streisand's Brice offers the funny girl's greatest gift: a reminder that no matter how bad it gets, be yourself. It will be OK or not, but you only have yourself either way. So, be as gorgeous as you are, and remind yourself when no one will. The role's comic clowning comes from this place and finds its power there, in and through the laughter that can reflect a woman's brilliance back at her.

For audiences in both the 1930s and the late 1960s, the representation of women's liberation from the constraints of men and marriage had the power to link the funny girl body with the promise of making it on one's own. The moment in the mirror could offer a radical kind of narcissism that signaled a private agency broadcast on the public scale. The ballet joke's break with bourgeois sensibilities stood in for the negotiation of new opportunities for Jewish women on and off stage, ducklings of Old World antics turned divas of do-it-yourself fame and upwardly mobile new wealth. As Brice and Streisand's unassimilable swans embodied similar themes in two periods, it is important to contextualize the backdrops against which they came into celebrity as cherished icons of a shared immigrant past. What else was going on around them that made these performances stand out as public favorites? In what ways did their dance humor take up or eschew the logics of their day, such that Jews and non-Jews alike could relate to them on such a large scale? And how does that help tell the story of Jewish assimilation through shifts in ethnoracial identity and feminist performance?

SOPHIE TUCKER, BETTY BOOP, AND THE BAWDY BODY BLACKING UP

In the same first two decades of the twentieth century when Brice's dance humor mocked middle-class aspirations through ballet and modern dance bloopers, Jewish comic Sophie Tucker presented a sexually frank style that provided a different kind of escape from increasingly tight controls on women's roles. Widely heralded by fans and reviewers of her time and after as "the Last of the Red Hot Mamas," Tucker became famous as one of a number of female performers known for their uncouth lyrical humor and banter in the late nineteenth and early twentieth centuries.[17] She got her big start in 1907 on Joe Wood's New England vaudeville circuit after having performed regularly at her parents' diner. It was Tucker's "blue humor," or jokes about sex, for which she became best known. Hit songs like "I Ain't Takin Orders from No One" and "Nobody Loves a Fat Girl but How a Fat Girl Can Love" indicated her address to a world untethered to heteropatriarchal logics and tied directly to her experience of her body. Tucker's sexual frankness was seen as a fact of her physical size. Because Tucker was known to be big and gawky, she was told she could sing sexy material that, if used by attractive performers, would seem salacious and offensive.[18] Using humor and self-mockery, she sang her "red hot" torch songs about women's sexual passions and romantic agonies: all women, even "big, ugly" ones, needed sex and love.[19] She contended that it was men's failures in bed and in marriage that denied women their due.[20] As Joyce Antler notes in *A Journey Home*, at a time when vaudeville and burlesque were becoming increasingly subdued to reach a broader family audience, Tucker managed to elude censorship; her "ugliness" was a new mask, one that gave her the freedom to transgress.[21] In an era identified by its first-wave tides in American feminism and early twentieth-century assimilation, Tucker's famously "blue" take on female independence was a bawdy banner for women's liberation beyond comedy circuits. In 1938 she helped found the American Federation of Actors and became its first president. Tucker's lead in vaudeville and the entertainment industry overall signaled major advances for women in mainstream channels, while joining the tide of Jewish female activism in American labor movements throughout the 1930s.

In joke-work that resisted puritan family values, both Brice and Tucker demonstrated how Jewish women could lead lives as forward-looking, unconventional, innovative moderns, as "Americans" unfettered by patriarchal constraints or traditional ethnic ones.[22] Tucker openly criticized marriage, taking shots at the dictum of the day that a woman couldn't be successful and be a good wife, and Brice would remarry three times. Both are remembered for breaking with tradition while talking openly about it. Yiddish theater, vaudeville, and radio provided new kinds of Jewish affiliation for a secular generation of American Jews with Tucker and Brice at the helm. It was a period when Jewish stage and screen women could find their places in a less separatist, more inclusive, pluralistic society despite rising tides of anti-Semitism and the crisis of the Great Depression.

A significant part of their generation's search for place was the performance of impersonation, which Tucker and Brice both deployed as plays on race and gender. Increasingly, a derivation of blackface minstrelsy called *coon shouting* became Jewish woman's territory as Jewish male composers took up the song tradition for their star counterparts. The broken English lyrics and diminutive cakewalks signaled white ethnic imaginations of slave history through fictions of failed love attempts and thwarted dreams. While Tucker would perform explicit coon shouting acts for a significant part of her early career, Brice is known to have worn blackface only once. Still, Pamela Brown Lavitt points to Brice's "broken-English" singing style as a more subtle form of coon shouting with layered connotations.[23] Indeed, Brice's Yiddish-inflected English and theme of failed love mocked immigrant Jews in ways that closely related to the coon shouting traditions, indicative of a time when the vocal and physical impersonations of Old World Jews were inextricably linked to the performance of blackface minstrelsy.

The humor spoke of its times. Lavitt argues that the humor of early twentieth-century vaudeville revolved around the concept of "open ethnicity," wherein "everybody played with being anything."[24] By the time Tucker and Brice established performance careers, coon shouting by literal and less literal means was already a play with the malleability of race, especially for white ethnics like Jews and Irish immigrants, who had light skin. Their deliberate move was to cartoon themselves as ethnoracial Others and also active assimilationists, a contradiction that was assisted by the "open ethnicity" frame.

This performance permission for a light-skinned "everybody" to play everything helps contextualize the range of impersonations that Betty Boop also caricatured in her cartoons in the 1930s. Boop began as a Jewish cartoon and a "Red Hot Mama," too. Aligned with Brice's girlish antics more than Tucker's adult humor, Betty Boop gave synthetic body to the voguish baby voice of Jewish actress Mae Questel, and her first cartoons were drawn against a neighborhood of Yiddish shops and immigrant personages. The embodiment of the Jewish "Ghetto Girl" stereotypes, Betty's naive discoveries were sexed up in gartered stockings and innuendo. In her 1934 animation *Red Hot Mama*, drawn by Dave Fleisher, Betty inks out the bad little good girl. Her ventures in hell and its freezing over appear sympathetic as Betty's innocence wins out against all odds. As opposed to the vulgar frankness of Tucker's milieu and Brice's defunct femininity, Betty's charms feminize her as an idiot-savant who unknowingly happens upon her sexiness while relying on it to get her out of trouble.

With roots in New York's Lower East Side and parents who clamored indecipherably with music boxes for heads, Betty Boop's flapper-teen years were spent dreaming of a life of adventure. In the 1932 cartoon, *Minnie the Moocher* (see figure 2.3), she and boyfriend Bimbo run away from home after Betty becomes fed up with her parents, who don't accept her carefree life and aspirations. The two end up in a cave, where a shadowy walrus sings to the voice of jazz star Cab Calloway, and moves as him too, as footage of Calloway dancing was rotoscoped for the cartoon. The appearance of various ghosts, goblins, and other scary creatures invokes the cast of Calloway's Cotton Club Orchestra, who provide the cartoon's musical accompaniment throughout, and play on camera at the beginning and end of the short. Media studies scholar Amelia Holberg's reading of the cartoon argues that it uses African American jazz music and movement styles to alternately entertain and frighten Betty and her boyfriend.[25] The cartoon animates Betty's Jewishness through a blackface-themed drama of desire and distance. As opposed to Tucker, who wore black cork makeup, or Brice, whose ethnic personifications never tried to grow up, Betty Boop escapes her ethnic roots for a liberated adventure. Finding herself among ghosts who stand in for the black male jazz ensemble that accompanies her flapper fantasy finally freaks her out too much. Trying out the life of the "red hot hoochie coocher" that Calloway sings about and deciding she doesn't want it, Betty ultimately folds and returns home, finding it all too

Figure 2.3: Screen shot, Betty Boop and her Yiddish parents in *Minnie the Moocher* (1932). Drawn by Max Fleischer.

overwhelming.[26] While the lyrics of Calloway's song are known to be non-sensical, it is telling that the "red hot" aspects of Betty's forays are imagined through black ones that she can enter into and opt out of at will.

Boop's cartoons shed light on the breadth of imitative performances in vogue at the time. In *Betty Boop's Bamboo Isle* (1932), Betty is Samoan. The musical group The Royal Samoans recorded the sound track and opening dance that Betty copies in a topless hula. She romances Bimbo, who blackens up to fit in and becomes the beloved leader of the natives. This trend of trying on otherness as a fantasy act to put on and take off was hardly her invention. Still, it is important to recognize the ways Betty Boop could cartoon a cultural phenomenon in vogue by other Jewish female acts at the time, such that the very play with identities was a Jewish female comic tradition already taking shape.

In Betty Boop's *Stopping the Show* (also 1932), a poster of Fanny Brice's portrait comes to life as Brice asks Betty in her signature Yiddish accent to "maybe giv[e] out a little 'personation of meeee, nooo?" to which the always-willing cartoon personage happily acquiesces. As Betty plays Brice's "Indian," the show-within-the-show humorously delivers an impersonation within an impersonation. A moment later, Betty also copies Josephine Baker's iconic Banana Dance as yet another impersonation in her repertoire.[27] Recalling the big names of female performance and their variant styles of dance, animator Fleischer situates Betty between impersonations of expressly Jewish acts and the other hugely popular ethnic and racial personages they loved and likely related to.

This ability to layer and change identities is key to the performance history of the early twentieth century and its influence on Jewish female joke-work to come. The racial and ethnic play of Brice, Tucker, and Boop reveals the morphability of their positions as Jewish women in the limelight. What made them so funny or even "red hot" was this fiery adoption of race and gender identities, whereby they enhanced their acts with more Othered personages as roles to inhabit and then discard. Their range of baby-ness and bawdiness is reflective of positions in-between ethnic Otherness and the white majority, revealing the salable techniques of celebrity women in male-run entertainment industries.

While varying in technique, the three figures foregrounded a tradition of impersonations and identity acts that threaded through the Jewish female comedy that followed, even as the public embrace of any sexy or raunchy references was forced to fade from plain view. The Motion Picture Production Code of 1930, which was strictly enforced by 1934, aimed to tame these ribald acts, protecting family entertainment through protocol that enforced restrictions on content with sexual innuendos. The new guidelines, referred to as the Hays Code, censored risqué material in movies, which now needed approval before their release.

Brice, Tucker, and Betty Boop were among the throng that strategized ways around the new controls. In Betty Boop's case, the Production Code effectively whitewashed her personage and desexualized her image. Betty was now limited to roles as husbandless housewife and career girl in a fuller skirt or dress.[28] While it was not written into policy that Betty should shirk her Jewish roots, Yiddish-language signs of the old neighborhood ultimately disappeared altogether, eventually disassociating the desexed star from any ethnic signs.[29] The imagination of Betty as a sexual figure was so intertwined with her Jewishness that desexualization was also de-ethnicization, and growing up also meant growing out of her immigrant roots, if not ignoring them altogether.

Despite this de-ethnicizing impulse, Jewish comedians who followed kept up the traditions of the early stars, plotting against patriarchal traditions in and out of Jewishness through stage and screen performances known to be more innocent, like Brice, or more bawdy, like Tucker. Braving the stage during World War II and unstopped by the conservative tide of the McCarthy era, Jewish female comics joined in to continue the tradition of parodying men, marriage, and a new category of American materialism within reach as they reiterated a model of the modernizing Jewish woman, at once both on her own terms and somehow ever-tethered to unassimilable traditions and their effects on the female body.

PARTY ALBUMS, POSTWAR AMBITIONS, AND
THE JEWISH AMERICAN PRINCESS

In the decades leading up to *Funny Girl*'s release, Jewish female comics kept up the joke practices of their predecessors while navigating shifting access to the American mainstream. Whether playing to Miami nightclubs of vacationing, retired, or transplanted Jews, new comics brought the punchlines of an older Jewish world to the growing Jewish suburbs. Jean Carroll rose to prominence in the 1940s and 1950s as one of the first women to perform stand-up; later, comics Belle Barth, Pearl Williams, and Patsy Abbott were so bawdy in the 1950s and 1960s—so "blue"—that clubs would only let them on for late night shows. "I'm 65, I'm fat, I can still take five guys a night," Barth boasted famously. "I pay them now, but it's okay."[30] Against the conservative tide of the McCarthy era, their explicit language, emphasis on sexual freedom, and candid remarks about Jewish culture earned them huge followings.[31] Known best for their party records that furnished the living rooms of the growing Jewish middle class, these enormously popular working-class Jewish female comics cultivated a lucrative Yiddish-laced humor that upturned social mores of quiet, sexually passive women.[32]

As culture and gender theorist Giovanna Del Negro writes, the fans of these women longed to escape the unquestioned blandness of white-collar existence and the climate of cultural conformity.[33] The femininity they constructed was far from the magazine images of women in *Playboy*, first published in 1953. Their bodily humor likewise offered a total reversal of the Kinsey Reports, released in 1948 and again in 1953, on the sexual behavior of thousands of interviewed women, which documented that women had less sex than men.[34] These frank and sassy Tucker-esque performers configured an altogether alternative realm of the sexually expressive female body for middle-class audiences.

Jewish female comic success during this period was directly tied to the social transformations of Jewish American life after World War II. As Jewish America left the ethnic enclave of the inner city and ventured out into white suburbia, the roles for Jewish women and the stereotypes about them shifted. The party albums and late night performances of bawdy Jewish female comics paralled this geographic and economic shift, and joke-work navigated these concerns in ways Jewish women could relate to while ushering in a postwar period of new Jewish access. In *How Jews Became White Folks*, Karen Brodkin outlines a postwar age defined by the promise of middle-class access through the GI Bill and its range of benefits for returning veterans. Able to get low-cost mortgages, Jews moved to the suburbs, and cash payments of tuition and school-related living expenses allowed a new Jewish generation to attend college. Tension around assimilation persisted, and so did its pressures to conform for young Jewish women. Plotting out that period, Brodkin recalls the effect of the shift on young Jewish women in what she calls the "blonde ambitions" of the late 1960s and 1970s.

It is in this context of shifting access and new wealth for American Jews that *Funny Girl* came out in theaters, first live as a Broadway musical in 1964 and then as a comedy-drama film in 1968. Teens of my mother's generation bought the sound track record in droves. For my mom, a ballet dancer with a professional career that was over by the time she was in eleventh grade, the swan scene saved her sense of humor, and likely her sense of self, too. A thyroid failure accrued through years of eating disorders had led to a total bodily shutdown that kept my mom in bed for her junior year of high school. In Providence, Rhode Island, she used to take the train to Boston after school each day, dancing her way into white ideals of womanhood, while back at home her mother supervised as she practiced diction in the mirror. "I smashed my camera on the way to Canada," my mom and her mother would work the long vowel sounds so as to undo the local ethnic accent. No doubt the funny depiction of Streisand's swan parodied the pressures to perfect ballet and unaccented English through its performance of active and aesthetic resistance. For my teenage mother, Streisand's funny girl had healing powers. To see a woman who looked like her on the silver screen, one who danced to dismantle the gendered and classist hierarchies at play, could tend to the deep wounds of anorexia and physical limitations brought on by ballet and exaggerated through other practices of assimilation she practiced just as often. I imagine my mom, realizing—if only for the fleeting moments on screen—that she could be like "Becky" and refuse to comply with the expectations of Jewish assimilation and ambition alike, failing them as if on purpose.

By going back to Brice- and Becky-like dance humor, *Funny Girl* cut through the comic material of its moment, which largely scapegoated Jews as economic opportunists, and the Jewish American princess as the worst extreme. In the mid-1970s the Jewish American princess joke met mainstream appeal, epitomized in Rhonda Weiss, Gilda Radner's television caricature for the first season of *Saturday Night Live*. In a well-known sketch called "Jewess Jeans," Radner wears high-waisted, skintight jeans in the style of the Jordache jean brand that was regularly seen in a similar commercial at that same time (see figure 2.4).[35] Radner's jeans feature an embroidered Jewish star on the pocket, a visual reminder of anti-Semitic badges worn by European Jews in the Holocaust and thus itself a symbol of changing times (see figure 2.5). The parody underscores the materialism of late 1970s America, while assigning its most conspicuous consumption to newly wealthy Jews. Furthermore, lyrics rhyme the Jewish look of designer clothes with a matching designer nose to link values around wealth and appearances. As matching designer schemes, the surgically altered Jewish face and new pair of Jewess jeans can outfit the new Jewish woman into the American mainstream.

Shuly Rubin Schwartz discusses Radner's "Jewess Jeans" parody in the context of a changing material messaging, in which clothing announced the arrival of Jewish women in the middle class.[36] While Radner's parody emphasizes clothing, it invites attention to her body as the more provocative material driving the joke. Radner's model-ready height and thinness and the ways that she moves make the parody possible.[37] She floats through the steps of her runway walk and a glam photo shoot with a lackadaisical go-go feel. Never hitting or landing too hard on the beat, her unmuscular movements stop short of full extension. Even Radner's gum chewing is lazy as if by choice, and she

Figure 2.4: Screen shot, Gilda Radner in "Jewess Jeans," *Saturday Night Live*, season 5, episode 11 (1980). Comedy Central.

Figure 2.5: Screen shot, Gilda Radner in "Jewess Jeans," *Saturday Night Live*, season 5, episode 11 (1980). Comedy Central.

never fully closes her mouth. The message is that Radner's body need not work too hard, except at this illusion of effortlessness. In this sense, she impersonates the spoiled daughters of upwardly mobile Jews, whose rising economic bracket can newly afford such luxuries. In contrast to Brice's "Becky," who worked in spite of her injuries, Radner's Jewess labors only for her looks.

With class parody in the foreground, Radner's commercial Jewess is the frontwoman of a multiracial trio of backup singers in the same jeans. Her fashionable whiteness is an image category within minority reach for Jews, as if in contrast to her black and brown backup singer-dancers, who may not so easily become white folks. When the male voice that comes in as the final tagline of the commercial says you don't have to be Jewish to wear the jeans, Radner adds with head turned back to the camera, "But it wouldn't hurt." The tone of her voice yields a familiar Yiddish-inflected cadence, even as the punchline signals a shift in what it connotes. In a period of new Jewish wealth, access, and mainstream recognition, to be Jewish and female is to have comfortably assimilated, such that it no longer hurts too much to be Jewish, and it wouldn't hurt to try to be like Jews.

Like Streisand's "Hello, Gorgeous," Radner's "It couldn't hurt" became the quotable nugget that spoke of its times through Yiddish inflection. A grandparent's answer to nearly any whether-or-not clause, "it couldn't hurt," is to say that more is more, not less. Where Streisand's reflexive moment in the mirror is a personal one to which a broader public can most likely relate, Radner's direct address to the camera offers this cultural dictum as if it were also up for grabs. Why not try it, the final line provokes, suggesting an acknowledged sense of achievement for US Jews who had moved from lowly ethnic immigrants into the white majority.

Unlike the ever-childlike impersonations of Brice and Streisand, and also unlike the bawdy bodily humor of Tucker and the party album comics that followed, Radner's era saw the rise of Jewish female comics who played with their celebrity platforms in ways that made fun of their fame and the money they made. In the context of ethnic assimilation, this meant the ability to comment on the newfound points of access they now enjoyed. Such representations broadcasted the upward mobility of Jews as an obnoxious and enviable stage of the American dream wherein Jewish women were funny and famous, and now because of that, somehow newly sexy, too.

SEXY JEWS AND LEGGY MOVES: BUNNIES, BABES, AND MERMAID MANEUVERS

By the time Streisand graced the cover of *Playboy* magazine in 1977, her celebrity image had been transformed from funniness to a less than obvious realm of newfound sexiness.[38] In the cover shot, Streisand wears tiny white shorts and a T-shirt emblazoned with the *Playboy* logo. All legs, she poses with the self-referential caption, "What's a nice girl like me doing on the cover of *Playboy*?" In Henry Bial's discussion of this career-affirming maneuver, the question reads like a thought-bubble for the unconventional cover girl and a boundary crossed for Jewish women. Asking with the title and scope of his article, "How Jews Became Sexy, 1968–1983," Bial contends that the celebrity successes of Jews in the mainstream account for a consummate shift in the US entertainment history. He cites Barbra Streisand and Woody Allen as key examples, and in doing so links a process of becoming sexy to commercial success. Bial thus pairs Jewish sex appeal with class affluence made possible by ethnic assimilation.

But whereas the terms of Bial's focus emphasize the increase in Jewish celebrity visibility, his discussion of sexiness deals with gender only peripherally. Even as he positions Streisand's *Playboy* debut as an "apotheosis of an evolution in the way the Jewish body is perceived by an American audience," Bial invokes a Jewish discourse around gender without fleshing it out entirely.[39] An opaque conflation of *Playboy* and Hollywood success leaves readers to fill in the blanks about the precise relationship between celebrity Jewish bodies and their newfound sexiness after 1968. In his estimation, the "gawky singer," together with "geeky comedian" Woody Allen, helped shift the way Jewishness was perceived as an element of sexual desirability.[40] As "sexy superstars of the 1980s," Allen and Streisand fulfilled materialist Jewish fantasies wherein money equals power and power equals sex appeal.

When Bial does address femininity outright, it is in relation to the ability of Streisand to manipulate her anxious Jewish looks. Even as Bial admits that the idea of what it means to "look Jewish" has varied significantly from context to context, he argues that women who do, stereotypically speaking, look Jewish can gain acceptance not by erasing, hiding, or avoiding their Jewish looks but by "acting Jewish."[41] Acting Jewish, as in Radner's parodied material girl and Streisand's self-doubting cover girl, becomes a way for Jewish women to openly acknowledge their non-normative feminine looks and reclaim their funny power as sexiness.

For readers who know this experience of going from outcast to performer too well, there is no doubt that this ability to yield a workable sexiness with funny power based on pained aspects of ourselves is not only convincing, but extends well beyond Jewishness. What is compelling about Bial's formulation, however, is less the possibility of a female sexiness that sources its own funny pain as part and parcel of its craft than his emphasis on economic mobility as a guiding factor in US performance history. The intersection of this celebrity sexiness with the performance of gender is especially revealing. In a mid-1990s interview with Linda Ellerbee, Streisand explained why she didn't approve the bunny outfit shot for the magazine:

I was the first woman actress to be on the cover of *Playboy* who was interviewed inside, and I posed in a bunny suit. The picture was great. Nothing nasty, just long legs. I'm sorry now I never allowed them to print it because I was so afraid it was betraying the feminist issue. I thought the women would get mad at me, but the truth is, if I can have good legs and also be smart and also be able to direct movies, why am I apologizing for this?[42]

Streisand reflects back on what guided her decision making at the time, when she did not want to betray "the feminist issue" by allowing the magazine to publish its trademark bunny-styled photos of her. Her comment offers insight into her generation of women, who had similar feelings about how they were willing to be seen and portrayed, given the political charge of the feminist movement at the time. To be heralded by *Playboy* was one thing, but to be bunnified was another. By the mid-1990s, when she made the quoted comments, Streisand was speaking of "the truth" of her legs, her intelligence, and her filmic career as if they were of equal status, from an older, and perhaps more self-resolved place, but also arguably from a postfeminist perspective. When imagined in the light of a funny girl gazing back—first at her *Playboy* readers, and later at her younger self in retrospect—the photo shoot reveals Streisand's struggle with her own representation in ways that speak to the story of funny girl bodies becoming sexy ones, and the ambivalence of her era in the shift from second wave feminism to the period that followed.

Streisand's original prudishness about the publication of the photos stemmed from her protection of the feminist position, which she understood as antithetical to the iconic *Playboy*'s bunny. Playing up her Jewishness on the cover photo would have offered a partial answer to the question of what to do. A similar sentiment circulated in other Jewish female acts of her generation even when they played with barely clad personas, but always within expressly Jewish contexts or "outsider" frameworks. Comic actress Madeline Kahn's performance of the sexy saloon girl was one such plot. In Mel Brooks's satirical Western comedy *Blazing Saddles* (1974), Kahn plays Lili von Shtupp, a German seductress-for-hire and a humorously mediocre lounge singer.[43] The scene sits within the larger scope of the film's revision of history and nationalist lore. Full of narrative, character, and musical anachronisms that mean to reverse racial stereotypes, Brooks's *Blazing Saddles* pokes holes in Hollywood's mythic personification of the American West.[44] The humor of Kahn's hypersexualized personification is only legible within a Jewish parody of German fascism.

In one scene, von Shtupp performs burlesque for the saloon boys (see figure 2.6). She enters dressed in the hypersexual look of lingerie and garter belt, stockings, and heels. Her blank expression comes across as too cool for the adoring catcalls of her cowboy audience, but we realize soon that it is because she is too tired to care. "I'm tired / tired of being admired," she sings, reaching for the wall but missing her grip. Her burlesque offers a show within a show, in which the stage number is yet further evidence of the role

Figure 2.6: Screen shot, Madeline Kahn as Lili von Schtupp in *Blazing Saddles* (1974). Directed by Mel Brooks.

von Schtupp plays throughout the film. *Shtupping*, cunningly, is a Yiddish obscenity for heterosexual male penetration, and thus encodes in the character's name the farce of Kahn's deliberate ethnicization of the German saloon girl and her shiksa sexiness.[45] The joke that she is tired of being admired suggests that the blonde seductress has been having lots of sex. And yet the physical humor of Kahn's excessive exhaustion comes across as if she cannot manage the role of saloon girl, as if she is done trying to play the part of a femme fatale and cannot be bothered. The boredom with sex is a familiar stereotype of the Jewish American princess, who is famously unenthusiastic about sex.[46]

The unsexy details of Kahn's exhaustion extend across the bit and come to speak for larger political satire. Her long, guttural "ahhhhhs" are more moan than tuned note, and the suggestive way she sits with her legs open is muted by a vocal lisp that slips into Yiddish inflections. At the end of the act, Kahn is joined by four backup dancers dressed as rifle-wielding German soldiers. They enter with the unison steps of a spoofed Nazi army to protect the star and her need to rest. Brooks's own voice dubs over a chorus dancer with the classic trope of the Jewish mother, pleading with a drunkard from the crowd who jumps onto the edge of the stage: "Don't you know she's pooped?!" A pooped femme fatale is funny for its inversion of the dangerous woman and its deflation of German virility. By acting Jewish and acting sexy, too, Kahn's German saloon girl, guarded by a Nazi entourage, simultaneously retaliates against German fascism and American anti-Semitism.

Kahn's characterization differed from Streisand's virile shtick for *Playboy* due to her non-Jewish looks, which let Kahn sex-up a fascist femme fatale who can only fall asleep. Both, however, underscored the impossibility of sex appeal even as they played it up, bringing back the humor of Brice's "Becky" in this way, Streisand through her duckishness, and Kahn through her embodiment of the ultimate shiksa threat/fantasy.

In the same years, Jewish (looking) stage sensation Bette Midler was drawing growing crowds for her Sophie Tucker–style performances. Coming up as a gay male icon in the bathhouses of New York City, Midler first performed with "Divine friends" Barry Manilow and Joni Mitchell at the Continental in 1971, getting her nickname Bathhouse Betty.[47] In her first steamy performance, she sang and sweated on a stage built for her by venue owner Steve Ostrow, entertaining with an hour of original and cover songs that revived a Jewish vaudeville tradition. One costume change had her dressed as Carmen Miranda, with a towel wrapped around her hair topped with plastic fruit. She egged on her audience of men, naming herself their Jewish mother who only wants them to have fun.

Midler soon established herself as a star with enormous success and a world tour, in which she first performed my personal favorite of her repertoire, Delores De Lago. Part island exotic, part swamp lady, Midler's mermaid muse, beached permanently in a wheelchair, evolved over a long and varied career. Initially conceived as a lounge act under another name, the bit began as a bipedal babe and reoccurred many times before its ultimate iterations as paraplegic fish out of water. In one early rendition made for television, Midler stars in *Hawaiian Oklahoma* on NBC, emerging in an oversized clam after having been fished out and presumably rescued by the singing and dancing natives.[48] The clamshell routine, and its comic reference to oversized vaginas, predates the De Lago role by some years. Possibly also a play on her *haole* upbringing in Hawaii, the island fantasy returns to the ethnoracial appropriations of Jewish vaudeville with biographical implications. At the end of a remixed "Oklahoma," she returns to the large shell for an onstage exit, pulling one of the conch blowers into the clam bed with her just as it closes, in time for the cast to hit its hood with happy blessings that send them back to sea.

In 1978 Midler went on her first world tour, appearing as De Lago for the first time. The anonymous island chorus and clam were replaced by a mermaid-in-a-wheelchair act with backup singer-dancers in similar getups (see figure 2.7). The romantic with bound legs became a regular act, with additions to costume and choreography made for each iteration. Performed by Midler throughout her career, the bit plays out the impossible sexiness of a washed-up, underwater nymph in a busty sequined bikini and chiffon accents. Always returning in highly aerobic roles, Midler's mermaid and the taper of the scaly tale regularly require her to jump through the entirety of song and dance portions, often with tricky dives and dismounts that stick perfect landings, even into her fifties. The dancerly skill is always evident, as she ends quite exhausting routines with just as routine a contagious smile and her characteristic gesture of one very graceful arm up overhead, exposing her early ballet training. Midler's ability to play well with her practiced dance body through verbal and physical punchlines is what drives the parody of this fish-out-of-water portrait of a woman.

Figure 2.7: Screen shot, Bette Midler in *Bette Midler in Concert: Diva Las Vegas* (1997). Directed by Marty Callner.

Midler maneuvers her bawdy body with dancerly grace, in contrast to Brice's and Streisand's practiced gracelessness. To compare these women's work is less to judge their prowess than to mark the ways they framed physical techniques of parody that carried out previous traditions while constructing new modes. How they approached the performance of femininity while looking or acting "Jewish" lends insight into the ways their embodiments responded to and helped constitute changing discourses around them. When viewed together, Streisand, Radner, Kahn, and Midler flesh out a generation of Jewish women who were fragile or flippant about men, but always in tune with feminist thinking. And yet as each emerges in the context of newfound access to white American mainstream, they play differently with being seen as viable sexual beings as if for the first time.

In one Delores De Lago number named "Ballin' with the Oldies," Midler and her backup mermaids mock up a Richard Simmons–esque workout with sexually suggestive, and as Midler explains, divinely ordained exercise balls. When used properly, the bit suggests, they sustain the bounce of her breasts to the beat of the song.[49] Mocking the exercise mania that best illustrates the 1980s and its associations with blonder icons like Jane Fonda, Midler's campy play contends with the desiring gaze presumed by the workout video genre and throws balls in its face.

Midler's career biography retains a queer appeal, with her having been actor, singer, and gay male icon since her younger performance years. Breaking with waspy ideals of demure femininity and overriding the role of heterosexual man, Midler makes visible and material reference to her own bawdy sexual power, treating his balls and her own breasts as playthings. To sexualize a hyperfemininity for homosexual men and their friends enacts a counterdiscourse on gender and sexuality, revising what it means to be sexy and even what it means to be feminine or effeminate (for herself or men in her crowd). Midler's signature blend of outlandish characterizations constructs her performance of femininity through camp, and with a sense of her own sexy star power. Flaunting her Jewish and female excess as godly gifts of a jokish divine ordinance, the flirtatious tail flapping of Delores De Lago's auto-impersonations seems to flip staid notions about the performance of gender upside down with choreographed control.

As Midler is confined in a wheelchair of chastity, she contrasts with Kahn's saloon performance, which straddles its inverse. Both acts spotlight the lower body, the legs and the female sex organs. How their low bodies move or fail to move makes fun of age old sacred-profane archetypes through the humor of Jewish female sexuality that is either too excited or too bored about sex to have any. The result in both cases punctures grand narratives about what a woman gets to do and how. It also foregrounds preferences for social and political satire in queerer spaces and Jewish movies. Like Radner's self-conscious display of her long and lean body, too, Streisand dangles a bared limb down her *Playboy* pedestal while questioning herself. Wondering what a nice Jewish girl like her is doing on the cover of *Playboy* magazine, she provides her leggy display as only part of the answer, having worked her way up and famously on her own terms. Those are the same legs that limped instead of leapt and so on in her chicken ballet, after all, which would forever remind us of her ethnic ties to lowlier roots. The self-reflexive bodily displays of Streisand's cover girl, Radner's princess parody, Kahn's seductress, and Midler's mermaid signal the funny girl body as one aware of its star power, sexiest when playing up, but unbound by, the ethnic excesses and gender difference they sang and danced about.

CONCLUSION

From Streisand's disregard for the *Swan Lake* Prince to Midler's ball play, Jewish celebrity icons of the late 1960s and 1970s subverted social codes with their ethnic and gender interplays. Jokes by women about men, about marriage, and about themselves return to tropes of domesticity and the business of the family as tied to class-consciousness and race anxieties. Heterosexist by design, the verbal and physical joke-work across these topics upturns masculinist scripts dominant in Jewish traditions and mainstream America alike that define a woman and how she moves. But as frontwomen with or without backup singers and dancers, Jewish comediennes have largely done this alone. In solo acts, Jewish female performers have reached for their audiences as covert accomplices in heist-styled takeovers. Divas of their own performance domains, they are larger than life and thus larger than the disappointments of love.

Reiterating versions of what Stacy Wolf described as Streisand's "beautiful ugly"[50] routine through various tactics, these Jewish female comics of the twentieth century either personified Jewishness as more raunchy than pretty or made it funny to play sexy. Between overbearing demands of the Jewish mother and sexually frigid materialism of the Jewish American princess, performers invoked stereotypes that variously downplayed their desirability or otherwise delivered it as bigger than life, too big for men. Drawing on the dancing humor and body talk of earlier comic women, they embodied caricatures of themselves as red hot and ballsy or defunct, desexualized swans. Playing up outsider status as Jews and women, performers in each case fleshed out a physical humor tradition that skewered social standards, especially regarding marriage and men.

In doing so, Jewish female comic women waged war against patriarchal codes key to their times. Cartooning their impossible feminine mystique and labeling it Jewish gave permission for Jewish and non-Jewish audiences to laugh at conventions throughout most of the twentieth century.

What distinguishes the works of Streisand, Radner, Midler, and Kahn from their predecessors, Brice, Tucker, and Betty Boop, is the proximal distance to white femininity that enacting something "Jewish" affords. "Red hot" torch songs and blue humor expanded Tucker's reach from early career blackface gender drag to sexually frank permissions for women of every size and creed to be and feel sexy. Her red and blue jokes became white ones as mainstream America made a place for Jewish women's joke-work to rail against domesticity and offer a temporary escape from middle-class blandness. Betty Boop's shapeshifting ghetto girl showed how malleable the performance of identity could be in the taste for "open ethnicity" through the 1930s. Vaudeville acts best known for their range of race and gender impersonations thus helped acculturate Jewish women into the urban American mainstream, both free of ethnic constraints and tethered to its outsider status.

As an embodied history of Jewish female joke-work took shape through these ribald acts, what it meant to be Jewish and female shifted in relation to cultural, economic, and geographic factors. The GI Bill in the postwar years and the growing women's movement of the 1960s and 1970s helped usher in a new generation of Jewish female comics who returned to joke legacies of the past as subversive interventions into the patriarchal controls still delimiting women's roles. Against this backdrop, Streisand's swan sang and danced of the jokish unassimilability of immigrants and their un-American antics. In a tribute to both past and present periods, the Yiddish swan looks at herself in the mirror, puncturing middle-class pretentions she also wishes were reflected back.

The enormous celebrity success of Streisand in that role put her on the cover of *Playboy*, asking jokingly what a nice girl was doing in a place like that, as her contemporaries rose nearly as high in the richly sexy 1970s. Enjoying lucrative popularity in mainstream television, movies, and world tours, Jewish comic women played roles that pierced anti-Semitism by stoking its flames, revising stereotypes of the Jewish male schlemiel by way of female fabulousness (Midler), oversexed exhaustion (Kahn), and effortless glamour (Radner). Midler's beginnings in the gay male bathhouses in New York City made her a queer camp icon, and Kahn's femme fatale couldn't care less about desirous men. Clowning the conventions of heterosexual love altogether, each riffed on the outmoded happy-ever-after, making happier audiences of the early 1980s who no longer subscribed to family values in the same ways.

Altogether, these performances outline a twentieth-century legacy of Jewish female comedy in which the range of physical and dancing humor constitutes a history of the funny girl body becoming sexy. The following chapters focus on twenty-first-century celebrity figures, but return again and again to these foundational techniques of voice, gesture, face, costume, and leggy maneuvers that move up the ranks of an American mainstream.

CHAPTER 3

Comic Glory (and Guilt)

The Appropriative License of Jewish Female Comedy

In the cherished dance legacy of Jewish female joke-work, Jewish women have continued to rehearse comic techniques of the yiddishized clown, the female misfit, and the unassimilable immigrant through the late twentieth and into the twenty-first centuries.

This extension across generations follows a reiterative model wherein the return to tropes of early comic stars accompanies context-specific shifts in performance tone and bodily tactics. It is this reiterative impulse that makes the best case for a postfeminist, postassimilatory framework, one that points simultaneously forward and backward in time. This chapter aims to help mark the reiterative shifts into these parallel "posts" through a focus on celebrity Jewish comics of the 1990s through the present. I argue that comic performers in this chapter foreground the continuous citation of Jewish femininity to license perverse slides between majoritarian and minoritarian points of view that both promise a progressive ethos around race justice and liberated sexuality and do so through their gross appropriations. In this sense, these performers embody the comic glory of celebrity platforms with enormous public reach and the guilt of mainstream white access, a tension that speaks to the performative capacity of Jewish female joke-work to physicalize and verbalize sustained "in-betweeness" on a massive scale.

The jumble of identities that contemporary Jewish women claim and critique from celebrity platforms adds kinks to Jewish female comedy imagined throughout the twentieth century. New joke-work leans on familiar premises of these performing women being not quite right, and not quite not, whether construed in racialized or sexualized terms, but does so with newfound access to the majoritarian mainstream. From this self-critical place of same-different, performers play up positions of power and alterity, access and alienation, center and margin. Performing self as, with, and dependent upon the Other, they present themselves by way of refusing any singularity of self-definitions or alliances. In this way, contemporary comics construct the twenty-first-century Sexy Jewess as an intersubjective figure hyperaware of her own layered racialization and sexualization, and one who stages these often contradictory identities upfront and center.

The performance analysis of this chapter starts with Sandra Bernhard's *Without You, I'm Nothing* (1990), focusing on her physical and verbal deployments of Jewishness as they relate to blackness, bisexuality, whiteness, and womanhood. The chapter compares the joke-work of Bernhard's film to a selection of works by celebrity comic counterpart Sarah Silverman from 2005, 2007, and 2008. Silverman's career has a much straighter hold on a heterosexual mainstream viewer base, even as it explores ever more oppositional content. Finally, the chapter draws on excerpts of Comedy Central's *Broad City*, which stars its cowriters, Abbi Jacobson and Ilana Glazer (2014–), as a site of millennial remixing in which deliberate misappropriations meet sexual freedoms in ways that signal the glory and guilt of the Sexy Jewess in all her extremes. I focus on these three decades of artists and performances because of their shared practice of interweaving identity acts and impersonations as intersubjective roles in their repertoire. I argue that the connections they animate among Jewish identity, race impersonation, and sexual freedoms leverage Jewishness as a comic appropriative license, a fast pass that drives into the wreck of white guilt, and with speed.

As these performers demonstrate, the contemporary reiteration of Jewish female "in-betweeness" occurs in large part through the intersections of identities that don't level out. This happens especially through double personifications of blackness and bisexuality, whereby performers call out race injustice while claiming sexual freedoms as part of their Jewish female shtick. This impulse arguably extends an early twentieth-century Jewish tradition of black impersonation though the twenty-first century and its associations with gender-bending performances for women, wherein women blacked-up as men to gain access to male-run entertainment circuits. In ways that resonate with the antiestablishment ethos of contemporary Jewish female comics, turn-of-the-century Jewish women joined immigrant waves of comic performers to skewer authority through personification of marginalized figures they both identified with and distanced themselves from in the very act of performance. For female performers, the practice granted access to a male-run industry by butching up through black cork makeup. Scholarship on Jewish male performers has cast the practice as reflective of interracial desire, but for Jewish female performers, has largely remained untheorized in relation to sexuality.[1]

Today's reiterations of the practice foreground the intersection of race play and sexual desires as a core part of their joke-work. In the analysis that follows, I argue that contemporary Jewish female comics turn to blackness to disavow postassimilatory whiteness and the guilty privileges it brings, while exaggerating postfeminist sexual freedoms. The performers discussed in this chapter imitate and parody whites impersonating blacks, all the while sourcing Jewishness to undiscipline sex and sex appeal. In doing so, they perform a host of appropriations they mean to deconstruct in the name of exposing racism and destabilizing whiteness. A large part of that destabilization is the invocation of same-sex desires that likewise do not and cannot resolve, but not for the same reasons or with the same effects. This paradox mobilizes physical humor that is at once self-reflexive and political, social and sexual, reappropriative and misappropriative. As performers recuperate repressed identities—in a tangle of Jewishness, blackness, and bisexuality—they work to dismantle racist thinking through surfacing same-sex desires, while repeating the erasure of black bodies and voices they approximate but never fully acknowledge.

When conceived in the context of celebrity comedy since 1990, in-betweenness embodies a unique take on performing identity with massive reach in a period when identity politics comes to matter more than ever before. As performers surface and criticize race, class, sex, and gender disparities that affect the country's most marginalized groups, they thus echo the nuanced work of amateur artists like the Schlep Sisters or Little Brooklyn (as discussed in chapter 1), but on a much larger scale. In contrast to the do-it-yourself dens of the neoburlesque performance circuit, celebrity female comics navigate a male-run industry that must always contend with its young, white, male base. Moreover, when celebrity performers take on identity as joke material, they serve up exaggerated selves and others as public personages informed by the sheer scale of audience and access to the major tools of popular culture's social impact. For such large-scale social actors, the entangled messes made of identity-based material necessarily blast beyond the personal. Understanding this public practice of self-referential performance and impersonation as an extension and revision of the comic history that preceded it, this chapter takes up where the last one left off, progressing chronologically through the next moves of the Sexy Jewess in the mainstream.

As accumulative points of access within and beyond the entertainment industry whitened America's Jews throughout the bulk of the twentieth century, the roles in which Jewish women performed themselves also necessarily multiplied. Surely the reverse formulation is also true, in which the performance of new techniques and personages invited audiences to see and think in new ways about Jewish female performers and themselves. Performers reiterated a familiar self-reflexivity, but with a kind of double consciousness that paired defunct femininity with the Jewish guilt of white privilege by way of heightening its blind spots and bad behavior. These are the self-conscious terms of the postfeminist, postassimilatory turn that this chapter's performances embody best. Abstract and nebulous as is any cultural turn, this one revolves around a new period of Jewish female comedy that moves into the murky postscripts of twentieth-century assimilation and women's liberation. In other words, these comics head into the age of identity politics face first.

The chapter thus begins in the significant period of the 1990s, amid the heated culture wars and the myths of multiculturalism. It points forward into the so-called postracial world of the Obama era, whose bubbles burst with the overt racial and sexual antagonisms of the inauguration that followed. What resounds over the stretch of three decades are the identity plays of Jewish female comics that, while extending comic traditions of those before them, toy much more with their own contradictions. They flesh out a mission of social justice spliced with the sourest of social misdoings; a representational discourse of stand-up comedy, sketch television, and funny dancing manifested through a deliberately appropriative tangle of identities. The results of their impersonation remain incoherent, and for this they tend to offer only partial apology. Inevitably, the funny thing of the Sexy Jewess in each case carries with it the violence of misrepresentation even in the name of its skewed opposite, empathy.

SANDRA BERNHARD AND THE I/YOU OTHER

In 1990, queer female comic celebrity icon Sandra Bernhard starred in her one-woman concert film, *Without You, I'm Nothing*. The show within a show marked a fictive return to her early days of performance in the smoky jazz dens of Los Angeles's supper club scene.[2] A mockumentary-styled movie, the piece is a filmic version of her Broadway act from two years earlier, reset for an all-black on-camera audience that performs its indifference to her fame, her soliloquys, and her intimate confessions, difficult as they are to swallow or follow. Bernhard's script consists of amorphous rants and diatribes that move from fragments of her own true-ish history (family trips to the World's Fair; tickets to see Barbra Streisand) to queer dreams of a better world without racism, sexism, and fascism, indebted to disco and funk, all of which she delivers with an iconic black spoken word effect to a black club that couldn't care less. [3]

Bernhard delivers her opening lines into the mirror in a backstage scene that reiterates Streisand's famous entrance in *Funny Girl*. More confrontational than Streisand, Bernhard addresses her viewers directly, "You know, I have one of those really hard-to-believe faces." Drawing her nose and lips together, she explains, "It's sensual, sexual; at times, it's just downright hard-to-believe. I wish you could kiss me right now. Just this side of my nose." The preference for which side of her nose she'd like to be kissed also recalls

Streisand, who famously preferred to be photographed in left profile. "Just a silly little peck, so to speak, as it were," Bernhard adds, layering her old-fashioned niceties like femininities past. With a tone of voice that implies anything but what she says, she continues, "I am so glad you can see how truly beautiful I am right now." The look in her eyes dares the viewer to call her bluff, as the cold, prolonged stare into the camera sets the stage for what's coming as the murky inverse of what it seems (see figure 3.1).

As the monologue's self-assurances address her out-of-film critics head on, Bernhard introduces her character as herself. She talks back to the barrage of commentary on her features, most notoriously her pronounced nose and lips. Called "la jolie-laide" or beautiful-ugly woman and regularly cited for her oversized features, by this time Bernhard had already made a name for herself as an impolite postfeminist Jewish female artist who broke with all standards of appropriateness through her attitude and her looks.[4] Later named in a 2012 issue of *Interview Magazine* as the original queen of punk-rock performance-art musical comedy, Bernhard states that she built her career on such emboldened platforms. Confessing in that interview that the most important, overriding arc of her three-decade career had been "a refusal to be self-deprecating," Bernhard claimed her postfeminist stance as a conscious break from the past, both in feminist discourse and in the kind of humor so familiar from women in comedy.[5] Citing the leading white and mostly Jewish feminist voices of the 1970s, Bernhard described the cultural background of her formative years as inspired by radical women and their public platforms.[6] The "new place" Bernhard envisioned was one that carried the torch of second wave feminism and its landmark wins for women's choice, while moving into

Figure 3.1: Screen shot, Sandra Bernhard's opening monologue in *Without You, I'm Nothing* (1990). Directed by Joseph Yacoe.

the period that followed. Bernhard's point of view looked forward and backward at the same time, intervening in social and stage discourses linked to Jewishness, gender, and comedy by way of their reiteration and revision.

That new place was be wickedly funny, and visibly Jewish, but moved away from the tenor of female comedians before her. Bernhard lists Jewish greats Phyllis Diller, Joan Rivers, and Totie Fields (who add to the cache of Jewish female comics discussed in the previous chapter) as continuing the traditions of self-mocking, inferior women. About these earlier comics, Bernhard explains, "It was like, 'I'm fat! I'm ugly! My husband has to put a bag over my head when he comes to bed!'" Bernhard remembers deciding, "I'm never gonna do that," to which interviewer and comic actress Roseanne Barr adds that she always felt the same way. The humor that the two agree to avoid is the near-classic trope of the Jewish female hag, who is too ugly to be desired by men and whose face must be covered to illicit proper arousal. A jokish mechanism imagined to shut a wife up and shut her down in the process, the bag symbolized the precise kind of censorship that came off for Bernhard's generation of liberated women's voices.

Trading out the old bag for a high fashion style that made her famous, Bernhard foregrounded her layered play with her high-low looks as core to her celebrity persona and creative power. Her nose, which like Streisand she never changed despite industry pressures, rendered her face both visually and politically provocative, waging its ethnic protest against facial standards of straight white womanhood. Also like Streisand, her long, lean white body could play with any number of feminine personages, and Bernhard also posed for *Playboy* at the peak of her career. A fashion icon and a funny face, Bernhard's identity acts and impersonations throughout the film cannot be viewed outside of this frame. Her opening monologue's heightened attention to the physical and symbolic dimensions of her images invites audiences into the film's race and sex representations.

When we see the club for the first time, it is in framed fragments of black lips and faces that fill the room with smoke and stand-up bass. Onstage, Bernhard is dressed in African garb—head wrap and large hoop earrings— singing Nina Simone's "Four Women." Her offenses increase with each stanza, as she sings of her skin being black, tan, and brown as if in solidarity with women of color through a song about suffering and recuperative self-image. Exultantly throwing her hands up in the air while belting the end of the song, "They call me Peaches," Bernhard then blinks rapidly to signal her self-ironizing lack of a clue as she waits for applause she doesn't get (see figure 3.2). The crowd is anything but interested in Bernhard's appropriative antics here and throughout the show, revealing the chasm between them and a darkly parodied Jewish-black alliance that she seems to say only Jews imagine.

The multiple impersonations of race and gender that follow are equally outrageous and self-mockingly one-directional, as they extend to a slew of other

Figure 3.2: Screen shot, Sandra Bernhard singing Nina Simone's "Four Women" in *Without You, I'm Nothing* (1990). Directed by Joseph Yacoe.

black, white, and Jewish acts, layered with equally changing confessions of sex and sexuality. Throughout, Bernhard upsets clear relationships between categories as if that disorientation itself is what matters most. Indeed, the very construction of identity and identification in Bernhard's film underscores the significance of their blurring. This is Bernhard's configuration and comment on the intersectionality of race, gender, and sexuality in the critical feminist spotlight of the early 1990s. Rather than smooth out or polish over the awkward misalignments of identity politics she brings to the surface, Bernhard stages the sinewy interstices in between. With a blend of bodily and verbal personifications that reflect the problems of representation, she signals the problems of intersection through the failure of their cohesion.

In this way the film ushers in a significant new stage of postfeminist, postassimilationist performance in which worse-than-faux-pax provocations form and are formed by a newfound Jewish entrance into the white majority. Bernhard destabilizes the privileges whiteness brings by exposing the worst of its extremes and does so through the embodiment of racialized, sexualized impersonations that her liminality and looks render Jewishly. Bernhard's self-conscious performance of Jewishness thus plays same and different as bodily conditions of her layered in-betweeness. Bernhard embodies her Jewishness as a kind of appropriative license that impersonates black tropes and experiences as both within her reach and always beyond it. Bernhard further blurs her position with intentionally obscure expressions of same-sex desire.

In the film's explicit conflation of blackness and bisexuality, Bernhard appears in an orange lycra onesie with bell bottoms to perform her gender-bending cover of Billy Paul's "Me and Mrs. Jones" (see figure 3.3). Introducing

Figure 3.3: Screen shot, Sandra Bernhard singing "Me and Mrs. Jones" in *Without You, I'm Nothing* (1990). Directed by Joseph Yacoe.

the song by sitting her "big, fat, lazy ass down," she pitches the timbre of her voice to sound stereotypically black, while gesturing to her own slender frame. The body and face continue their joke that is both overtly and deliberately racist as Bernhard limps her wrists while lifting her eyebrows as if with too much effort. She and the camera pause for a suspended look at her long, curled red nails. Before singing, she explains that she's been all over the country with her Jewish piano player, who in reality is the African American Vanessa Burch who is not Jewish. The inversion passes unnoticed in the film, but signals Bernhard's excessive racial elisions and erasures. It also sets up the bisexual indications of the song to come, as Burch seems to become Mrs. Jones in this instance. The racial reversal suggests an interracial relationship that indicates Bernhard's appropriative deployment of blackness as a critical part of her known yet not publicly declared bisexuality.[7]

The act blurs sexuality while exaggerating its racial play. In doing so, it renders Bernhard's Jewishness the bodily factor that slips between both bisexuality and blackness, but only incoherently. This failure underscores the dark humor of such a conflation that can only cause more harm. In a stab at the white sexual liberation discourse of her era, and her own participation in it, Bernhard exposes the gross claims to universal womanhood that left women of color out of the conversation and problematically drew on civil rights discourses to render movements against racism and sexism as equal emancipations.[8] Bernhard's act thus mucks up the logic of lesbian desire and identity theft, as she steals the race of her pianist while singing her a love song. The love and theft recall the core premise of the seminal scholarship on turn-of-the-century blackface performance, wherein white ethnics engaged in similarly doubled expressions of a one-way imagination of the more othered other.[9] In the context of the postfeminist, postassimilationist shift Bernhard's movie makes manifest, this invocation of love and theft is foregrounded less as the psychosocial condition of anxious assimilation and more as the ironic, self-critical humor of Jewish femininity after white entry.

In addition to her black impersonations, Bernhard's exaggerated Jewish personages occur by way of appropriating and approximating a slew of identifications that can only offend or bore her black onscreen audience. The first of these stands out for its sheer obliviousness. After shaming herself and her black audience through her Peaches rendition, she re-enters as a stereotypical Jewish woman from New York. She wears a maroon velvet pants suit and bright pink lipstick and has her hair blown out in an outmoded style. She sings "Hinei Ma Tov," a Hebrew song generally saved for religious schoolchildren, and invites everyone to clap along. They don't, and she doesn't seem to notice. Instead, she launches into a non sequitur diatribe about a family vacation to the World's Fair the year that *Funny Girl* came out. Her father tried to get tickets, but they were sold out. "Barbra Streisand, Barbra Streisand," the name, delivered with the reiterative weighted gravity of a Jewish pop cultural past by now most cherished by gay white men, punctuates her indecipherable story with vocal impersonation of an archetypal black spoken word poet.

This bit formulates the causal relationship of her own awkwardness among those without whom, as the title suggests, she's nothing. And in important ways, it happens through the problem of her white body and Jewish face. The camera comes straight in on the issue of her physique for the first time, in a rolling close shot that moves up from her feet at the base of the microphone. She stands flat to the mic in an unexpected second position, her legs turned out with awkward confidence. Bernhard's bodily display here is that of the dominant but socially oblivious Jewish woman who uses the monologue like one-way talk therapy. Bearing all by talking too much and too openly, she overlooks the dulling effect of her oversharing. When the camera gets to her face, she looks up from the dead silent crowd to see that no one cares. The face itself wears Bernhard's near-permanent expression of displeasure, rendered by the downward drape of her lips and nose. Does it care what it sees or does? For audiences on-screen and not, she works her expression so that it is never possible to know.

As recognizable a face as she may have, Bernhard's use of her face in and as joke-work also extends to the ways she performs her set of racialized impersonations (i.e., blackface, Jewface, and whiteface), which though naming themselves after the face, in Bernhard's case implicate the entire body. It is her recognizable face and its Jewish excesses in relation to mainstream celebrity (read: white) women's faces that allow her to signal her play with and distance from the *in*appropriate appropriations she undertakes to undo. Her Jewish face—the inappropriate thing she wears front and center—allows her to slide into black impersonations differently than other white women would or could. And yet it is her body that allows her to engage with whiteness in ways that work through her race privilege with humor.

Her whiteface bits make fun of prudish white women who appear entirely unaware of their audiencess or themselves. Stretches of her monologues recall Christmas fantasies as fake snow falls, while musicians join her onstage dressed in costumes from various points in Western history while a Christmas choir accompanies them with Freddie Kruger claws. "May all your Christmases be white," she tells the crowd, mocking the racial *mal entendre* that excludes Jews and blacks alike. Then, impersonating whiteness again, Bernhard plays a young woman recounting her first day on the job and the thrill of a date that night with the boss in San Francisco. Sensualizing the office misogyny that sustains the glass ceiling for women at work, Bernhard lies passionately, "I have never felt straighter!" To exaggerate the irony further, she describes the feeling of caressing her "huge breasts" as she does it, forcing attention to her breasts, which are barely there.

In a world where nothing is true, everything is up for grabs. What that means for Bernhard's world of impersonated identity acts and cultural appropriations is that she performs whiteface, blackface, and Jewface impersonations while also showing the ways these roles do not and cannot carry equal weight. Any effort to distinguish among gender, race, class, and sexuality is blurred by Bernhard's repertoire of roles and the ways they knot webs of identity categories through exaggerated movements in and between them. Keenly aware of the heightened identity politics of her day, Bernhard's funny girl persona was an extension of Streisand's era and yet a different story altogether. The intersectionality of race, gender, and sex discourses was a topic more and more pressing in the public realm, largely made possible by the work of black women pushing the feminist conversation forward. The conspicuous white consumption of blackness and the offenses of white second wave feminism were especially charged in the multicultural rhetoric of the period, and Bernhard's film was both part of that pushback and the pushback against that pushback.

Garnering the nuanced criticism of some of the greatest contemporary feminist writers, *Without You, I'm Nothing* made a huge impact with its ironic engagement of critical race and gender consciousness as much a part of 1990s scholarship as public discourse.[10] In her reading of the film, bell hooks recognizes the important incongruity of Bernhard's racial play, where race and cultural appropriation is always imitation and therefore always fake. And yet, though she appreciates Bernhard's layered critique of race that punctures terrorizing grand narratives of white social thinking, hooks argues that the film ultimately absents the black people it purports to support. As Bernhard identifies herself with marginalized Others, hooks argues that she sources her Jewish heritage as well as her sexually ambiguous erotic practices as experiences that place her outside the mainstream. I agree with hooks that, in conflating sexuality and Jewishness as outsider identities, the film fails to clarify the nature of Bernhard's identification with black culture.[11] This failure is arguably the central problem of the film, which Bernhard's exaggerations self-parody most powerfully.

In one segment Bernhard's manager implies that black women icons like Nina Simone and Diana Ross stole from Bernhard's creative work. The ironic inversion of appropriative music industry history calls attention to the way white women have stolen from black women without acknowledging the debt they owe.[12] While acknowledging the humor of this revision, hooks reminds us that Bernhard's interventions, however corrective they may seem in such a light, do not account for actual black people or their perspectives. In an incisive critique, hooks offers the key criticism that "black women have no public, paying audience for our funny imitations of white girls." Indeed, hooks continues, "it is difficult to imagine any setting other than an all black space where black women could use comedy to critique and ridicule white womanhood in the way Bernhard mocks black womanhood."[13]

The film's ending highlights this asymmetry of race representations in a deliberate displacement of desire and identification. Bernhard comes onstage wrapped in a hooded American flag, like a prizefighter addressing the crowd in a press conference confessional: "Without me," she intones, then cuts herself off and starts over. "Without you, . . . I'm nothing." She tosses off her patriotic robe to reveal sequined pasties and a flag-patterned G-string below a black-styled wig, relaxed and then curled. During the length of the full Prince recording of "Little Red Corvette," all of the black audience members leave the club—with the exception of "Roxanne"— an avatar of sorts for the African American audience, played by the young, attractive Cynthia Bailey.[14] Roxanne sits by as Bernhard stages her strip tribute to the liberatory America she says she wished for but "never was" (see figures 3.4 and 3.5). When Roxanne finally does leave, it is after writing "fuck Sandra Bernhard" in lipstick on the white tablecloth. Dressed in billowing white chiffon, her fabric creates a wing-like effect as she struts out the door and into a bright white light, a vision of superior beauty and mythic dignity. This final scene effectively diminishes Bernhard and her performance as the "nothing" her title invokes. Bernhard ultimately does not and cannot do anything to undo her whiteness except make fun of it.

Critical reception of this ending scene considers the failure of the film to disrupt diminutive racial logics, even as it blurs whether Bernhard wishes to be Roxanne or be with Roxanne.[15] Considering those two possibilities as mutually constitutive, Ann Pellegrini asks, "What if identification is one of the ruses through and by which transgressive desires are rerouted?"[16] In other words, what if identifying with blackness through its impersonation allows Bernhard's same-sex desires to surface in ways not otherwise possible? And how does that happen through ruse? Bernhard's film foregrounds the idea that identification and desire go hand in hand, rather than being antithetical

Figure 3.4: Screen shot, Sandra Bernhard's burlesque striptease in *Without You, I'm Nothing* (1990). Directed by Joseph Yacoe.

Figure 3.5: Screen shot, Sandra Bernhard's burlesque striptease in *Without You I'm Nothing* (1990). Directed by Joseph Yacoe.

to one another. There is a kind of translation from one marginalized identity to another, wherein the former acts to license the other, however impossibly. Moreover, Bernhard's layered acts of racial and sexual desire can be conceived of as transgressive identifications made powerful through their legibility as ruse, or in other words, their legibility as joke-work. Yet if for joke-work to be legible as such is largely an issue of audience and address, Bernhard appears to undertake these very topics as ones to blur at best.

In the context of an embodied realm of Jewish joke-work, the muffled lesbian desire Bernhard invokes is both a force of her social and sexual politics of visibility and also a dark joke—a ruse—that foregrounds its own misappropriation. Bernhard thus camps up an entire cast of white, black, and queer characters only to highlight the alienating effect of their exaggeration. The queer maneuvers of Bernhard's filmic stage show present an emboldened bisexuality that in its radical celebration of sexual desire and gay club life also painfully misappropriates blackness to make fun of white womanhood and Jewish liberalism. She does everything a white, Jewish woman is not allowed to do and should never do; in doing so, she outs herself as both progressively rebellious and guilty of crimes for which she is only sorry enough to stay provocative.

The postfeminist, postassimilationist Jewishness of this formulation has to do with its intersectionality, and as a personal politics of self-representation, its intersubjectiveness. The "I" in Bernhard's title, as Pellegrini writes, "whether mine, hers, or yours" is the "intersubjective site" or the place of entanglement between marks of desire and identification. Ascribing this intersubjectiveness into Bernhard's Jewish female body as its impersonations, Pellegrini determines that Bernhard articulates the specificities of her body by speaking through another Other's terms. In doing so, the comic remains "caught up in the endlessly repeating and repeated logic of identifications found, lost, and found again at someone else's address."[17] Aligning with hooks and Pellegrini in this reading of the film, I agree that Bernhard finally only disrupts monolithic whiteness by reconsolidating blackness.[18] Bernhard's dark humor relies on this point. It is this attention to the deconstruction and reconstruction of race privilege that can speak, albeit differently, to her culpable white feminist and head-shaking black audiences. Importantly, the theme is one she underscores through a self-mocking representational license of her Jewish looks and liminality.

Ultimately, while *Without You, I'm Nothing* simultaneously teases and frustrates identifications, it may be the film's intention for its audience to contend with the difficulty of recognition, and more important, self-recognition.[19] The audience on camera does not get Bernhard, and Bernhard does not get her audience. But as Pellegrini so smartly argues, the very misrecognition compels the performance.[20] By showcasing the missed connections between Bernhard and her audience, the film thus permits the cinematic spectators to gain some distance on themselves.[21] This capacity of ironic joke-work effectively requires that we, as audience, accept and examine our roles, our commitments, and our complicities.[22]

This body that performs through impersonated and appropriated terms while leaving their implications entirely up to the viewer lives at the incongruous core of the postassimilationist, postfeminist phase of contemporary Jewish female comedy. In her ambivalent interplays of race and gender, Bernhard sets the stage for the Jewish female acts discussed in the rest of this chapter, but in other ways, the boldness of her ambivalence became some-thing more legibly mainstream in the decades that followed. Why and how this shift happened accounts for the changing valences of the Jewish female comic across a comedy industry zeitgeist known for its growing support for women and race diversity.

Nearly a decade after *Without You, I'm Nothing* was released, Sarah Silverman took the spotlight for Jewish women in comedy, with the effect of catering more deliberately to the white male mainstream. In the next section I argue that Silverman sustains a familiar Jewish female self-consciousness that, like Bernhard's, foregrounds its failures of identifications through ceaseless self-conscious claims to being the worst social offender. Without a funny face, however, Silverman's Jewishness is more conceptual than visible; her Jewish identity works as content and context in ways that let her source an always-understood alterity while passing with visual authority into white womanhood. This is enhanced by her spoken and embodied professions of straightness that help her maneuver through the heterosexual matrix of a mainstream fan base. As she embodies a less-than-visible position in-between, Silverman sources her Jewish female body in different ways than Bernhard does. Embodied invo-cations of black and bisexual content showcase this best. The ways Silverman slides from racial to sexual content through vocal and bodily impersonations frames a significant shift in the ways the performance of Jewishness came to license provocative joke-work on identity politics into the first decade of the twenty-first century.

RACE, SEX, AND THE SARAH SILVERMAN EFFECT

Comic writer and actress Sarah Silverman first gained national attention on the 1993–1994 season of *Saturday Night Live*, then received many TV, stand-up, and film accolades. She debuted her television sitcom *The Sarah Silverman Program* on Comedy Central in 2007. The show aired as a critical part of Comedy Central's efforts to stay viable after viewer numbers tanked following the major mergers of companies like Viacom and Time Warner in the 1980s and 1990s. The shift toward what comedy scholar Nick Marx has called "oppositional" content like Silverman's reflected a successful strategy of commercializing more "edgy" content that could reflect on racism and sexism without alienating a core base of white middle-class viewers.[23] As opposed to Bernhard's mockumentary film, Silverman's reach was definitively less queer, though the content of her joke-work played just as readily with race, gender, and sexuality.

Silverman's satire is well known for its plays with social taboos and con-troversial comments. Famous for her uncouth comic edge, Silverman's ver-bal sparring leaves her most often looking up to the side, biting her lip, and

Figure 3.6: Screen shot, Sarah Silverman in "Face Wars," *The Sarah Silverman Program*, season 2, episode 3 (2007). Comedy Central.

slightly confused. As if aloof in her attack, Silverman envisages the self-conscious play of twenty-first-century postfeminist, postassimilationist comedy through her childlike delivery of controversial punchlines reminiscent of earlier comic women, but with a tomboyish crassness more like Bart Simpson than Fanny Brice's Baby Snooks.

Like Bernhard, Silverman made a name for herself as a Jewish female comic who outs racism by way of performing blackness through impersonation and appropriation. But whereas Bernhard did it with a kind of reflexivity that announced itself outright, Silverman's blackface ruffled feathers for its conspicuous lack of complexity or commentary. In one episode of *The Sarah Silverman Program*, the comedienne's "Face Wars" showcased a modern-day extension of blackface performance.[24] Made up in blackface expressly to look like notorious actress-rapper Queen Latifah (see figure 3.6), Silverman is stumped to find out "how cruel white people can be" when they express outrage at the sight of her. She enters a black church to be among "her own people" (see figure 3.7). Exaggerating a slowed, stunted run in place with arms swinging on bilateral pendulums up to the pulpit, she effects the iconographic minstrel step and appears shocked to be forced out and pushed down the stairs by a crowd of angry people. "This is literally my darkest hour," Silverman says into the camera, playing up the intended pun of her black makeup, her minstrelsy, and the sad fate of her rejection.

The race dummy parody continues throughout the episode, as Silverman, who has been arrested and is speaking on her own behalf, addresses a

Figure 3.7: Screen shot, Sarah Silverman in "Face Wars," *The Sarah Silverman Program*, season 2, episode 3 (2007). Comedy Central.

cork-painted crowd of supporters as a self-identified "angry black-faced woman." Scholars Lori Harrison-Kahan and David Gilotta discuss this instance of Silverman's blacking up in relation to the question of whether it works to mark her more Jewish or more white.[25] Their thinking harkens back to the questions posed by Michael Rogin and Eric Lott, who underscore the performance of whiteness through the impersonation of Otherness for turn-of-the-twentieth-century blackface performers. But in Silverman's contemporary context, there is a more deliberate use of irony that performs at least two additional functions simultaneously.

If it is true that Silverman performs her postassimilatory Jewish whiteness through this exaggerated impersonation of blackness, it is also evident that Silverman uses blackface as a tool of ironic reflexivity. She plays up her signature simpleton expression while physicalizing a role that reads as race aggression. Like Bernhard and *Broad City* do (as I demonstrate below), Silverman's blackface reiterates white appropriations of blackness through parody. And also like them, Silverman's black impersonations happen alongside and through an imagined and unfulfilled bisexual fantasy. Silverman's ironic romanticism of Queen Latifah, the singer-actress known for her place at the prized top of the music and movie industries and her bisexuality, reifies a racialized construction of the comic's self-conscious whiteness that also relies on a sexualized appropriation. Silverman invokes Queen Latifah's celebrity and sexual identities as power roles she wants to play and possess. Their layered appropriation offers Silverman momentary escape from the dulled, straight white womanhood she mocks as hypernaive, if also well-meaning.

The doubled interest in blackness and bisexuality echoes Bernhard's complex desire for Roxanne in *Without You, I'm Nothing*. But where Bernhard brings this tension front and center, revealing the awkward and unrequited premise of her desire for Roxanne's approval, interest, and intimacy, Silverman's blackface plays dumb, exaggerating her outrageous lack of awareness as an only-implied wink to the audience.

In subsequent interviews, Silverman identified the plot line from 2007 as one she regrets. Admitting that it has become embarrassing in the age of social media, she told Kelly Connolly of *Entertainment Weekly* that in addition to sending up common, offensive stereotypes of both Jewish and African American people, she had added insult to injury by tweeting out a still from the episode for her fans. "Now it's forever there and it looks [like] it's totally racist out of context, and I regret that," Silverman said. "But there's nothing I can do about that."[26] The regret Silverman has experienced, however, is that the image was taken out of context. The comic does not describe any remorse about the blackface bit itself, which Silverman herself explains presumably in context: "Me and the waiter in [a] restaurant, played by Alex Désert, switch [races]," she recalled. "I say it's harder to be Jewish and he says it's harder to be black and we switch for the day. And it's really aggressively stupid and we're both idiots. I'm in like the most racist blackface and he's wearing *paius* and a *yamacha* and a big fake Jewish nose and he's wearing a T-shirt that says 'I Love Money.'"[27]

Assuring her fans and critics that the sketch was "great" on the show *Watch What Happens Live*, Silverman assumes that her audiences get her play with opposites. Her self-conscious performance of white privilege means to stand in for white guilt. Still, without addressing the blackface itself, she shines light on the illogic of racism by reiterating racist stereotypes, positioning herself as its worst perpetrator. The ironic performance switch-up is one she admits is aggressively stupid, but still "great" when understood as an exercise in exposing the idiocy of stereotypes. While the apology follows suit with other contemporary Jewish female performers who have gone too far (Amy Schumer as a recent example,[28] and to a different extent, Lena Dunham, for her all white erasures of blackness altogether[29]), it doesn't fully account for the impact of the "Face Wars" episode and the race (and to a lesser degree, sex) warring it waged on a mainstream scale.

If regularly taboo about race as it relates to her white, straight Jewishness, Silverman has sourced her political incorrectness as a tool for leftist campaigning. Boosting Barack Obama's 2008 presidential election campaign via her seriocomic Florida swing vote video "The Great Schlep" and its viral web distribution, Silverman outlined key commonalities between aging Jews in Boca Raton and young black males, including the shared prevalence of friends dying, interest in material wealth or bling, and love of track suits and Cadillacs.[30] Basing her humor entirely on stereotypes, Silverman feigns an innocent naiveté in the name of an earnest campaign advocacy. Squaring off to the camera lens in the middle of the frame, Silverman sits right in front of the camera, leaning in. She addresses a Jewish generation of young voters, whom she implores to take action, joking that they should convince their Florida grandparents to get to the polls. She makes fun of older Jews who distance themselves from blackness and of young Jews who appropriate it to the point of identification, thus campaigning for the swing vote by way of a jokish black-Jewish alliance overlooked by Florida's comfort-seeking Jews. Like Bernhard, Silverman makes fun of a leftist Jewish-black alliance by exaggerating her own asymmetrical savior complex. Like Bernhard, too, she does so at the cost of parroting derisive black images rather than including black voices. Where Bernhard loses her on-camera audience through going too far and risks doing the same with viewers at home, Silverman constrains her power to offend through her girl-next-door persona that tranquilizes her risky material on race for much larger and more mainstream audiences.

The face wars Silverman waged on her television program resonate with her whiteface and Jewface impersonations in her 2005 stage show *Jesus Is Magic*. In large part a throwback to the stage shows of Jewish female comics before her, Silverman's solo show, filmed for television, draws on the dancing and vocal joke-work of the Brice-inspired idiot savant while inciting the Tucker-esque politically incorrect. The reiterative return to early Jewish female acts comes with important revisions. She blends these traditions with a markedly different brand of bodily comportment that competes with lowbrow humor and butthole jokes.[31] The comedy hour begins with an attempt to impress her friends, comic Brian Posehn, and her sister, actress Laura Silverman. She tells them her scheme to make a one-woman show in a day. The show's first moments thus establish the self-derogatory narcissism of its protagonist and her mix of hubris and procrastination. It also signals that the material need not be taken too seriously, advice she gives her audience again at the end of the show. Like Bernhard's confession at the end of *Without You, I'm Nothing*, when she reveals that it all was a lie, Silverman's I-wrote-it-in-a-day routine makes a similar admission. As Silverman reveals that every bit of her stage show has in fact been painstakingly worked through, she acknowledges the labor of comedy that, while deliberately contentious, cannot be overlooked as "just" a joke. It is right or wrong, funny or not funny, but she worked for it, and therefore, as the logic implies, so can we.

Still, with the signature childishness that marks her career, Silverman pretends to dream it all up with her opening song, as the living room–writer's room skit becomes an animated odyssey of Silverman driving through the clouds. The journey leads to her entrance onto a proscenium stage with a large theater audience and full band. Sitting in front of a vanity mirror, placed onstage as opposed to Bernhard's private backstage, Silverman situates herself within a familiar Jewish female performance lineage in its reference to Barbra

Streisand as Fanny Brice in *Funny Girl* (1968). Where it may have been a more subtle citation in Bernhard's act, here Silverman goes right for the reiterative shout out to Streisand's opening line, "Hello, Gorgeous," but flattens its layered reflexivity with one-dimensional narcissism. "Me," Silverman whispers into her image reflection. "It's me. You're beautiful." Leaning in to kiss herself, she stops short, saying into the mirror, "Not now, not like this." Silverman perverses the self-affirming tone of Streisand's original line for comic effect. Like with Bernhard, Streisand offers Silverman the ultimate Jewish female performance citation. Like for Berhard too, it is Silverman's battle with her own image that sets the tone from the outset.

Silverman's stand-up makes fun of the Jewish body she identifies as inappropriately hairy and awkward about sex. In one joke early in her set, Silverman seems to ask seriously why everyone thinks Jewish women aren't sexy. She then insists that yes, they *can* be sexy, pretends to put on lingerie, and accompanies a Yiddish-inflected "*Yeidel deidel deidel*" into a minstrel-like dance, to the crowd's enormous delight. She shrugs her shoulders, pushes forward and pulls up her pelvis, and sends her folded elbows one at a time to each side with a matching hop on each foot.[32] Even for those less familiar with the quintessential Yiddish shoulder lift and catch-all expressive shrug, "*Nu?,*" which this clownishly mocks, the effect is clear enough. Silverman's version of the Jewish woman's sex appeal can only reaffirm its unsexiness. The joke implies that *yeideling* Jewish women are too noisy even in negligees to turn anyone on.[33] The Yiddish-sounding noise (*Yeidel deidel deidel*) contrasts with the feminine sighs and silences that supposedly happen in regular white sex. Like the most self-deprecating of the performers included in this book, Silverman reiterates how comically unfeminine the funny Jewish female can be.

The moment sustains assimilatory expectations of normative, white heterosexuality at the core of Jewish female imagination. With this formulation intact, even just a few seconds of the dancing joke achieve its minstrelsy of abject Jewishness and its haggish femininity. Rather than remain the degraded hag body, however, Silverman restores her charge with her signature deadpan expression, which she sustains throughout the laugh. As opposed to Bernhard's antics, which seem altogether unfazed by her crowd, Silverman's impersonation of unsexy Jewishness remains entirely self-conscious, evidenced even more so as she awkwardly adjusts the waist of her pants after the bit, pulling them up as if pulling herself together.

She takes the joke further, introducing a song she would like to sing and asking for the lights to dim. When the stage goes fully black at her request for "sexy lighting," the audience laughs as Silverman wonders aloud, "Is there anything on me at all?" The joke is that, in order to be convincingly sexy and Jewish and to make space for erotic fantasies, the lights would have to be out completely. Making fun of herself in this way, Silverman embraces a masculinist smut joke tradition, in which laughing with her is actually laughing at her.

And yet the self-reflexive moments of standing in the dark make visible the reality that her female stardom is still mitigated by male-run industry whims. Her fame could be taken away at any moment, not just because of her Jewish unsexiness, but also as soon as she is either too old to be quite so cute or too successful to be convincingly sexy in the ways her act requires.

The film then interrupts this self-criticism with a cut to Silverman in a velvet red dress and a blown-out perm à la Dorothy Vallens in David Lynch's 1986 neo-noir film, *Blue Velvet*.[34] The prerecorded segment features Silverman's long, shapely figure poised in contrapposto, characteristic of a femme fatale icon at the microphone. The camera zooms in on her face, as she sings in a low, soft voice. Her sexy red lips never close completely, and her eyes command authority with directed focus that sustains for the length of held notes (see figure 3.8). As she affects a vibrato with slowed words that build anticipation, the close-up of Silverman's more made-up face figures her as a genuine sexpot.

But before we can indulge, the camera cuts back to Silverman onstage in full dork affect as she embodies the honky-tonk tenor of her original song, "Put the Penis in the Hole." Adding arm gestures that match the excrement and anal sex lines of the lyrics, Silverman adopts a cartoonish voice akin to Bart Simpson's before switching briefly back to sexy singer once again. Pointing the index finger of her long black-gloved hand at the camera, she asks in a line, "Have you ever done drugs so that you could have sex without crying?" She accents the "yea yea" with jazz hands framing her breasts, contracting her chest in time with the beat.

While such camera cuts ask the viewer to shift back to the live Silverman as quickly as she does, her cartoonish exaggerations overshadow the sexier Silverman incarnated just instants before. And yet the real and symbolic

Figure 3.8: Screen shot, Sarah Silverman in *Jesus Is Magic* (2005). Directed by Liam Lynch.

capital her sexy seconds provide cannot be overlooked. Competing with popular male and female comics, Jewish and not, Silverman's joke styling has to be viewed in the context of market salability and its roles for Jewish women. It is within this context that her persuasive performance—however brief—of the heterosexual lounge singer fantasy buys her more clout as a mainstream comic; ironically, it is the very thing that sells her act. Strikingly, Silverman's on-camera audience is unlaughingly quiet during Silverman's sexy singer routine. Silverman asserts hetero-sexiness as a role in her repertoire, and in its exchange for the coarser joker, proves she could pull it off if she tried. This doubled ability to fulfill both a role and its reversal is precisely her postfeminist, postassimilationist bodily ability.

Tall and ambiguously Jewish in the stereotypic gauges of Eastern European Jewish appearance (large chest, big nose, frizzy hair), Silverman can play with acting Jewish differently than Bernhard and the earlier Jewish female comics that inform her act, made famous by their non-normative looks. As if in reference to those women, Silverman makes fun of her body, but the Jewishness of such humor and its assumption of an inappropriate femininity are more clearly a choice than a visual mark. Playing this up, Silverman brags about her swanlike neck, which by all means is not a Jewish feature. Reversing the body-effacing tradition of her Jewish industry mothers, she claims the whiteness, purity, and classical ballet aesthetics that Brice and Streisand so brilliantly eschewed. Acknowledging her white looks, Silverman perverts the chaste swan image with a sex joke, assuring the audience that her long, perfect-looking neck measures six inches at its most flaccid state. She says between waves of laughter that she is measuring "from the balls up."

As Silverman boasts about the size of her neck in reference to her balls, she measures her white looks and Jewish female body against male ones. Her phallic neck competes with a penis, she means to say, as her noteworthy source of bodily power. Showing off her celebrated feature that outdoes her (Jewish) male counterparts, she claims a physical authority through a jokish gender inversion. She both digs at the issue of women having to compete with men to be in comedy and draws attention to the long-standing joke of Jewish males' effeminacy construed through their famously circumcised penises. In this way, Silverman both joins and disses her broad audience of men who compare dick size and Jews who forever occupy this schlemiel stereotype. And yet the effect works to undo her subtle femininity, too, already on the line because of her general tomboyishness, childlike persona, and always-masculinist ambition to climb up the mainstream comedy ladder.

Silverman's gender and sex jokes are always also about her whiteness, most often delivered through seemingly honest confessions that she twists upside down. In one joke, when she wishes not to be labeled gay or straight, Silverman adds that she prefers to be seen as the white woman she is. And in a segment delivered later on about Asian men, Silverman defends herself against criticism about her lack of racial sensitivity. She apologizes without apologizing, "I don't care if you think I'm a racist. I just care that you think I'm thin."[35] In both instances of irony, Silverman says the opposite of what she means, with the signature incongruity that sells her brand of joke-work. And yet these lines perform a kind of reverse psychology, which when read against, her white, thin body, reveal the guilty pleasures of heterosexual white womanhood that Silverman accesses with authority. Her irony emphasizes the absurdity of the race privilege that she regularly occupies and yet, because of her Jewishness and her ethics, cannot willingly embrace.

The show's title, *Jesus Is Magic*, perhaps outlines this best, as it jabs at white evangelist thinking as a critique of whiteness altogether. The phrase "Jesus is magic" comes up in the set when Silverman addresses the issue of intermarriage. Stoking the fire of Jewish cultural fears about intermarriage, she talks about her Catholic boyfriend. But undercutting the power of a non-Jewish partner's perspective, she adds that her would-be children will "just have to understand" that Mommy thinks something rational, while daddy thinks that "Jesus is magic." The joke makes fun of an American brand (more than a Catholic one) of blind faith by way of debasing a belief in a magic Jesus. It also frames the idea in gendered and ethnic terms, as Jewishness stands in for a more rational "mommy," in opposition to an irrational, goyish "daddy." The marriage joke riffs on the white America that she can access through intimacy, and even lifelong commitment, even as it makes fun of a country whose over-riding cultural belief is a religiously justified irrationality.

When she re-enters the stage as the male Pentecostal preacher in a full-staged pants role against a projected backdrop of animated penises and rain-bows, the magic of Jesus is taken to a spectacular extreme. Not only is daddy irrational, Silverman says with this joke, but he is all powerful in a society that ascribes to a make-believe world of neon imagination. Dressed in a baby blue suit and tie, Silverman parodies the misogyny and racism of the ultraconservative. In this way, she exaggerates a white, Christian dominant logic that she means to subvert, and like Bernhard's holiday wishes for a white Christmas, aligns herself further with the audiences her characters also alienate.

Silverman's magic Jesus jokes thus affirm her play with incongruity, wherein she can become one thing to position its opposite, constructing only to deconstruct. Jumping back and forth between identities, she demonstrates an ironic dexterity that plays racism and sexism from multiple sides. In Lacy Lowery, Valerue R. Renegar, and Charles E. Goehring's reading of *Jesus Is Magic*, Silverman's blatant capitalizations on white privilege, postfeminism, and the trivialization of serious events allow her to challenge behaviors and attitudes she finds questionable.[36] That is, by adopting an onstage persona of childlike innocence, Silverman is able to discuss controversial and edgy social topics in a distinctive way that makes these issues more palatable to audience members. The authors celebrate Silverman's use of "meiosis" or what is known as "comic minimization," which reduces the apparent significance of a topic in order to highlight its true gravity and importance.[37]

The embodiments of this joke-work fall within the discourse on irony, including Kenneth Burke's foundational writing on the comic use of incongruity. From Burke's perspective, irony can be understood as a "situated instance of perspective by incongruity" or a "perspective of perspectives" that allows multiple and even competing ideas to be held together at the same time.[38] Building on this theme, communications scholar Dustin Bradley Goltz adds that irony "mobilizes a twiceness that rubs" against what is being said and meant, creating and negating simultaneously what is doing and what is done.[39] When considered in the context of Silverman's Jewish joke-work and the comic license of its identity play, this "twiceness" is multiplied on a few important levels.

Silverman's face and body behave together and apart, as do her whiteness and her difference, her straightness and her only partial dismissals of it, and her attack and apology. These incongruities layer one over the next as ever more evidence of the intersubjective I/you that Bernhard's film brings to the surface. What reading the two comics together makes clear is that it is this paradoxical nature of ironic performativity and its "perspective of perspectives" that so assists the postassimilatory, postfeminist comic commentary on insider and outsider positions. Both Bernhard's and Silverman's Jewish female bodies stand in and take the blame for the worst of white thinking while working (failing and flailing) to undo it. In each case, Jewishness acts as a kind of appropriative license that means to out racism and sexism through their exaggeration. As bathroom humor and glamorous girl come together in Silverman's joke-work, however, she rehearses and revises a new Jewish guilt: that of the Jewish woman's white pleasures. For Silverman, this means to look and live like the majority and still claim a selective and salable marginality with market savvy.

Building on this success of Silverman's self-conscious, dorky-sexy Jewish woman in the celebrity spotlight, the next section analyzes how *Broad City*'s costars and show writers, Abbi Jacobson and Ilana Glazer, have risen to the top of a mainstream industry (like Silverman) while sustaining a niche appeal with more progressive social and sexual implications (more like Bernhard). Having started on a web series before catapulting to stardom through Comedy Central programming, the costars enjoy privileged positions on postnetwork TV, thanks to the major support of the most successful women in comedy, including producer and comic actress Amy Poehler. Millennial menaces, their plots play out elaborate schemes that most often peak in epic failures, whether harmful to themselves or others. As if accustomed to their own foibles, their narrative and physical comedy returns to the self-deprecating joke-work made famous by earlier Jewish comic generations but always points to its limits when it comes to the interplays of race, gender, and sexuality. Blurring black impersonations and bisexuality with the culpability of any number of other misappropriative conflations, the costars claim postassimilatory, postfeminist Jewish identities with equal parts poor taste and progressive ethos. As they manage to offend nearly everyone, they render their race privilege accessible and comically only somewhat aware of itself. The humor softens the blow for white audiences who might wonder if and when they themselves are to blame for similar social blindness; for other audiences more in the loop, it likely invites laughter at the recognition of how much more work needs to be done within white, liberal (Jewish) circles to understand and undo racism, even and especially when sexuality is already so opened up.

BROAD CITY'S BAD GIRLS GETTING BI IN-BETWEEN

Three decades after Bernhard's film, Comedy Central's *Broad City* is once again tied up in the intersections of whiteness, blackness, and bisexuality, but with millennial twists and references. Centered on the friendship of two self-proclaimed "Jewesses" in their postcollege years, the show is aptly named for its emphasis on both comically unclassy young broads and the broad lens of its progressive representational scope. The show playfully shocks bourgeois sensibilities as costars navigate work, weed, and anything but straight sex in New York City's queer and multiracial world. It undertakes these themes through an in-your-face set of identifications and impersonations that make fun of the characters who perform them as much as the social problems they provoke. And it does so through a new technique of comic parody, one that Glazer herself called "vulnerability as strength" and arguably something akin to sincerity.[40]

My delight in watching the first season stemmed from the recognition of a refreshing level of sincerity, which seemed to out its outrageous offenses while naming them part of everyday white privileges that Jewish girls enjoy and eschew. While drawing on Jewish comic traditions of self-mockery and irony, the show did it in a way that positioned feminist charges as still very much under way if always problematic and Jewish identities as likewise on the line, in transition, and under regular review. The postassimilationist, postfeminist premise of *Broad City* envisions a pastiche of references bent on normalizing difference rather than sameness, wherein the bounds of either reach beyond a black-white racial logic and do so through depicting a range of sexual freedoms. The cast of core characters broadens the possibilities of who and what topics can be funny on mainstream television. Ilana's roommate, Jaime (Arturo Castro), is an openly gay Cuban immigrant who secures citizenship in season two. Ilana's African American boyfriend, Lincoln (Hannibal Buress), plays a quirky dentist who likes Ilana despite her narcissistic flaws. In a reversal of traditional TV gender roles, he prefers monogamy, but supports her polyamorous sexual whims so long as he doesn't have to know too much about them. Ilana's crush on Abbi is a fixture of nearly every episode, though the sexual tension between them is more often expressed as comic relief than unrequited love. Ilana tries to pull Abbi into a threesome for much of the first season, a theme introduced in the first episode as it opens with Ilana having sex with Lincoln while skyping with Abbi. Ilana's promiscuousness is made a facet of her funny femininity, a level of hilarity about life that is alternately driven by ego and empathy taken to exaggerated extreme. The mix is a carnal construction of her postfeminist, postassimilatory Jewish American liberalism, portrayed as a general joie de vivre that appears to know no bounds. In the context of identity performance and racial impersonation, the open sexuality allows the costars to construct new versions of the Sexy Jewess in pop culture. Together the two exist in earnest and perpetual pursuit of a millennial happiness that hinges on a broad vision of social justice that they invest in but fail to ever fully understand.

According to *New Yorker* writer Emily Nussbaum, "Jacobson and Glazer's take on identity politics—and their characters' well-intentioned but barely informed fourth-wave, queerish, anti-rape/pro-porn intersectional feminism" is an "intricate matter, both a part of the show's philosophy and a subject of its satire."[41] Within this frame, the liberal play of Ilana's Jewess libido slides with uncomfortable ease to cartoonish adoptions of urban black and brown aesthetics by way of street wear, emulated vocal style, and dance. As Nussbaum points out, this undercurrent risks "finding something intrinsically funny about white people talking like black people."[42] Such discomfort plays out in the show's dialogue as Abbi says to Ilana, "You're so anti-racist, sometimes, that you're actually really racist." Later, when Ilana's elaborate masturbation ritual includes donning gold-hoop earrings complete with the cursive "Latina," it is clear that who that joke was on, and who got to make it, reflect the appropriative license of comic Jewish femininity. Resonating with critical readings of Bernhard's film by hooks and Pellegrini, Nussbaum writes of *Broad City*: "The show's secret engine . . . may be its willingness to tiptoe close to failure."[43]

The show's cultural appropriations accompany economic ones, as the narrative premise of slumming it after college without steady work—or work ethic—underscores the gentrifying erasure of disenfranchised bodies, whether in the Brooklyn neighborhoods where Ilana and Abbi now live or the service jobs they compete to keep. At the same time, Ilana's parents are Jewish New York liberals whose lifestyle invokes a supportive middle-class family. Her Jewish mother (Susie Essman) spends her time in the underground dens of the city's black market, where a taste for knockoff purses takes the stereotype of always-frugal-but-ever-wanting Jewish women to its darkly funny, illegal extreme. For this habit, both Ilana and her mom speak what Ilana calls in a later episode Yiddish-Mandarin. The returning plot line calls on the familiar trope of a Jewish love for all things Asian, revising orientalist fantasies with economic ties to a Chinatown underworld. While rendering Asian characters through stereotypes, it does so with a joke on equally extremist Jewish material desires.

Regularly depicting Ilana and Abbi as privileged white women with no money, the show exposes where those points of access break down because of Jewishness and in spite of it. Explicit references to their Jewish identities come up in almost every episode of three seasons, often in either opportunist plots gone wrong or as a means of underscoring social premises they find difficult to digest. In the very first episode, Abbi and Ilana scheme a way to make $200 to go to a secret pop-up Lil Wayne concert and create a Craigslist ad as "two Jewesses just trying to make a buck." When they show up at the first caller's apartment, hoping to make easy money, they encounter a creepy character (played by Fred Armisen) who hires them to clean his apartment in their underwear for an hour (see figure 3.9). After a montage of the two scrubbing floors to Little Wayne's "Milli," Armisen's character refuses to pay them, saying he is a baby who has no money. They scream and trash his place in revenge, taking bottles of his alcohol and a fur coat on the way out. They offer up their half-naked Jewishness as a ploy for his sick amusement, naming a "Jewess" scheme as one they willingly exploit so long as they get paid.

In episode 5 of the third season, Ilana outs herself as culture vulture extraordinaire, busking for money by tap dancing down the center aisle of a subway car. Recontextualizing a script and practice of black subway performers, she tells the crowd that she's recently fallen on hard times, having lost her job at deals, deals, deals after graduating from NYU. An older woman rider rolls her

Figure 3.9: Screen shot, Ilana Glazer and Abbi Jacobson in "Cleaning in the (Half) Nude," *Broad City*, season 1, episode 1 (2014). Comedy Central.

The Case of the Sexy Jewess

eyes and snatches the single dollar bill Ilana makes right out of Ilana's zippered backpack pocket. Wearing a coconut shell bra and bold block color vertical striped pants, Ilana is the image of the queer Jewess clown, her hipsteresque hyperconsciousness so conspicuously uncaring, it's chic. Her tap shoes, worn throughout the day as if she is always prepared for impromptu dancing, allow her to walk, bike, and perform for tips in the footsteps of the down and out as she clearly makes fun of the white postcollege Williamsburg poor who busk on the Bedford stop platform.

Like Bernhard and Silverman, whose spotlighting of white privilege also reinforces it, Ilana takes the spot of the black entertainers who most visibly dance on the New York City metro. Whereas largely African American male crews create hip-hop-styled spectacles of dance acrobatics for the length of the L train from Brooklyn to Manhattan, Ilana's dance up the A train reroutes the racial and spatial blackness of the format and the form she rips off, while adding insult to injury with tap's white history of black appropriation. This lack of racial awareness plays out throughout the show's multiple seasons as its unique brand of social conscience and self-consciousness. Cartooning her white blindness, Ilana leverages her liberated sexuality to justify the joke of her offensive black appropriation. A male rider records the dance on his iPhone, only to realize it's Ilana, his younger sister, and calls her out about needing a real job. She flips on the railing and center pole as her brother—also gay—reprimands her, saying that she's homophobic for not listening. The mention of homophobia stops her straight away, and she is horrified by the thought. "It is?!" "No, just kidding," he says, "but you still need to get a job." The fear of sounding homophobic outweighs the eye rolling of riders disgusted with her class and race privilege, which she fails to even notice. The joke here is that homophobia poses a greater offense to Ilana than the abuses of her race and class privilege. Writing this blind spot into the show, the performers and collaborating writers of the show expose the asymmetry of white progressive maneuvers, wherein claims to intersectionality risk flattening distinct politics of representation, or worse, forgetting them altogether.

Like Bernhard, Ilana offends her on-camera audience, which doesn't get her and doesn't care to try. In doing so, both performers create deliberate distance from both their audiences and their material. Through this ironic distance, they allow themselves and what they really think to be transparent and then not. As they mix their messages, self-conscious projects of impersonation underscore liberatory premises rife with paradoxes. Both sexual and racial expressions lean on a familiar Jewish in-betweeness to push the edges of acceptability, where flamboyance around sexual freedoms parallels efforts to visibilize race injustice. And yet by messing with social fears of bisexuality and blackness alike, performers take identity politics that do *not* work in the same ways and then draw a false equivalence between them. While joyfully offering break-through renditions of bisexuality that upturn social thinking about what's allowable on camera, their black impersonations conspicuously disenfranchise black bodies and voices. And yet to celebrate the former while admonishing the latter misses the significant intersection of how Jewish identity seems to license black appropriations alongside sexual freedoms. This theme for Jewish comic women in pop culture has sustained at least the last thirty years, if not for a much longer Jewess twentieth century.

Apart from the show's jokes on white privilege, its portrayals of Jewishness are opportunities for sexual enlightenment and of the Jewish female body as one to embrace in all its awkwardness. In important contrast to Silverman's *yeideling* Jewish woman, the Jewish traditions that *Broad City* brings to light often foreground sexual openness and acceptance. For example, when Ilana's family is sitting shiva for Grandma Esther, observing the traditional Jewish funeral rite, Abbi shows up with a dildo in her purse, which Ilana's mom insists on inspecting (remember, she is obsessed with bags and knockoffs). Ilana quickly asks if Abbi "pegged" her new male lover the previous night, and Abbi nods shyly in affirmation. Ilana screams that it is the happiest day of her life, and Abbi's recent sexual experience becomes the whole family's business. As Ilana's brother and parents take the cultural trope of a Jewish family's lack of boundaries to a new level, Abbi loosens up and adds that she was channeling Grandma Esther's no-holds-barred quest for life. The family weeps in an instant of Jewish pride and hugs in an open embrace of living without regret.

This type of celebrated self-discovery resounds as the show's most sincere lesson, trading out rote determiners of acceptability standards for the efforts toward personal resolve. This sincerity about being oneself no matter what manifests not only through open sexuality, but also through funny dancing. In an episode called "Abbi on the Edge of Glory," Abbi lip-syncs the Lady Gaga song of the same name with the freedom of an impromptu naked dance alone in her apartment, baring all for the camera, and convincingly, on her own terms. The camera pans the empty hallway as Abbi bolts out of her room on musical cue. Holding her face just centimeters away from a piece of wall art that is presumably one of her own, she performs for the imaginary audience of her own creation: "There ain't no reason you and me should be alone / Tonight yeah baby, tonight yeah baby." Winding her arm overhead in circles with the downbeat, she ventriloquizes the pop star: "But I got a reason that you-hoo should take me home tonight." She rushes into the living room, mouthing a strong-willed: "Tonight yeah baby, tonight yeah baby." With her breasts and pubic area blurred for the camera, she moves with a stiffness that becomes her signature throughout the show's three seasons, but with evident elation that is funny because it appears to feel so good, rather than embarrassing or shameful (see figure 3.10).

Rocking back and forth on too-straightened legs, winging her locked arms in and out with the club beat, she sings: "I need a man that makes it right when it's so wrong." A quick glance at her arms suggests a recognition mid-scene of

Figure 3.10: Screen shot, Abbi Jacobson naked and rejoicing in "Abbi on the Edge of Glory," *Broad City*, season 3, episode 5 (2016). Comedy Central.

the erectness of her limbs, and she plays it up more, walking like a toy solder up to another piece of wall art. "Right on the limit's where we know we both belong tonight," she promises a crowd of none while beating her arms up and down. As the stanza swells with feeling and Lady Gaga belts, "It's time to feel the rush / to push the dangerous," Abbi runs to the window and jumps with an exclamation. She clenches her fists with commitment and pulses them to the music.

By the time she grabs the tripod as a microphone and gets up on the couch as her makeshift stage for "I'm gonna run right to, to the edge with you," the self-satisfaction is palpable and contagious. The pure moments of feeling good exalt the viewer with the chorus, "I'm on the edge of glory and I'm hangin' on a moment of truth." The premise of one's own truth empowers the performance. She sings for herself, "Out on the edge of glory, and I'm hangin' on a moment with you." Ending the scene, she rocks out with righteous confidence: "I'm on the edge!" The loveably embarrassing choreographic soliloquy climaxes with believable female self-expression. It's dorky, self-helpy, and an enormous relief for watchers who can (and should) laugh at themselves by relating to this ultimate embrace of self-acceptance. With hipster prowess, the moment's resounding message reminds us of Fanny Brice's 1930 role in *Be Yourself*, when funny girls were emboldened female leads and sacrifices made for others were finally less important than being oneself. This is ultimately the liberatory promise that *Broad City* invites for the twenty-first-century Sexy Jewess and her friends. Self-acceptance ultimately softens the sting of the pair's comically skewed sense of boundaries, whether about race or sex. While this risks smoothing over the misappropriative aggressions toward the impersonated bodies and voices it leaves behind, it does so with a sense of its own vexed power.

Between Ilana's tap dancing and Abbi's self-affirming living room solo, the show foregrounds the impact of its humor through dancing joke-work that conjoins appropriative and affirmative Jewish female identities. While sharing these attitudes and antics between two characters throughout three seasons, the comic duo works to draw both positions together as complementary parts of all that the show means to parody.

Racial impersonation and sexual liberation work as complementary self-expressions for millennial Jewesses looking to make a buck in a popular television show when they rarely do. Playing up contiguous parts of white privilege while wading in its guilty muck, they make their own rules, which can only power their own stoner worlds. Ultimately sincere at the end of each episode, they profess their unconditional love for friends and family and for each other more than anything else. In doing so, their cartoonish aggressions are exaggerated reminders of what work still needs to be done.

CONCLUSION

Revealing a mainstream embrace of race and gender diversity that capitalizes on Otherness in the name of recuperating it, comic female performers of the last three decades highlight a range of appropriative plays as self-conscious Jewish projects of race, gender, and sexual representation. Their joke-work blows up in a proliferation of comedy programming referred to as a mainstream comedy zeitgeist, wherein Jewish women maneuver celebrity roles as allies for diverse identities they impersonate and alienate, and for which they offer different kinds of onscreen apologies or moves toward self-acceptance.[44]

Together, their periodization patterns a Jewish female self-consciousness in which the representation of "insider" and "outsider" identities—and their gross appropriation by various means—becomes the hypersensitive material of self-parody. As Jewish female performers participate in a larger cultural shift toward irony as central comic device, they perform incongruous acts that reveal a new era of ambivalence about identity as it relates to Jewishness. Where ethnic and gender difference afforded to assimilatory Jewish female performers of the twentieth century their distinct outsider identities to recuperate, the embodiment of contemporary Jewishness and femininity reveals a new trajectory of contentious jokes more and more critical of the access to white privilege and white guilt.

Inciting the politically incorrect as core to their comic personas, these performers source Jewishness as excuse and apology for derisive racial impersonations, most prominently, and the gender comments that accompany them. Jewishness offers a category of liminal experience that allows these performers to act as if they are on the margins in order to critique the center. In regular citations of their inferior status as women, too, these comics recuperate positions of gender difference to satirize delimiting representations of women. In doing so, they impersonate women in unflattering ways: Jewish women are unsexy and out of touch, white women are classist prudes, and black women emerge only by proxy, as appropriated alter egos that are either angry or hurt.

Claiming a social and sexual outsider-insider status to different degrees, performers reveal their offensive appropriation and authenticity as social weapons of their comic craft. Bernhard and *Broad City*'s leads draw similar attention to the interrelated experiences of their ethnoracial and bisexual in-betweeness but reflect the bodily concerns of their different decades. Performing this in-betweeness as comic device and negotiation of coterminous identifications, all three comics deploy an ironic mixed messaging that means to dismantle racist discourse while playing out its worse extremes. Compared to Bernhard's film and *Broad City*, Silverman's comic celebrity reaches far beyond niche comedy markets. Her use of black cork makeup in the "Face Wars" episode of *The Sarah Silverman Program* distinguishes her performance from the racialized embodiments of the other two examples, moving the focus from the comic body to the corked-up face. The explicit use of blackface also helps to historically contextualize the damage of her identity play beyond the self-reflexivity of Bernhard and *Broad City*. In a plot line that compares the plights of Jews and blacks, the "face wars" Silverman wages end in too big a defense of the straight white world she aims to criticize.

Starring in high-visibility acts that they help write and direct, all of these artists flesh out the terms of a Jewish female humor that relies on the layering of contrasting affects to simultaneously do and undo the impact of their jokes. Bernhard becomes the grotesque master-appropriator whose partial apology falls on no-longer-listening ears. Silverman and *Broad City*'s Jacobson and Glazer wave the banners of a new mainstream, joining a comedy mania that presumes to make fun of everybody equally in an era that many claim is postrace. In going for jokes that ironize themselves with more or less sincerity as much as the subjects they take on, all three comics create incongruous personas of distance and intimacy with both their audiences and their material, allowing themselves and what they really think to be known and then not, brought forward and then blurred over. Their chosen tropes lean on citation and reference, playing with key moves of the face and body in wicked ways that are deliberately less lovable than their predecessors'. In doing so, they toy ironically with sex and sexiness, race and imitation in ways that both depart and develop from the legacy techniques discussed in the previous chapter. Through competing expressions of face and body, they mix their messages with comic craft and increasingly viable commercial success.

In these missives directed at both social order and its prudish appropriateness, physical joke-work relies on Jewess identification with blackness and bisexuality that stages a break with pernicious race supremacy and hetero-sexuality in the same breath. In sliding between one idea and the other, per-formers walk bell hooks's "critical tightropes" of white destabilization through black appropriation, while undertaking Pellegrini's aim to "reroute" transgres-sive sexual desires. As performers leave their on-screen audiences apathetic, or worse, totally offended, they stage the appropriative limits of the queer comic license that they employ so liberally by getting away with too much, and all too knowingly, not so much at all.

The next chapter further develops this racialized and sexualized logic for Jewish female in-betweens through Darren Aronofsky's mainstream ballet movie, *Black Swan* (2010), which I read as a Jewish horror film. The personi-fication of the Jewish female monster drudges up race and sex dramas from the repressed margins of social thinking in ways that make significant transla-tions from humor to horror genres.

Both the social queerness of the Jewish female body and its explicit dis-plays of bisexual desire returned as major motion picture plot hauntings, in which Portman's sin of swan sex no doubt helped her win the Academy Award as Best Actress of the year.

CHAPTER 4

Black Swan, White Nose

Jewish Horror and Ballet Birds by Any Other Name

What happens when Jewish female humor is revised as a Hollywood horror plot and the clownish joke of the Jewish swan is reworked as a doomed figure of the repressed come back to haunt the ballet stage? When the Jewish female body is made the agonizing symbol of ambivalence or of ambition taken too far and aspiration taken too seriously? And what happens when the appropriative racialization of desire, as discussed in the previous chapter, returns to terrorize the protagonist's world, but only in her imagination? These are questions posed by Darren Aronofsky's *Black Swan* (2010) and its contribution to a study of Jewishness, gender, and sexuality through the ballet movie and its monstrous swans.

In its all-out atavism of a "wereswan" lead, the film's leading girl loses all hold on reality as she dances the solo swan lead in a scary take on *Swan Lake*.[1] Far from the duckish ponds of Fanny Brice and Barbra Streisand's swan send-ups, *Black Swan*'s Natalie Portman and costars Winona Ryder, Mila Kunis, and Barbara Hershey terrorize viewers and each other as a four-way face of the Jewish female monster. The Jewish actresses in competing diva roles cast a dark pas de quatre over the classical ballet and its lakeside scenes. Gone are the funny girl swan's winking self-delusions and near-classic unassimilabilty. Instead, we see the breaking points of ballet dreams reflected in the psychological thrills of a passing ethnoracial act and its dramatization and domestication of deviant female sexuality.

As female egos crack and derangement ensues in pursuit of dancerly perfection, *Black Swan*'s lead ballerinas offer dark parodies of traditional *Swan Lake* conventions, recasting the White and Black Swan roles as psychological thriller figures, and as I argue, horror-style femmes. And yet in reading the film for its representation of sexualized ethnoracial symbols, it also becomes possible to consider how the movie reiterates traditional social codes of White Swan femininity through conservative recontainment of her excess femininity, ethnicity, and sexuality. As swan alternatives surface through popular film adaptations, however, they only offer bits of representational difference or Otherness. Ultimately, swan alternatives shore up the aesthetics of white femaleness encoded in the original White Swan. This simultaneous emergence and erasure of alternative identities patterns a fairly standard politics of filmic representation in Hollywood that pulls from the margins to entertain with what it ultimately dismisses, domesticates, or kills off. We may think of minority and women characters across a range of mainstream movies cast as comic relief, hypersexed hazards, or tragic figures. How these characterizations and narrative components play out in the ballet movie comes to stand for its politics of visual and bodily representation.

Framing the film's representation of ambiguous ethnic and sexual identities at work, this chapter asks: In what ways does *Black Swan* use ballet to appropriate repressed social identities with tenuous relationships to the mainstream? How might these appropriations amount to an ultimate domestication of the very identities the film puts forward for thrilling appeal? As *Black Swan* uses classical dance and its swan imaginary to unearth and then rebury psychosocial dramas linked to race, gender, and sexuality, the film sensationalizes professional ballet and its damaging pressures on the female psyche. It makes way for monstrous returns of the same repressed identities rendered funny in the previous chapters: the ethnic Other, the woman, and the sexual deviant. Skewed intersections of these deviled identities come out from under the surface of social acceptability, but only to sabotage themselves as monsters of self-demise. As I argue throughout this chapter, lurking in the film's fictional ballet company, character development, and plot entanglements are the horror plots of Jewish racial passing and sexual deviance. These plots are key to both the movie's central story of swan monstrosity and its potential to link horror and humor genres as related expressive modes of managing Jewishness, gender, and assimilation in relation to the body.

SYNOPSIS AND SETUP: THRILLER BALLET AND JEWISH SWANS ALL SEXED UP

In *Black Swan*, aspiring ballerina Nina Sayers (played by Natalie Portman) competes with the newest company member, Lily (Mila Kunis), for the two-part role of Odile, the White Swan, and Odette, the Black Swan, in the film's fresh twist on the traditional ballet. Though Nina has all the pure qualities of the White Swan, she struggles through the film to convince the company director, Thomas Leroy (Vincent Cassel), that she has what it takes to play the

Black Swan role. Reconceived in the movie as a break with the original ballet plot, the Black Swan must reflect the fully liberated White Swan, a deviant second self of the pure swan and the dancer who plays her. Nina's obsessive pursuit of the Black Swan's fierce sensuality grows increasingly delirious. Her sick competition with Lily climaxes in a same-sex scene that signals Nina's surrender to all things bad, bodily, and Black Swan–like. All the while, skin lesions, unexplainable sores, and an eventual attempt to kill Lily backstage turn out to exist only in Nina's mind.

Such psychological thrills throughout the film reflect a world of bodily gore, repressed sexuality, and murderous revenge where nothing is entirely certain for the protagonist ballet monster and viewers alike. While plot twists and imagined occurrences create ongoing uncertainty about what is real or not real throughout the film, one crucial aspect of the storyline and its ballet remake is clear. The classic *Swan Lake* love story between prince and princess is upstaged by the hypersexualized battle between the film's leading women and the swan symbols they embody. This conflation of ballet and deviant sexuality parallels an ethnoracial representation implied throughout the film. As I argue in this chapter, an assimilatory narrative is troubled by the ambivalent Jewish identities of its characters and actresses.

From the look of it, *Black Swan* is not the most explicit Jewish movie. The characters are not stereotypically Jewish looking, ballet is not a familiar Jewish filmic theme, and the melodrama of Nina's self-sabotage does not especially address religious identities at all. But in the context of an assimilatory century of Jewish American representation on stage and screen, the narrative trajectory is rife with familiar, if skewed, Jewish cultural resonances. The spacious quarters and tall ceilings of the Sayerses' New York apartment signal the prewar buildings typical of the predominantly Jewish Upper West Side. Iconic stereotypes of the overbearing Jewish mother and self-obsessed Jewish American princess play out to their extremes, and the terse relationship between mother and daughter unmistakably evokes the classic Jewish American trope.[2] Nina's mother, Erica Sayers (played by Barbara Hershey) pressures her daughter to succeed, forces her to eat, lives vicariously through her, and comforts her through infantilizing rituals. Nina, a good (Jewish) daughter, appears at the start of the film as obeisant, disciplined, and successful. When Nina cracks midway through, it follows that she ignores daughterly duties of every sort. Such a break with filial duties causes the greatest offense to the mother-daughter mirror game. The Jewish mother is emotionally cut as Nina surrenders to the seductions of the Black Swan role.[3]

In addition to narrative components and setting, a Jewish reading of the film and its emphasis on dance roles makes it significant that all four actresses who play the film's female leads are Jewish, and most have changed their names for Hollywood. Portman was born Natalie Hershlag, Barbara Hershey was originally Barbara Herzstein, and Winona Ryder was first Horowitz. Mila

Kunis's non-Anglo name perhaps never needed fixing. In roles like Lily, the sex appeal of the actress's spray-tanned "Otherness" may well sustain Hollywood stereotypes of unspecified (but not familiarly "Jewish") female exotics. Kunis is also the youngest generation of dancers and actresses in the film, which adds to her signification of sex appeal.

Here, I read the Jewish identities of the actresses alongside the implied Jewishness of the characters they represent in order to highlight how their bodies function as sites of representation in which boundaries between performer and performance are blurred. Indeed, what distinguishes dance from other expressive forms may be its inseparability between doer and the thing done. As in live performance, dance in narrative cinema perhaps too easily slips between the look of the body that dances and the dancing that body brings to a role. Thanks to the camera close-ups that create the fragmented effect of Portman's head, arms, and bust as the upper half of her dance double's (Sarah Lane's) lower half, it is Portman's expressive performance of Nina and her own celebrity face that audiences see and perceive in dance and non-dance scenes. In that same sense, the threat and the thrill of Nina's breakdown in pursuit of perfection also reveal the public pleasure of defacing Portman's pretty girl image. The monstrous appeal of Nina's sexual deviance, conceived most graphically through her lesbianism, and her Jewishness, personified most by her assimilatory aspirations, may then be seen as dangerous thrills enacted by ballerina and actress alike.

In this way, *Black Swan* dredges up race and sex dramas to make monsters of its female leads. Wild identities of ethnic and sexual Otherness, however, are only fit to die off in ambiguous ways in the film's domestication of the monster femmes. Conceiving of "domestication" in this way implies a declawing or taming, of "wild" or monster identities depicted as dangerous threats to normalcy. *Black Swan*'s domestication of monster embodiments in both dance and nondance scenes amounts to the film's final perpetuation of swan-styled white femininity so familiar to ballet traditions.

Indeed, since the first staging of Tchaikovsky's *Swan Lake* in the late nineteenth century, the White Swan has embodied the promise of transcendent perfection: the divine, ethereal, and impossibly light female form. Forever entrapped as a wistful werewoman under the jealous spell of an evil sorcerer, the fate of a princess-turned-swan lives in the kiss of Prince Siegfried, who must love her back to full life. A fairy tale of infinite proportions with an infamous set of 32 *fouettés*, the ballet's charm in countless remakes extends from the codified appeal of its classic aesthetics.[4] To disrupt those classic codes, as in the case of Brice and Streisand's comic parodies, discussed in chapter 2, is to expose the damaging cultural values of Western fairy tales so often overlooked. [5] In contrast, where *Black Swan* appears to disrupt those codes through its horror-style femmes, it constrains those monsters through a reinstatement of a white, straight world typified by ballet.

Billed as a psychological thriller, *Black Swan* capitalizes on the thrill of see-ing characters in unstable emotional states. While the film certainly fits this category, it arguably borrows its central villain from the horror film genre. The ambiguously Jewish, questionably lesbian female monster adds to a rich discourse in horror film theory, wherein the figure of the monster is a popular characterization that stands in for all that is socially and politically repressed in society. Film theorist Robin Wood names three categories of the repressed that can return in the form of the horror monster: the ethnic or racial Other, the woman, and the sexual deviant.[6] It is explicitly this mix within the horror figure construction that makes it relevant to the ballet film's layered appropri-ation of repressed identities. *Black Swan* takes advantage of these identity cat-egorizations to project the film's protagonist, Nina Sayers, as a Jewish female monster with deviant sexual desires, and by horror definition, deadly ones.

The Jewish background of *Black Swan*'s protagonist and megastar may sur-prise some. Portman's career-launching stage role as Broadway's Anne Frank notwithstanding, those who follow a bit more closely know the movie star as a modern-day Jewish poster girl for fair play. After having been selected by Christian Dior as the "new face of fashion" for the popular designer's fall 2010 season, Portman made headlines that year with her public statement against Dior designer John Galliano. Galliano's anti-Semitic remark among friends in a bar in Paris went viral, and Portman responded with outrage, rescinding her contract with the company.[7] But if her Jewish persona is potent enough to boycott the bad-mouth couture boys, Portman's onscreen image in unabash-edly un-Jewish roles is the passing Jewish face of a much whiter movie world.[8]

Portman's ability to read as unambiguously white, feminine, and perfectly desirable is her biggest contribution to Jewish visual representation and the small-nosed condition of her white swan femininity. Indeed, it is Portman's unmarked Jewish nose and its visual promise of "perfection" that offers a cen-tral tension when reading the film "Jewishly." Nina's monstrous hypersexual-ity, masculine ambition, and emotionality extend from Portman's perfectly petite, contained figure, and, I am arguing, her nose specifically (see figure 4.1. All figures in this Chapter are from *Black Swan* (2010). Directed by Darren Aronofsky.).

The stigma of the Jewish nose, which has stood in for all that is inferior, sickly, and meek about the Jewish body, is well documented in Jewish jokes and jokes about Jews.[9] Known as the Jewish phallus, the Jewish nose has come to signify the circumcised penis and Jewish male effeminacy, from psy-choanalysis to cultural studies discourse. For Jewish women, its presence has meant equally unflattering reflections of diasporic identity, homely roots, and defunct femininity. Like an ethnoracial coat of arms, such a nose has remained antithetical to assimilation, to American standards of beauty and status quo

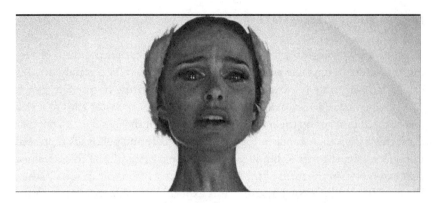

Figure 4.1: Screen shot, Natalie Portman's strained face of perfection.

gender norms. The fact that Portman passes out of Jewish appearance so easily is part and parcel of her unstereotypical Jewish face.

If Jewish actors have long renounced ethnic names, there is more to be
said about the corporeal dimensions of such de-ethnicization projects and the
possibilities of Jewish female bodies playing roles designated by mainstream
films like *Black Swan*. As far as noses are concerned, Portman and Ryder are
widely believed to have had nose jobs, and some websites reveal that Kunis
also has had one.[10] While not the only indication of a Jewish body, the nose
plays a central role in the representation of Jews in American TV and film.
The infamous nasality of Fran Dresher's voice in *The Nanny*, to give a popular
television example, as well as the "nosy" affectation that shapes her character,
arguably stems from her Jewish female nose. The more recent Jewish female
TV talent, Rachel Barry on HBO's *Glee*, fretted for at lease one episode over
whether to get a nose job in an all-too-familiar Jewish female drama. To do
away with the nose on the Jewish face erases the visual mark of stereotypical
Jewish looks that would more explicitly render her the ethnic Other.

As is discussed in each chapter of this book, the presence or absence of the
Jewish female nose tells an important history of Jewish assimilation throughout the twentieth and twenty-first centuries. Still, it is significant to note
that contemporary screen representations of Jewish-looking characters are
reserved almost entirely for effeminate men, or what is known as the schlemiel
character.[11] In contrast to the Jewish male face and its embrace as the mas-
cot of misguided American masculinity, the Jewish-looking female had long
been pushed off screen by the time *Black Swan* came out in 2010.[12] Despite
the decline of Jewish-acting actresses, or maybe because of it, an obsessive
log kept by countless Jewish sites had by that year invested nearly exclusively
in those celebrity personalities who "pass" into white roles, just like Nina,
Lily, and Beth.[13] The presence of "perfect" Jewish women who do not look
stereotypically Jewish reflects the monstrous threat and thrill of ethnoracial

passing. When *Black Swan* is read as a Jewish horror film, the haunting prov-ocation revolves around whether it is scarier for mainstream audiences for new-century Jewish girls on camera to look "Jewish" or not.

The white passing of the *Black Swan* cast serves as a microcosm for ques-tions of passing through classical dance more broadly: How do the ballet movie role and realm work to alter or hide the Jewish body? And back to Rebecca Rossen's question, "How can dance act like plastic surgery?" To consider these questions, this chapter also asks: How much does the citation of a classical dance canon and context already cover over or cut off a visual, embodied identification of ethnic Otherness? In addition to her good girl persona, it is because of her looks that Portman and her character Nina are both made to innately know the White Swan's attributes. Before Nina devolves fully into darkness, she appears so "normal" that the viewer has little cause to question her ability to dance the White Swan role. Normal for a ballerina, that is: stiff, erect, and pinkish.[14] In the casting rehearsal for the lead role of the season's new ballet, Thomas asks Nina if she'd like to be the Swan Queen, to which she responds, "If you want me to be" while at the ballet barre, obediently and full of desire. Leaning in closely, Thomas replies, "Well, if I was just casting the White Swan, she'd be yours . . . but I'm not." When the accompanist then plays the Black Swan coda and Nina begins to dance, Thomas yells with hands pull-ing at his hair, "Seduce us! Not just the Prince, but the court, the audience, the entire world! The *fouettes* are like a spider spinning her web. Come on! Attack it! Attack it!" Just at that moment, the door clangs open as Lily marches in late with iPod headphones on and completely throws off Nina's focus. Nina stumbles, several spider spins short of finishing.

Throughout the film, Thomas reiterates this point. "I honestly don't care about your technique; you should know that by now," he tells her when Nina comes to ask for the part. "Truth is, when I look at you, all I see is the White Swan. Yes, you're beautiful, fragile, fearful. Ideal casting. But the Black Swan . . . it's a hard fucking job to dance both." Nina answers with a feverish kiss to prove her deviant dark side, going so far as to bite his lip and surprise them both with her boldness. He sees how badly she wants the role—that is, how willing she is to be bad in order to fully embody the Black Swan's dark surrender—and he casts Nina after all. By the time the list is posted for the company to see, Nina has begun her transformation from good (Jewish) girl with dreams of swan assimilation to vicious female monster willing to slay for prima perfection.

In the company's gala scenes later, Thomas makes a public announcement of Nina's new role as Swan Princess (see figure 4.2). The ceremonial toast is a traumatic trade-off for the previous soloist, Beth (Winona Ryder), who copes by drinking too much and ends the night in the hospital after a crip-pling injury that looks deliberately self-destructive. This near-fatal accident merely foreshadows Nina's own lethal fantasies of upward mobility within the

Figure 4.2: Screen shot, Nina Sayers (Natalie Portman) and Thomas Leroy (Vincent Cassel) announcing the new swan soloist.

company and in the public eye. In Nina's moments standing alongside Thomas at the top of a cascading stairway, she peers down from a literal and symbolic high point that marks her tenuous ascendance to the ballet throne and its assimilatory achievement of an impossible social climb.

The figure of rising success in floor-length, designer white looks down at her dominion of balletomanes, funders, and fellow company members. Next, the abrupt camera cut to Lily laughing (see figure 4.3) mirrors Nina's anxious place at the top.

As is expected in this misogynistic world of whacked-out power plays and gender norms, Thomas invites Nina home with him. Nina is too timid for sex or even its suggestion, and Thomas instructs her to go home and "touch herself," as if the masturbation will release a valve of freer sensibility and its translation to a more desirable, looser carriage. This loyalty to role honors their mutual interest in Nina's success, though one that both characters understand must also meet Thomas's own sexual desires.[15] Nina's prudish inexperience helps typecast her as fit for the White Swan, an asset Portman's white nose and high cheekbone features make possible. And yet, to whatever extent this white racial passing allows the Jewish actress access to one-half of the coveted swan lead, Nina/Portman must slander her supreme prudishness to secure the role.

Paradoxically, the lenses of the film ascribe an opposing rhetoric of natural dance attributes to Kunis's character, Lily, whose more liberated embodiment better suits the Black Swan role. When Lily first dances on camera with other corps members, Thomas and Nina watch from the studio balcony as he

Figure 4.3: Screen shot, Lily (Mila Kunis) laughing at Nina's expense.

admires Lily's sensual passion (see figure 4.4). A visible tattoo of lilies across her back suggests an edgy, bad girl twist on the uptight ballerina, and her hair, worn loose, likewise betrays the traditional bun-head look and the floral white imagery of her name (see figure 4.5). But it is the "imprecise, but effortless" movement itself, as Thomas describes her dancing, that most threatens Nina and assigns Lily's lack of technique a personal freedom. "She's not faking it," Thomas explains, referring to her genuine sensuality and typifying the film's equation of dancing ability with naturalness.[16]

This personality-driven premise of dancing ability barely veils its racialized opposition of white and black symbols. This conflation of the ballet villain's blackness with epidermal blackness occurs so explicitly that Lily reads as the darker-skinned, exotic foil to Nina's white patina. As Nina impersonates Lily's sexiness in several attempts to get the part, she tries on the racial and sexual "Other" in symbolic ways. In a pinnacle example, Nina lets Lily take her out dancing at a nightclub the night before stage rehearsal and agrees to wear Lily's sexier black tank top over the white one she's already wearing. After some condescending persuasion, Nina lets Lily stir an ecstasy pill into her drink at the club. The two dance with Lily's typical abandon, and Nina's tight control slips into oblivion. This lusted-after "badness" sensationalizes a too-familiar trope of hypersexual black femininity. And even as Thomas tells us that Lily is "not faking it" in her freer, floppier dancing, Lily's deviant behaviors appear as nothing more than practiced plays with being bad. An act to be put on and taken off, the badness of blackness works to further whiten both characters and the actresses who play them. The "dark side" is a role to step

Figure 4.4: Screen shot, Lily in rehearsal.

Figure 4.5: Screen shot, Lily in rehearsal with her hair down.

into by will, a party drug, and a measure of their white desire for Otherness and distance from difference.

This ease of adopting sexual and ethnic markers of Otherness allows Nina and Lily to embody certain differences, like sexual deviance, and to deny others, like overt Jewishness. More specifically, the racially symbolized Nina/Lily double exaggerates a legacy of Jewish participation in black impersonation and extends its historical investments in securing whiteness. [17] Blackface performances by turn-of-the-twentieth-century Jews marked critical American beginnings for immigrant outsiders. The act of putting on black cork makeup and dancing black minstrel tropes effectively distanced Jews from yet more othered Others (black people) by way of performing Otherness as a made-up thing to put on and take off the face and body at will. *Black Swan*'s central dramatization of Nina's manic dark side continues this troublesome, if also strategic, history of black impersonation for Jewish performers.

As Portman's character travels from innocent White Swan to fatalistic Black Swan through racialized and sexualized impersonation, a monstrous trajectory toward animality and all things dangerous, primal, and bad sustains white-black stereotypes still so forcefully at play in Hollywood and beyond. Moreover, as Nina's ego double, Lily is a foiled shadow of Nina's ambivalent Jewishness. Seen as two halves of an assimilatory Jewish whole, the imagination of passing female bodies entangled in spiteful lust sexualizes both characters along revealing binary lines. Securing positions in whiteness by performing blackness as badness, the Nina/Lily dyad contrasts assimilatory aspirations with lecherous, libidinous acts. In doing so, the constant doubling of the two melds the characters into a singular body, a two-headed Jewish female monster that Nina and the audience see repeatedly in the movie's multiple use of mirrors.[18]

As Portman and Nina convincingly oscillate between characterizations of a naturalized White Swan role and devious Black Swan dark side, the Jewishness of actress and character surfaces in-between as not quite white and not quite not. This liminal position sustains the assimilatory threat central to the horror plot: that the Jewish female monster just might be part of a white, mainstream "us" and no longer an outsider, ethnic "them."

JEWISH SWANS, QUEER CONTEXTS

Narrative and character components in *Black Swan* overlap Jewish and queer discourses. In developing how these frameworks may work collaboratively, it is useful to underline their points of intersection. Cultural studies scholar Jon Stratton directly relates Jewish and queer viewership in *Coming Out Jewish*.[19] Making the discourse of "coming out" an explicit link between American Jews and closeted queers, Stratton's text focuses on Jewish material that comes out of hiding and into popular entertainment forms. Stratton writes that a Jewish "coming out" is part of the discourse of assimilation; one "comes out" as Jewish when others may not know by looking. He links this uncloseting to the acknowledgment of Jewish racial passing, based on the premise that neither Jewish nor homosexual identities may be entirely visible on the body.[20]

How Jewish moments play out and to what ends differ from case to case. But the recognition of double-coded contexts is sustained throughout Stratton's book, in which certain audiences might experience the material Jewishly, while others less familiar with ethnic tropes will not. Especially relevant to this chapter is Stratton's understanding that Jewishness can be understood as "a variable textual attribute" not necessarily tied to characters explicitly identified as Jews. Furthering the connection between Jewish and queer discourses, Stratton bases this malleable capacity of "Jewish moments" on Alexander Doty's similar theorization of "queer moments" that are not definitively linked to queer-identified characters.[21] The intimacy between a Jewish and a queer coming out extends scholarship that has historically looked for the overlaps between theories of ethnic and sexual difference.[22] That said, where queer Jewish scholarship has largely focused on effeminate male subjects, its application to a reading of *Black Swan* contributes a focus on women's roles and the act of coming out to thrill audiences with "wereswan" scariness.

To name and question the liberatory potential of *Black Swan*'s "queer" bodily characterizations accounts for how bodies move in and between static notions of the racialized, sexualized white feminine regime so familiar in Hollywood portrayals. As in the preceding chapter discussions of neoburlesque's homosocial potential, the social queerness of the "funny girl body," and the contemporary comic interplays of race and sex freedoms, the project of viewing filmic bodies in queer ways might include a search for the resistive potential of dance in narrative cinema. In each of these contexts, a queer reading upsets or otherwise intervenes in patriarchal structures of power and normative gender roles. It is this counterhegemonic, agentive power to mobilize seemingly fixed assignments of coded social roles that holds the power to push queerness beyond a strictly sexualized meaning without entirely divorcing itself from orientations of alternative sexuality.

And yet at play in *Black Swan*'s representation of these sexual and ethnic differences, whether deliberately embodied or denied, is their commercial appropriation. Conservative permissions of plot line and character demise determine what can be seen and how. This may come as no surprise to audiences familiar with Hollywood's habit of pulling from the margins only to fortify white tropes. But the case of a movie so manic about classical dance contributes novel means of making such manipulations legible. *Black Swan*'s alternative takes on traditional swan princesses through queer and Jewish psycho-thrills raise questions about to what degree repressed identities and ideologies can surface in a mainstream ballet film. Such thinking opens up new questions: In what ways does the raw, creative queer power of nonstraight, nonwhite identities corrupt and/or carry forward the ballet plot in *Black Swan* and other ballet films? To what degree can the ballet body play with and discard sexual and ethnic identities in dance and nondance scenes? And how does the film conflate stage, screen, and behind-the-scenes worlds such that hypersexualized characters within the ballet and the passing Jewish female actors who play them may only be differentiated along blurry boundaries at best?

Adding a bodily or physical dimension to this layered "coming out" entangles the repressive aspects of classical dance in a queer and Jewish reading of the ballet horror genre. Indeed, the repressed female monster "returns" from the margins of the socially acceptable as if called forth by the unyielding demands of the classical dance world *Black Swan* depicts. In order to meet the expectations of Thomas's *Swan Lake* twist, Nina must "come out" of her protective, prudish shell. In this central plot line, ballet itself ruptures Nina's pink adolescence. Her naiveté is native to her white swan training, and she grows up clearly closeted by the protective bubble of her mother's assimilatory dreams. And yet the seductive promise of ascendance up and out of these repressive controls is what ultimately beckons the monster forward to wage her unshackled attack. Only harming herself, however, the failed return of the monster ballerina ultimately renders impotent any of Nina's creative, constructive power to change her circumstances or those of the film's conservatory ballet world.

Black Swan thus uses its monsters not to dismantle notions of normalcy linked to race, gender, and sexuality but to maintain them. In doing so, the film reinstates the White Swan figure as a standard symbol of hegemonic, balletic beauty. Perfection provides a pleasure-nightmare of those passing in-between ethnic and white identities via false eruptions of the sexual queer. Ballet becomes the means and the material through which the hypersexualized, racialized edges of culture can be managed and marketed for mainstream audiences. Unpacking the film's remake of *Swan Lake* as the sphere of repressive social and political thinking and staid legacy of ethereal bodily perfection ultimately reaffirms a layered pathology of whiteness. The queer edges of culture creep into the spotlight to doubly entertain and then be recontained by the conservative logic of the film. The monstrous ambivalence of an assimilatory ballet body, in striving to be perfectly white by playing with symbolic blackness, meets only the ballerina's own manic end through the selfish, sick sabotage of her own bloody toenails, guts, and gore.

LESBIAN SEX AND SWAN SIN: THRILLS FIT TO FORGET

As assimilatory depictions of class and race mobility are coded through the representation of classical dance desires, the film relates the dangers of a Jewish racial "in-between" to those of the bisexual woman. In this sense, the film draws on themes familiar to comic genres, as in the previous chapter, in which Sandra Bernhard, Sarah Silverman, and Ilana Glazer link expressions of bisexuality to the impersonation of blackness by way of an appropriative license that their Jewishness affords them. What both humor and horror representations make clear is that distinct from the homosexual, the "bi-" further underlines the ambivalence of a position between goodness and badness. In *Black Swan*'s intended ambiguity regarding ethnoracial and sexual identities, the threat of the Other's ability to pass in and out of "difference" is vague enough to ensure that neither the Nina/Portman confluence nor the film as a whole poses any real threat to hetero-patriarchy. Perhaps nothing in the film says this better than the crazed cunnilingus that, according to the film's conservative cover-up, never really happens.

In a stoned stupor masterminded by Lily, the two characters return to Nina's apartment after an evening of clubbing. Securing a door against Nina's mother's aggressive surveillance, they immediately kiss, and Lily initiates oral sex; a pas de chat, as one blogger punned, that exaggerated the cattiness of the enemy-lovers.[23] The same-sex scene is a blurry hallucination of self-pleasure as self-sabotage, as Lily's face appears on-screen as Nina's own for a split second. But even beyond this mirroring effect, the plot muddles the lesbian encounter through its immediate erasure the following day. Nina arrives late to rehearsal the next morning, only to find Lily dancing the Black Swan role. Any clinging hope that the two women would rise up through homo-romance against the evil choreographer's manipulative plot is crushed by a "just a dream" justification. When Nina brings up the night before with Lily at the first water break, Lily's response ensures for Nina and the audience that no such sex ever happened. Lily mocks Nina for her monstrous mix-up, teasingly asking, "Was I good?" The impulse to side with Lily, the more sexually resolved of the two, is meant to win out for the viewer.

This painful slap in the face makes the manic monster look almost human. Nina's vulnerability interrupts the horrible transformation that she undergoes throughout the film. While reeking of middle-school mean girls, this episode of shame and self-doubt offers a queer pause as well. This sympathetic portrayal makes legible the tensions between what is understood to be "real" as aligned with oppressive norms of socialized sexuality.[24] Ambiguity over whether Lily is tricking Nina or Nina has officially lost her mind is not only prescribed by the plot, but also is evidence of the film's representation of sexual queerness. The sex that supposedly didn't really happen, *did* for Nina, as much as it did for the viewer. A critical opportunity exists in watching for this episode of homoeroticism as even vaguely sympathetic the morning after. In reconsidering the wet dream as a queer moment, there may be power in its ability to puncture the overwhelmingly misogynistic grand narrative.

The potential of the lesbian sex to feel as real for the viewer as it presumably did for Nina might shift the film's representation terms. According to horror film theory, however, once the female monster expresses sexuality, moving from virgin to whore, she must be killed off. The idea is that in ensuring her demise, a film contains the real threat of female sexuality. But despite Nina's sexual exploration and the psychological deterioration that results from it, *Black Swan* leaves its fatal ending less than clear. The last scenes of the film show Nina between onstage and backstage scenes, switching between the two with choppy camera cuts that seek to match Nina's own emotional state.

Fully deranged by the pressure of opening night and her obsessive possession of the doubled swan role, Nina thinks she sees her nemesis, Lily, in the vanity mirror of her dressing room and reacts by strangling Lily (see figure 4.6), breaking the mirror and stabbing Lily with a shard. Nina drags the slain body into the bathroom and wipes up the blood as it seeps under the door. She attempts to regain composure, continuing to get ready for her next entrance despite the broken mirror just beside her (see figure 4.7).

Just as in the same-sex scene, the viewer watches from Nina's view the murderous death that *does* happen, only to find out shortly thereafter that it was only her horrible imagination. When a few scenes later Lily comes to the dressing room door to congratulate Nina on a well-danced Black Swan, the small blood pool beginning to stain the white mesh of her swan bodice makes (only semi-) clear that Nina has wounded herself, and not Lily as previously depicted. Nina does or doesn't notice her own madness, and in her return to dance the final act, continues to bleed through her bodice, to an equally uncertain death (see figure 4.8).

As the film leaves its ending unfinished in this way, it knocks our swan off a literal and symbolic balletic perch in a single, final gesture that climaxes with the thrill of her ambivalent demise. It is this unfinished fall behind the stage set that may best identify the limits of repressive representational fantasies and Hollywood's ambivalent willingness to see them at front and center. The sexualized acts of murderous swan-sin finally only demolish the protagonist herself, indicating most pointedly the utility of a repressed-monster analysis to the ballet movie plot. *Only* harming herself, the representation of

Figure 4.6: Screen shot, Nina strangling Lily.

Figure 4.7: Screen shot, Nina in the vanity mirror beside the mirror she has just broken.

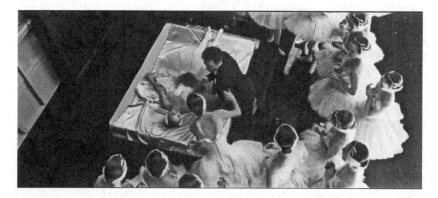

Figure 4.8: Screen shot, Nina's uncertain death.

monstrosity is a matter of Nina's own self-derailment. It is this assignment of psychic disfigurement to the female body that renders the female monster only fit to be contained.

SWAN QUEEN KILLS HERSELF, SAVES BALLET?

Evidenced in the matching sentiments of film reviews by dance writers, as well as *Swan Lake* reviews written in the wake of the film, is the monstrous offense of *Black Swan*'s butchering of ballet's repertory classic.[25] Several reviewers took issue with the doubling of Odette and Odille as alter egos, insisting upon the necessity of swan roles as two distinct characters, though regularly performed by the same dancer. *New York Times* dance reviewer Alistair Macaulay said audiences would surely be disappointed when they came to the Metropolitan Opera House if they came to see something akin to *Black Swan*, and admonished the ignorant crowd as much as the fourth and final act of American Ballet Theater's poorly envisioned flop.[26]

Underlying many of these perspectives was a public anxiety about Portman's dancing itself, which elicited significant defense of her stunt double's uncredited contributions.[27] The host of news media and blog commentary on Portman's uncertain dancing credits added to the film's appeal, of course. But more critically, media interest in the subject collapsed the space between fictional representations and the reality of dancers and their labor. Once again, the distinction between actors and their roles is murkier in dance movies than perhaps in other film genres.[28] The concern for dancer credit paints Portman in yet another position in-between opposites, wherein her status affords her access to both positions. She is both the more assertive, galvanizing opportunist getting away with artistic murder and the damsel in distress in need of saving from Lane, her lesser-acknowledged dance double.

In light of this chapter's focus on dualities and their layered appropriative pleasures, this money-making media trap pits one woman against another in ways that engender yet another swan doubling. The uncertain dance credits speak to the film's framing of the dancing itself. As the camera fragments the figure into short, severe cuts, the dancing body in motion is rarely fully visible. Conglomerate dancing of Portman and her stunt double splices the ballerina's body into quick edits that disfigure the dancer into variably signified, fetishized segments. Moreover, the notoriously torturous aspects of ballet training boasted in shots of Nina's painfully smashed toes remain off camera. A fictive separation of labor, body, and psyche in the film finds it sufficient for technique to be alluded to but not seen.

This partial view of the work of dance pieces together the whole girl from a composite of two women's variant limbs; in doing so, it dices up the body in ways that heighten drama but interrupt the possibility of viewing full dancing sequences. Perhaps the most pointed blow to the ballet community is the camera's conspicuous concealment of the ballet's central climax: the 32 *fouettees en tournant* at the coda of the Black Swan pas de deux. The topic of the coda comes up two times in the film. The first time is after Nina's audition for the Black Swan was sabotaged by Lily's late entrance into the dance studio. Nina returns home devastated, but more determined to practice the *fouettees* in the triptych mirrors of her apartment ballet barre. The second time is as Nina feverishly dances the part on opening night, accompanied by the final growth of her full feathers at the near orgasmic point of insanity. In both cases, the camera splits the body into top (Portman) and bottom (Lane), and the horror of her mania moving at full speed replaces any pleasure of viewing the ballerina at work.

The lack of intact *fouettees* or any on-camera balletic feat draws critical parallels for other less than fully visible matters of the movie. The conspicuous absence of *fouettees* disregards the athletic mainstay of any serious *Swan*

Lake reconstruction. It not only disappoints dance viewers familiar with the ballet, it also distorts the dancing body beyond the body-chopping camera cuts. Even if the film makes no claims to be true to the ballet, camera trickery and claims of Portman's training still appear to construct a dancerly authenticity. More than merely hiding the actress's lack of dance technique, the invisible *fouettees* sever the dancing of the dance movie from actual bodies in ways that resonate with other passing or ambiguous race and sex identities in the film. Playing the dancer without having to dance allows the actress and character to impersonate a perfect White Swan and set the stage for her monstrous devolution.

The conservative logic of contemporary ballet cinema and its passing roles for white Jewish women thus constrict around the strained depiction of dance itself. The degree to which dancing may be seen on-screen resonates with other ambiguous identities, like Jewishness and lesbian sexuality, approximated and impersonated through the film. Just as the camera conjoins the upper and lower halves in questionable percentages, so too do physical and psychological thrills pull from the margins only to blur the angst their presence provokes. Lesbian sex supposedly never happens; narrative Jewish themes are invoked as visual Jewishness is unmentioned and unmarked; and the protagonist's body, when the camera lets us see it in full, is but a bloodied corpse falling from grace, only to find no certain fate in life or death. In these in-betweens, *Black Swan* constructs the Jewish monster ballerina's ultimate threat to self. Reinforcing the danger of ethnic, sexual, and female identities, the Jewish monster swan sickens with pleasure, and pleasures with her inevitable demise. Finally, the protagonist's erotic surrender to madness effectively thrilled mainstream audiences unambiguously, earning the film a nomination for best movie of the year.

THE FUNNY THING ABOUT HORROR: MOVING ACROSS GENRES

The horror of the Jewish female monster offers a critical counterpoint to the humor of the Jewish female comic and her funny girl body. The lack of intended humor in *Black Swan* insists that viewers regard the severity of ballet's (white nose in the air) disciplines with utmost seriousness. In doing so, the film imagines concert dance and the suspense genre as complementary zones of strict, high art humorlessness. The combination of the monster thriller and ballet's insatiable demands creates the effect of a world so intense it quite literally hurts. Where for some this painful personification of psychic and physical burden produces empathetic, kinesthetic viscera as if it were happening the same for Nina as for the viewer, others may sustain a critical space of distance from the realm of feelings within the film as unconvincingly over the top, and laughably so.

While horror films often invite laughter for audiences who seek out a campy, cult movie appeal, the Academy of Motion Picture Arts and Sciences's reception of *Black Swan* refused this impulse altogether, pitching the film as the year's most respected high drama. But in a screening of the film among colleagues and friends less convinced of the film's art appeal, viewers laughed variably at parts that they later explained felt sensationalistic, disingenuous, or just plain *bad*.[29] As opposed to rote reflexes, the instances of laughter offer their own space of resistance. Mikhail Bakhtin writes that "laughter has the remarkable power of making an object come up close, of drawing it into a zone of crude contact where one can figure it familiarly on all sides, turn it upside down, inside out, peer at it from above and below, break open its external shell, look into its centre, examine it freely and experiment with it."[30] In other words, laughter can queer repressive controls, and quell the power of its psychological thrills as mere cheap thrills of the sexually and artistically bored.

The space of laughter here, rebellious in its refusal of the film's emotional trajectory, reconsiders the power of the film through its active resistance. As the jaded attitude of my focus group scoffs at the film's incredulous affectations, it also disregards the overarching logic the film puts forth. By laughing at the film, presumably instead of gasping, the commentators reveal an ineffectuality of the film's performative gestures; in other words, they argue that it doesn't do what it says it's doing. To laugh at the horrible moments of Nina's gruesome cuticle tearing, for instance, refuses to fully enter the contract of spectatorship and its requirements of blind acceptance. The laughter at bad acting, bad dialogue, unbelievable sex, and equally unpersuasive splicing of Portman and dance double stunts resists complacence about the film's dismissive premise of an excessively female struggle for success blown—as usual—way out of proportion.

In the other chapters in this book on Jewish funny girls, *bad*ness offers a self-consciously Jewish, intentionally queer dance impulse. When my own colleagues found Jewish burlesquers danced "badly," I had fun tracing all the reasons why scantily clad, fleshy Jewish girls in sexy Jewish acts would never try to be "good" dancers as long as standards of dance were tied to appropriate femininity like the White Swan Queen. The very name of the cabaret showcase discussed in chapter 1 of this book, Nice Jewish Girls Gone Bad, suggests as much. That they have willingly gone bad parodies an expectation of prudish religious chicks by trading in pious ethics for sexy fun. Funnily enough, the group's founder and ringleader, Susannah Perlman, offered *Black Swan* as a perfect example of what her Nice Jewish Girls were railing against.[31]

Where the bad Jewish girls of *Black Swan* couldn't seem to be having less fun with themselves or one another, it is significant that the rhetoric of their "badness" similarly pivots around unresolved sexual politics and the representation of Jewish female bodies as the performers outlined in the previous chapters. Notably, the badness of *Black Swan*'s cast accounts for a similarly intended badness of their deviant experiments in homo-curious eroticism—a going bad. The unintended badness remarked upon by my peers is perhaps more interesting in the sense that it invites knowing laughter at that which falls privy to mainstream logic in the name of the innovative, the fresh, the new thrill of the year. Whereas Jewish burlesque and related comedy formats acknowledge that they react against Hollywood's weak depictions of women in similar ways, films like *Black Swan* make monster-house pets of those same queer portrayals.

In addition, an analysis of what is unintentionally funny in *Black Swan* versus parodic ballet renditions by Streisand and Brice described in chapter 2 lends itself to an important historical critique of humor and horror in relation to period-specific Jewish whiteness. Both films reflect not only when the Jewish female body may be depicted as same (white) or Other (Jewish), but also how her representational break with ballet's white institutional milieu may wage conservative or radical social critiques. The Jewishness of *Black Swan's* characters, writers, and directors is overlooked in the white/black world of ballet's demands for perfection, as opposed to the deliberate duckishness of *Funny Girl's* "perfect imperfections." A significant link between horror and humor may exist in the potential for a horror film to express hostility in ways similar to the devices of a joke. Both are seen as nonthreats despite their subversive potential to bolster or break with social norms. Ultimately, when the female monster makes her own joke, the joke may not as easily make a monster out of her.

Portman's "white nose" constructs a good girl image via the White Swan the same as it does for her celebrity appeal. Her face of perfection, and its absence of a Jewish nose, becomes the source of incongruous humor too. In one *Saturday Night Live* sketch written and directed by Adam Samberg, Portman parodies her own perfectness in a black and white gangster rap music video.[32] The refrain, "Shut the fuck up and suck my dick," substitutes the irony of a "white nose" for a pretend penis-phallus. Playing with the implausibility of a badass persona for Hollywood's sweetheart, the humor highlights the whiteness of her image through the video's distance from actual blackness. As a riff on the so-called Jewish-black alliance that now makes its way into so much of Jewish written and directed humor (see chapters 3 and 5), Samberg and Portman's comic debut makes laughable the anxious Jewish appropriation of rap.[33] As it commodifies blackness as a guilty white pleasure, the skit also works to heighten the gap between the media-soaked masculinity of black cultural forms and Portman's white femininity. Were she to be more Jewish looking, this parody of the black, male rapper would not work with the requisite white good girl and black bad boy implications. For Samberg, of course, the Jewish nose marks his mainstream appeal in a moment when Jewish male faces are widely embraced in American entertainment, especially in comedy.

While the story of "Jewish looking" figures on television and film records an important history of Jewish assimilation, it is significant to note that today's screen representations of Jewish-looking characters are reserved largely for men. Scholars of film and television have remarked on the recent resurgence of Jewish visual representation, and in particular the contemporary creation of a postmodern self-reflexivity made new by its self-conscious repetition of old insider-outsider tropes.[34] The widespread popularity of this emasculated putz circulates well beyond Jewish-oriented circles. Stratton argues that its recurrence in Hollywood suggests an overall Yiddishization of American culture.[35] But where references to Jewishness are explicit for some, Stratton argues that schlemiel characters often offer the viewer the possibility of being read as a Jew (via looks, behavior, name) but no certainty.[36] Stratton finds evidence of an ambivalence of representation that a gender-sensitive reading makes even more explicit. In the case of the sketch with Samberg, his more stereotypical Jewish features, falsely masculinizing Viking helmet, and gender-reversing backup role help make the farce legible as a Jewish (male) joke less accommodating of Jewish-looking women.

As if announcing the race and gender anxieties provoked by Portman's white passing, horror roles and garish humor deface her perfect image. To the extent that a stereotypical Jewish nose is monstrously funny good or funny bad, Portman's power lies in her perfect lack of such a bodily mark. Defacing her image is at once tied to and in substitution for a process of de-facing (as in a literal detachment off the face) the nose from the Jewish actress. In the case of *Black Swan*, this absence amounts to an invisibilization of Jewishness in the film's narrative and cast components. Moreover, the presence of hot, and horrifying, Jewish chicks who do not look Jewish complicates the idea of a so-called Jewification of American film and Yiddishization of American culture. As ballet roles assist the passing acts of Jewish female actresses in mainstream film, the psychological thrills and horror appeal of a Jewish female monster take on these scary and sexy implications for Jewish and non-Jewish viewers, although arguably in different ways. Just like jokes that read differently for those they represent, so does Hollywood's dance horror thrill differently when identities are at stake.

CONCLUSION

As I have argued throughout, analysis of *Black Swan* reveals its layered domestication of the "Other" that housetrains the homoerotic alongside the racial passing of the film's Jewish actresses and ambiguously Jewish characters. Through an exaggerated American dream turned nightmare of mismanaged sexual discovery, the film imagines ballet as a way to transcend the Jewish female body's ethnic excesses. It likewise sources those excesses as pleasurable bits of derangement, rationale, or justification for why characters aspire perfect the white balletic idyll. Passing out of classically unwanted Jewish female stereotypes of the mother, the hag, and princess that dominate film and TV roles played by Jewish performers over the last several decades, Portman, Kunis, Ryder, and half-Jewish Hershey wade into the muck of perfect prudish swans gone wild and wrong. By dancing defiantly with yet more othered Otherness, imagined and embodied through the Black Swan, the film unearths its monstrous figures of lesbianism and Jewishness, only to rebury them through the logic of ballet dreams.

What it means to dance defiantly toward one's own demise in the name of ballet dreams breaks through a purist professional dance veneer only to bolster its prudishness, its exclusivity, and its white patriarchal imaginary. Worse, it relies on a treacherous racial logic of black and white that deploys white-passing Jewish bodies to play up blackness and its long-standing tropes of untamed physicality, raw sexuality, and unchecked emotionality. More than a dramatization of psychological symbols (i.e., a character's light and dark side), the black and white premise of Aronofsky's film plays out a racialized, sexualized imagination that speaks to social fantasies and fears while ensuring that their place remains unstable and unclear. So long as the ballet conjures up contradictions of ultimate beauty and ultimate repression, so will the social threat-fantasy of an oppositional force come out from under to entertain with its monstrous re-emergence. The degree to which the monster reaches to take over but only truly harms herself satisfies the public urge to see the horrid creature fail.

The task of teasing out dance and politics thus adds a meta-monstrous dimension to the realm of ballet thriller-horror, ferreting out the movie's entangled implications for the fate of Jewish female actresses. Hollywood continues to imagine the balletic ideal through the portrait of stringent discipline and a damaged self-image. The ballet as elite cultural institution maintains its sturdy hold on mainstream movies as the ultimate emblem of high art and concert dance scenes. And like the return of repressed identities that refuse to fully resolve in the film, the murky potential of yet more taunting threats looms for *Swan Lake* remakes to come.

In the comparative whiteness of Jewish performers in roles like those in *Black Swan* and the Jewishness of *Funny Girl*, an important distinction between visual representations of Jewishness and its embodied efforts at whiteness is construed in bodily terms. The Jewishness of *Black Swan*'s characters, writers, and directors is overlooked in the white and black world of ballet's demands for perfection, as opposed to the deliberate duckishness of *Funny Girl*'s perfect imperfections and Brice's joke-work that it references. In both cases, the implications of ethnic visibility or invisibility bring to light mainstream ideas of where and how Jewishness can or should be seen in relation to the female ballet body or filmic depictions thereof.

As horror and not humor, *Black Swan* makes scary and only queerly funny the monstrosity of the upwardly mobile passing act. And yet it thrills audiences with the lethal improbability of any effectual damage beyond that of the monster to herself. What *Black Swan* repeats as horror and *Funny Girl* presented as humor is once again the crisis of unassimilable difference. The fear and dark fantasy that follows is that the altered noses will grow back, the name changes will regress to ethnic originals, and the filmic and nonfictive careers among Hollywood's ballet elite will be made moot by muddy signs of unpassable Jewishness.

Laughing at and laughing with may ultimately distinguish the performance that intends to be funny from the one that poorly executes its opposite aims at seriousness, but both scenarios offer a space for viewers to resist dogma in more or less radical ways. Comedy and horror lend themselves to parody in comparative ways, as both construct worlds of funhouse social commentary on the mundane concerns of their respective audiences. What is funny, as what is scary, forces a reframing of the familiar wherein Jewishness exaggerates its moves in and out of mainstream scripts. Taken to their absurdist ends, Jewish jokes may frighten, and ambiguously Jewish horror may look pretty funny. Releasing the steam valves of social insecurities, either approach bedevils through self-conscious roles of the not-quite-white star and the thrill of her excessive desires.

The next chapter plays out these tensions of excessive desires via sexual deviance by taking them to their logical extreme: pornography. Spotlighting the parody films of adult film company Burning Angel and its direction by lead performer Joanna Angel, the analysis highlights a punk porn genre through a focus on its Jewish female boss. In dialogue with the Sexy Jewess tropes of the postassimilatory and postfeminist contemporary period, and as a master of self-display, Angel's approach reflects an alternative take on the next steps for Jewish female comedy. In it, Jewface jokes and black appropriations are identity acts of the world's richest industry. Bookending the arc of chapters that moves from the downwardly mobile all the way up, Angel's impersonations and self-reflections perhaps most fully bear the themes raised throughout the book. From twisted Jewish mother jokes to the horror of doppelgangers in haunted mirrors, popular references and claims to her unorthodox new Jewishness become the cultural material which Angel makes both most sacred and profane. Outing her internal struggles with the form that she finds feminist but isn't always sure why, she lets us know, maybe more than any other woman covered in the book, just how blurry the representational stakes can be when profiting off roles in-between.

CHAPTER 5

Punk Porn Princess Joanna Angel and the Rise of Jewess Raunch

The award-winning Burning Angel Studios website prominently features Jewish company founder and film director Joanna Angel among the two hundred pierced and tattooed female models whom she calls her "army of hot punk chicks." Since 2001 the self-described "original home of hardcore punk rock emo porn" has contained ever-growing pages of video and photo content, event listings, and interactive chat forums against a mostly metal soundscape. Photo galleries of hyper-coiffed, inked-up bodies depict straight sex, same sex, and group sex, while band interviews, comic book discussion threads, and snickering parody categories sell antiestablishment images for a lucrative porn industry.

From niche categories of video content like "Gonzo," "Goth," Horror," and "Glasses" to more familiar drop-down options like "BDSM," "College," and "Anal," the site guides its viewers who want to find sex entertainment in any number of ways, more novel or not. The most listings are found under the banner "Tattoo/Piercings," a priority that is not surprising given that the company modeled much of its punk aesthetic from the Suicide Girls.[1] Like that site, too, Angel and a growing number of young women who work for her appear to manage their own correspondence with site visitors as much as their own images.

It is Joanna Angel's visual, textual, and embodied address to women as porn agents that makes her enterprise such a significant addition to a study of Jewishness in the context of gender and sexuality. In dialogue with feminist porn history and the evolving opportunities for its female directors and performers, as well as Jewish humor aimed at the contemporary generation, the website reflects the values of its genre that both court and challenge accepted norms, rousing new dimensions of the Sexy Jewess.

By directly addressing women visitors, Burning Angel promotes an ethos of female agency, as Angel invites female site users who are "having way too much good sex . . . behind closed doors, for no pay" to join her team of models and "help take over the world." The invitation indicates, first, that good sex is worth good money, and second, that women interested in the kind of porn her company makes are promising candidates for the job. Such an open call suggests a for us, by us mentality even as Angel admits that the site's biggest demographic is twenty-five- to forty-year-old white males and male-female couples, groups likely turned on by the premise of women-friendly porn.[2] Angel advocates for her female viewers to bring the sex work they already supply out from behind closed doors and get paid for it.[3] This "outing" is significant in that it likens the bedroom door to a kind of closet behind which women have repressed their inner pornographers. The Internet interface opens that door as wide as the site's massive online reach. What "world" Angel wishes to take over remains unnamed, but it is clear that the site's punk ethos and its branding of porn offer a partial answer to how she and her models stake their claim to its riotous nonconformity as a subcultural aesthetic for the commercial mainstream.

As part of its liberatory vision, however, the site constructs a conspicuously *white* world, with only a scattered few performers of color, and while lesbian scenes are prevalent, the site hosts almost no depictions of gay male or transgender sex. In this sense, Angel's company sells sex outright for an adult entertainment industry that, while always growing in number and scope of niche markets, remains predicated on the hypersexualization of cisgendered white women and their coed sex partners. A significant part of this chapter investigates how Burning Angel's brand of sexy girl power promotes a sex-positive freedom that markets a radical takeover by an army of hot punk chicks while maintaining a white, heterosexist imaginary, and why. In this sense, the discussion links back to questions of pop cultural Jewish joke-work in the context of gender and sexuality raised in previous chapters, wherein Jewish female performers in celebrity spotlights reach toward ever more "edgy" subject matter and embodied material to satisfy a mainstream appetite for oppositional content without threatening a white, male fan base (see especially the discussion of Sarah Silverman in "Race, Sex, and the Sarah Silverman Effect" in chapter 3).

The conspicuous whiteness of Angel's company competes with her openness about Jewishness and her regular use of Jewish joke-work. Known best for her "XXX parody," Angel stars in films she directs while making use of verbal and physical comedy that seems to derive directly from women discussed in previous chapters. The Jewishness she references calls on many of the ethnic, cultural, and religious themes deployed by mainstream comedy and stand-up such as Sarah Silverman's and Jewish-themed neoburlesque such as the Schlep Sisters to do and undo stereotypes about Jewish female sexiness and lack thereof, while satirizing race and gender identities. Angel's Jewish joke-work and sex-positive persona come together most poignantly in her spoof of a Jewish holiday as well as her foray into interracial sex films, in which Angel invokes blackface as part of her race plot. As Angel stars in her own religious and race dramas, her porn persona extends and departs from expected tropes.

Drawing parallels between Angel's altporn edge and her unorthodox embodiments of Jewish joke-work, this chapter traces how her work engages mainstream and subcultural porn markets, using her Jewishness to do so. The analysis takes as its premise that pornography makes hardcore raunch its core concern and, in doing so, raises questions about the difference between actual sex on camera and the funny suggestion of it so ubiquitous in Jewish female joke-work. To flesh this out, I turn to Ariel Levy's configuration of the female chauvinist pig, whose enormous influence on the American mainstream drives raunch culture, but not generally in the progressive ways that it says it does. I borrow also from studies on pornography that frame the debate around the genre's representational politics, championing a queer and feminist movement of pornography that celebrates the liberatory potential of porn made for and by women. Tying the conversation back to Jewishness, the discussion contextualizes Angel's circulation through the Jewish culture magazine *Heeb* to help frame the way her appeal excites a new Jewish audience otherwise turned off by the cultural Jewishness of their parents' generation. A close reading of Angel's interracial compilation video finally returns to themes raised throughout this book on the performance of blackness as a gendered and sexualized Jewish imagination. In direct comment on racist archetypes in and out of porn that inevitably dial back to sex, Angel refigures the appropriative terms of desire and distance through a black/white drama that she parodies with graphic effect. Sliding between joke fantasies of phallic power and feminist progress, she becomes the Sexy Jewess extraordinaire.

FROM THE PORN WARS TO POSTFEMINISM

To enter the virtual realm of Burning Angel's tattooed porn stars and XXX parodies, site visitors agree to fairly typical terms: they are over eighteen, they won't show the content to minors, they will take measures to ensure that minors don't see the material, and they believe that sexually explicit material is not offensive or obscene. This last item, by design, would seem to contradict a central tenet of porn for the sake of legalese. The premise of porn, after all, may be that it makes sexual desire perverse in the name of pleasure.

Still, such parameters are mandatory as some semblance of social control when hard-core sex and its uncontainable access are on the line, online. The issue of obscenity is paramount for pornographers, who must work in accordance with mandated obscenity laws. What is obscene in the legal sense follows basic guidelines open to juridical interpretation.[4] In a nonlegal sense, however, many find porn obscene by its very premise of selling sex on camera. For antipornography camps of all kinds, porn's sexualization of relationships, pop cultural references, and other filmic content offend on principle. Indeed, more than the subject matter of previous chapters in this book, the topic of pornography and its ethics raises moral panic as a key component of its performance agenda.

At stake in these morality debates has been the issue of censorship of First Amendment freedoms. Peaking in the 1980s, the porn wars, also known as the sex wars, debated the role of sexualized representation in society. The debate grew into a full-scale divide among feminists that continues in 2016. Feminist writer and antipornographer Robin Morgan's famous slogan, "Porn is the theory, rape is the practice," argued that pornography amounted to the commodification of rape. Under this banner, the group Women Against Pornography (WAP) began to organize to ban obscenity.[5] Others viewed such efforts as evidence of an ill-conceived alliance between the conservative Reagan administration and the Christian Right, in which feminist activism served the aims of a conservative moral hygiene and public decency movement.[6]

By the 1990s hugely successful efforts by key female porn stars effectively impacted the mainstream adult industry. Candida Royalle's Femme Productions single-handedly created a "couples porn" genre that reflected softer, gentler, more romantic porn with storylines and high production values.[7] In the same period, the emergence of alternative porn, also known as altporn, made way for a genre of online and print pornography oriented toward alternative subcultures like punk and goth and has grown more popular ever since. While many argue that altporn challenges mainstream pornography and its hypermasculinist content, others disagree with the view that the growing for-profit niche has succeeded, or even has truly aimed to succeed, at this mission because of its continued objectification of bodies and sex, and especially women's bodies and sex. Whatever the moral stance, it is clear that the exponential growth of the Internet has since created more supply and demand for porn categories that increasingly blur boundaries of what is mainstream or subcultural, progressive or not.

Still, relying on punk aesthetics, Burning Angel signals its alternative sensibilities as a countercultural position, even as the company maintains a place at the top of mainstream porn listings. It blurs the lines between the conservative and radical subgenres of porn that paved its way, participating in several of them at once. While cohosting the 2016 AVN Awards (known as the Oscars of porn) in Las Vegas with popular porn actress Anikka Albright, Angel took home trophies for personal Best Porn Star Website for the fifth year in a row, as well as the company's Best Amateur/Pro-Am Movie award, for *It's My First Time 2*.[8] Winning in categories from the most professional to the best amateur, Angel's approach strikes the salable balance between mainstream and subculture through effects that are both glossy and do-it-yourself. On top of previous awards acquired over the past ten years, Angel and her company have been nominated for Best Director, Best Parody, Best Editing, and Best Group Sex Scene for Angel's *Making the Band*; Best Non-Sex Performance for Angel in *Dirty Deeds* by Wicked Pictures; Best Screenplay for *Killer Kleavage from Outer Space*; Best Screenplay for *Dude, Am I a Slut?*; Mainstream Star of the Year; and Best Web Director.[9]

A later offshoot of the AVN Awards is the Feminist Porn Awards, established in 2006. Created by sex-toy shop workers and open to films that meet certain criteria, the Feminist Porn Awards aim to "showcase and honor those who are creating erotic media with a feminist sensibility that differs from what porn typically offers."[10] The idea of the awards is to cater to a female viewer and what she likely wants to see, defined as active desire, consent, real orgasms, power, and agency as opposed to what, categorically, she doesn't want to see: passivity, stereotypes, coercion, or fake orgasms. The guidelines give a nod to "women taking over control of their own fantasies (even when that fantasy is to hand over control)." As a performer, Angel was one of six featured leads in a film directed by Tristen Taormino that won a Feminist Porn Award in the awarding organization's first year.[11] Angel herself, however, is absent from the dozens of female directors listed on the Feminist Porn Award site. Why this may be is not immediately obvious.

In a phone interview with Angel, she described trying and failing to win a Feminist Porn Award, explaining that despite being seen as a "black sheep" of the mainstream porn world because of her punk aesthetic and parody films, her work has been consistently viewed as too mainstream for the Feminist Porn Awards. Resolving to be "happy with [her] place in the industry," Angel explained that she has identified "very much with being a feminist" and views the business as an extension of her women's studies major in college.[12] In an essay she published in *Naked Ambition* early in her career, Angel described herself as "an honest-to-God feminist," while admitting that she struggles with what that means. Describing the initial stages of the site's development, Angel noted:

I struggled with feminism for so long, I even wasn't sure I knew what it meant anymore. I wracked my brain for all those important issues I'd talked about in my gender studies classes. I thought about Take Back the Night, sobbing on my ex-boyfriend's doorstep, and my brief, not-so-empowering experiences with lesbianism. I tried to put it all together, but it didn't add up. I couldn't explain how, but I knew deep down that I was, and always had been, a seriously real, honest-to-god, hardcore feminist. If anything could ever tie up these loose ends of politics, rage, and sensitivity it was going to be this Web site; I just didn't know how.[13]

Angel's difficulty in determining the bounds of feminism reveal how layered and complex the term's implications are for her and probably many of her generation, who sought out gender studies classes only to find themselves caught between their own lived experiences and the banners of feminist victories (e.g., "Take Back the Night"). Angel admits the ambivalence that accompanied the rapid growth of Burning Angel before she found her "hard-core feminism" in hard-core porn: "I was bombarded with questions I didn't know how to answer. People really expected me to stand for something, and truthfully, I knew I did, but for what I wasn't so sure."[14] While the boundaries of what is definitively "feminist" are as debatable and as personal as what is sexy or what is funny, it is clear that Burning Angel moves beyond the antipornography debates of second wave feminism and their influence on the various waves of feminisms that have followed, in order to conceive of a way to bring raunch together with ideas of egalitarianism. As Angel's claim to feminism moves temporally and ideologically beyond the censorship debates, Burning Angel site and accompanying Joanna Angel site contribute to a postfeminist, twenty-first-century context that centralizes feminism's paradoxes for women, as reflected in Angel's early ambivalence.

PIGGISH AUTHORITY AND SEXUAL COMMODIFICATION

Not quite feminist and not quite not, Angel's brand of female desire burns up censorship wars of the past while marketing itself to a masculinist, heterosexualist world of raunch. Ariel Levy explains this tension in her popular but also contested periodization of the rise of raunch culture and the female chauvinist pig,[15] whom Levy introduces as today's shameless perpetrator of sexual commodification. From fieldwork among camera crews filming *Girls Gone Wild* to the confessions of sex industry stars, Levy marks a turn away from the women's movement of the 1960s and 1970s toward the questionably liberatory attitudes of a postfeminist era. Among a range of female expressions of femininity that accompany just as diverse a set of sexualities, Levy finds a single common thread: a consuming, all-powerful desire to be "like men."[16] The critique pointedly suggests that the very premise of empowerment amounts to a brutish force of change, and not generally for the better.

Only thirty years ago, as Levy reminds her readers, "our mothers were burning their bras and picketing *Playboy*, and suddenly, we were getting implants and bunny logos as supposed symbols of our liberation."[17] The gap Levy describes marks the ideological gap between the second wave of feminism and the era that emerged in its wake. It also mirrors the shift noted in the similar comments made by Darlinda Just Darlinda (in "'Polyester Feminism' and the Stakes of Self-Display" in chapter 1) and Barbra Streisand (in "Sexy Jews and Leggy Moves: Bunnies, Babes, and Mermaid Maneuvers" in chapter 2). Not as an indication of the death of feminism, but rather serving as evidence that the feminist project had already somehow been traded out for something bigger, Levy includes herself in the generational shift, "We could outdo Male Chauvinist Pigs and become Female Chauvinist Pigs: women who make sex objects of other women and of ourselves."[18] The question of women making sex objects of themselves and other women is at the core of Angel's Sexy Jewess routine. And yet the female chauvinist pig that Levy describes is somehow both more pernicious and more powerful in popular culture, as her primary concern *is* power. Articulating this pig figure more fully, she notes:

We decided long ago that the Male Chauvinist Pig was an unenlightened rube, but the Female Chauvinist Pig (FCP) has risen to a kind of exalted status. She is post-feminist. She is funny. She gets it. She doesn't mind cartoonish stereotypes of female sexuality, and she doesn't mind a cartoonishly macho response to them. . . . Why try to beat them when you can join them mantra.[19]

Within this formulation of the female chauvinist pig, Levy names a "funny," "postfeminist" power position akin to Angel's, whose "exalted status" as a woman who "gets it" portrays her as someone unscathed by "cartoonish stereotypes" of female sexuality and the macho responses they invite. But what should one make of this theorization of female power as the propensity to want to be like men? Levy's thesis is that many of the conflicts between the women's liberation movement and the sexual revolution were left unresolved during the thrust of second wave feminism in the 1970s. "What we are seeing today is the residue of that confusion," she contends, in which the rise of raunch culture is not essentially progressive, but commercial.[20] This isn't free love, she argues. Raunch culture is not about opening our minds to the possibilities and mysteries of sexuality. It's about endlessly reiterating the commercial impulse as "shorthand for sexiness."[21]

Though Levy is careful not to scapegoat pornography as bad, even if it is grounded in the roots of raunch, she is clear that it lacks the potential for female sexual liberation in its pursuit of money and power. What Levy seems to find most twisted is the supply and demand for women with damaged egos, "erotic role models" that she likens to shark attack victims.[22] Bemoaning the lost feminist idealism that epitomized a "future that never happened," she leaves the reader wondering what's left for women's liberation in this version of raunch feminism.

Whether overly slutty or gluttonous, the concept of female pigs brings to mind the image of indulgent swine.[23] But as a capitalist, and a chauvinist one, the female pig provokes social problems it doesn't care to resolve.

Levy's problem with selling sex is its commodification of female pleasure that covers up for actual pleasure. In her words, if we were to acknowledge that sexuality is personal and unique, it would become "unwieldy," perhaps in the ways feminist porn and queer porn movements are aiming to open up. Instead, characterizing sexiness as "simple" and "quantifiable"—concepts she ascribes to raunch—makes it easier to market.[24] Hotness means "fuckable and salable," in Levy's scheme, categories she finds devoid of actual passion and pleasure.[25]

But many scholars and pornographers alike take issue with the sad fate Levy outlines. Among the most vocal is women's and gender studies scholar Jane Ward, who writes that while Levy is ultimately "a champion of genuine female desire," her argumentation falls back on the delimiting logic of the early censorship debates.[26] To argue that marketable hotness is empty of passion and pleasure only points to age-old feminist fears about cooption and commodification. Ward regards this as a foreclosing on the creative potential of female pornographers and especially female porn viewers who seek passion and find pleasure in a range of depictions of sex on camera. To push this even further, Ward risks standing up for mainstream porn as a source of alternative pleasure from the perspective that viewers can make choices about what they view and how.[27]

Viewers can find queer and feminist meaning and feeling while viewing mainstream porn with the same old scripts, Ward writes. She offers the prime example of her own queer viewership of the highly mainstream "college reality porn" and the experience of noting her own desire as a pleasurable practice of critical self-study. She, a self-described feminist dyke, admits to finding pleasure in what she calls unambiguously nonfeminist, nonqueer scenes. Actively pushing back against the premise of censorship, Ward defends the idea that inconsistency between preferences and politics may live at the core of one's sexuality, as it admittedly does for her. Open recognition of this, rather than condemnation, invites more rather than less transparency in the way sexuality works within the sexualization of culture.[28]

Angel approaches many of the tensions Levy and Ward raise in her self-reflexive essay ". . . On Being a Feminist with a Porn Site," writing that she knew she was doing something feminist, but didn't know how. Where Levy and Ward may set the two perspectives apart in the name of advocating diverse entry points into porn practices and meanings, however, I find that the conversations necessarily come together in Angel's brand of Jewess raunch. The contradictions themselves between embodied expressions of empowerment (by performer or viewer) and their commodification require both analyses. Angel herself appears to play with both ideological perspectives as part of her postfeminist pig persona. She is both empowered and commodified, feminist and lucratively chauvinistic. The next section discusses specifically how Angel constructs such a layered point of view through the Sexy Jewess performance of race and gender joke-work.

It is telling that even as the company continues to expand in size and scale, models and online users report feeling "at home" at Burning Angel. Many such comments are posted throughout the website's "Forum" pages, by film models and members alike. BellaVendetta wrote of her experiences working for the company on April 5, 2010: "I've formed some really intense, lasting relationships with some of the girls and I am proud to call them my friends." A member named Cody wrote that among many reasons that Burning Angel rules is that "they don't treat new people like crap or put them through humiliating games like the [Suicide Girls] chat did to [him]."[29] This feeling of being at home and at ease with Angel and her friends, juxtaposed against the hard-core porn they collectively stage, creates a softer space in ways that noninteractive porn cannot. Site users are likely also at home while posting such comments from bedroom devices, adding to the feeling of intimacy the Net-porn genre makes plausible through interaction.

Angel invokes this kind of realness with an additional website especially devoted to getting to know her. Accessible from any Burning Angel page, Joannaangel.com offers a running dialogue with her visitors: "This website is for my special fans who want to know the REAL me. . . . It's the next best thing to carrying me around in your pocket." Promising full accessibility to those fans who carry her around all day, presumably through downloadable member apps on smartphones, Angel and her virtual body propose a fantasy of authenticity and its ability to function as an erotic stimulant. Members who join her cadre of viewers gain access to the full websites, unlimited video downloads, and chat forums. With membership options that range from a three-day trial to a monthly or yearly membership, the organization takes care to court its viewers through trial periods without pressure to commit.

This in-your-pocket flirtation, together with Angel's invitation to be known by fans, blurs Angel's status as porn celebrity icon. Net-porn theorist Niels van Doorn writes that the desire for "real" authentic sexual practices is a response to the increasingly spectacular, silicon-enhanced artificiality of commercial feature-length pornography. In opposition to big-budget productions, alternative porn that blurs the distinction between pro and amateur evokes a sense that the bodies onscreen could be your neighbors.[30] Even at the top of the best-of list in her industry, Angel is still the girl next door.

Still, even as Angel invites fans to know the "real" her, there is little written on her personal site that makes explicit reference to her Jewish background. Instead, she reveals that she is five feet tall, wears a size six shoe, weighs one hundred pounds, and was born on "Christmas Day!" She lists all tattoos to date and their locations, as well as turn-ons like intelligence and humor, and turn-offs, which include guys who ask her on Myspace how to get into porn and people who follow Phish around like it's their job. No mention of Jewishness. And yet as a Jewish female celebrity in her industry, she has stirred significant interest among Jewish online communities as a female porn entrepreneur in a long line of Jewish male pornographers.

While not claiming Jewishness in her bio, she makes strategic use of Jewish tropes in deliberately funny acts that either reference Jewishness outright or suggest it through inference. In this way, she joins in the verbal and gestural Jewface traditions discussed in previous chapters, while also performing impersonations of a whole host of identities that continue a tradition of Jewish female joke-work. Known for her porn parodies especially, Angel thus joins the cadre of Sexy Jewess comics who constitute a contemporary discourse of Jewish femininity. "I love making people laugh, and I love laughing myself. I think people need to realize how silly sex can be. . . . Some people in the porn industry tend to take things too seriously."[31]

Angel does "out" her Jewishness in one holiday-inspired spoof video that stars her and a cast of eight men meant to signify the eight nights of Hanukkah. The video opens with a point-of-view camera angle as the male voice behind the camera identifies a sexual gift he wants to give Joanna for Christmas. She replies with a flirtatious laugh, "But I'm Jewish and you're Jewish, so why not celebrate Hanukkah instead?" The voice behind the camera admits that it is a great idea and suggests they go downstairs, where the rest of the men are waiting. Downstairs, Angel makes a show of counting only seven men and asks into the camera about the missing eighth. The voice answers, "What am I, chopped liver?" Angel laughs freely at her hidden boyfriend behind the camera and his gender-bending reference to the quintessential Jewish mother's refrain. Asking her whether she thinks he is less than real meat, he outs his Jewishness as an inside joke and a flirtatious gesture.

As the group sex scene begins, Angel directs the "menorah of men" to circle her. She lowers to her knees and verbally invites the camera in on her face, which is now eye level with the eight anonymous penises. Sustaining at center frame of all that happens next, Angel blows off the candelabra of white men, whose faces are rarely seen or heard. Camera edits move the short film along, cutting from Angel's seduction of one male performer to the next. As in typical heterosexist imagination, the men do not touch each other, but only themselves as they wait for Angel's individual attention. Untypically, however, it is Angel who is in total control of this "gang bang" reversal.

Directing the thirteen-minute movie from inside it, Angel calls the shots as the action progresses. She issues all movement directives of male counterparts and camera, indicating with vocal and physical cues where the camera focuses and what audiences see next. Shifting her gaze between the camera and the rotating penises in front of her, Angel's director's eyes work the attention of audience, cast, and crew. Her filmic enjoyment carries the action in audible moans and facial swooning that cut across edited segments. Compared to the silent male cast and their contained movements, Angel's vocal body and its expressions of creative control accentuate the pleasure of pleasuring that she gives in excess to the group, as a key part of her performance.

Playing both director and star simultaneously, Angel empowers both parts as female roles. Like the pleasurer and the pleasured roles, the doubled director-porn star position renders Angel the subject-object in Jewish ways, too. In the context of Jewish joke-work, Hanukkah holiday traditions are an easy target, and no less as a gang bang scene, reversed as a Jewish girl's power play. As Angel explains it, "That was a way for me to show off my Jewyness . . . 8 dicks, like 8 gifts of Hanukkah."[32] Rendering perverse Jewish family gift-giving traditions that even secular American Jews still hold dear, the act derides the expectation of the Jewish woman: namely, her mothering. Scenes that stage Angel in total control over sex, and with so many, reroute her reproductive role. That her Jewish boyfriend's gift is initially his body and "whatever [she] wants to do with it" returns to tropes of the dominant Jewish mother/wife of the passive, effeminate male. When depicted through the promiscuous pleasure of eight lovers, this directly upturns stereotypes of the Jewish woman bored with sex, so common to Jewish male joking, and its basis on traditionalist assumptions of marriage and monogamy.

Still, the embrace of Angel's Jewishness hasn't always been as pleasant. "Everything's hot except her huge nose," one viewer commented on an unaffiliated porn site that reposted the video.[33] This kind of response, while nowhere found on Angel's own sites, is familiar enough regarding Jewish female noses on camera. Even as it indicates the kinds of criticism her Jewish face may raise among those outside the in-crowd of her online world, however, the comment raises no issue of the video's Jewish content and its Hanukkah theme. Mediating her variously conceived Jewish parts in ways in and out of her control, Angel's holiday reel thus spoofs her Jewishness, to mixed reviews. It may be argued that in joking about Jewishness, like the other comic performers in this book, Angel invites this kind of laughter "at" in addition to any laughter "with" her. But as long as her own "huge nose" interrupts her hotness, such reception renders Jewish-looking women a problem for porn.

Angel's version of the Sexy Jewess has to strike a mainstream balance between recognizable humor and equally familiar anxiety about Jewish female looks. But no matter how much Angel makes light of her Jewish identity, passing it off in spoof films at only the most widely known dates on the Jewish calendar, the idea of a Jewish female pornographer has caused concern for Jewish and gentile viewers alike. In an online article in December 2009, "The Rise of the Hot Jewish Girl: Why American Men Are Lusting after Women of the Tribe," *Details* reporter Christopher Noxon notes that Jewish pornographers had only just begun to actively "out" their Jewishness. He cites Angel stating at that point that, "I never thought my Jewishness would be an asset." The comment is revealing in its presumption of a Jewish closet outed by the potential of financial opportunism. The reappropriative potential of porn as the space to out an unwanted identity is thus conceived of as the next act of Jewish upward mobility, and from an economic point of view is a direct contrast to the downward mobility of neoburlesque as discussed in chapter 1.

Regarding the question of ethico-religious boundaries, Noxon reports that Angel rejected offers to perform in a holiday-themed adult piece called *Dr. Suzy's Porn and Purim DVD Bacchanal*, which mixes group sex with *hamantaschen* (triangular cookies shaped like the three-pointed hat of Purim's antagonist, Haman). "I've desecrated Christian traditions before," said Angel. "In one video, I put a cross-shaped dildo inside me, but I'd never do that with a menorah—that's just creepy." The sentiment is consistent with my own interview with Angel, when she explained that people have tried to encourage her to have sex with a Hassidic guy on camera. Explaining that she had many Hassidic family members whom she would not want to offend, she added that she also didn't find it funny or exciting to think about.[34]

Whereas Angel's army of hot punk chicks markets a commercial aesthetic of punk's antiestablishment sensibility, her personal confession of Jewish ethics sterilizes any serious attempt at hard-core sacrilege. A subtext of Jewish self-reflection thus mediates her hypersexuality, taming it through self-restriction. Angel's prudish decision not to desecrate ritual paraphernalia stands out among her host of female models, who do not assume such moral Jewish responsibility. This ethical aspect of her Jewishness is in contrast to the largely white cadre of women she casts. In the world she creates as a home for sexy freaks and geeks, no other performer is picked for the part of the Jewish female joker who must decide when it all goes too far.

Even when viewed through Angel's punk rock hard-core aesthetic, her Jewish female body may never achieve what cultural and media critic Laura Kipnis has called the "Hustler body"—one that rails against the establishment with hypersexualized images of pregnant women, amputees, transvestites, and the like, all meant to shock or scandalize bourgeois sensibilities in some way.[35] As Kipnis explains, invoking the familiar second wave feminist slogan, the porn star's body is always a "battleground." In Kipnis's understanding, porn makes room for opposing sexual and cultural forms such as religious morality, class pretentions, and feminist consciousness to duke it out with the armies of bodily vulgarity, kinky fantasy, and "unromanticized fucking."[36] If Angel's armies readily step into this battleground of feminist consciousness and bodily vulgarity, the company's head herself remains apart, balancing contradictory schemes of moral panic and responsibility, working the in-between as always funny about her sexiness.

Gracing the cover of *Heeb Magazine* in spring 2005, Angel blew up, so to speak, after the magazine published an article on her and her blow-up doll, complete with an online link to Angel's website. Also posted were the announcement of a cash prize for the winning two-minute video with the doll and a punning "dry" review of the sex toy. One of the magazine's young male interns speaks into the camera and about the doll as he holds it next to him. He wears a typical Israeli tourist's T-shirt, with the Superman logo replaced by the Hebrew letter lexicon for "S." The choice of shirt seems to play up the contrast of his user review as he discusses his antiheroic sexual encounter with the inflatable prop. The back hole, he says, was much too small, and the unlubed front failed to satisfy. The intern's attempts to stifle laughter make clear that the toy disappoints. It interrupts the heterosexual male encounter by giving nothing back. But rather than blaming himself, the intern blames the inanimate sex partner. She is the unmanageable one that remains impartial to him, making her the root cause of his dysfunction. For audiences familiar with the castration complex of Jewish male sexuality, the joke blames the effeminizing effect of his failed erection on her. She neither attends to his orgasm nor accommodates his sexual needs.

As a copy of Joanna Angel, the toy offers a proximate version of pleasure with the porn star herself, a fantasy that is simultaneously out of his reach and precisely the premise that the site's interactive forums and "at home" heirs seem to make plausible. And yet in joking that the doll is not amenable to sex, the intern renders the encounter with her entirely unsexual. The tenor of his boyish humor is all smut, in that it reaches out from Jewish male to Jewish male, deflating the female object as best he can. The doll itself, however, is Angel's own joke. It is her toy, her proxy, her product made and sold in her own image. Like it or don't, she and her doll seem to say without saying. They could not care less.

The doll's impartiality stands in for Angel's position in important ways. However much she brands an intimacy with all of her fans, the doll reveals the manufactured reality of it all, puffed up with air. As sweet as Angel is known to be by countless fans and coworkers, she is the boss of a hugely lucrative domain and an evident source of envy for men. She has sex whenever she wants and with whomever she wants, and without the trouble of getting it up. In the context of Jewish joke-work, *Heeb*'s simultaneous promotion of Angel and demotion of her doll delivers the smut joke but between self-deprecating confessions of folding under the pressure of a woman, person or plastic. As the magazine makes fun of the artificial body by way of feigning objectification of an actual woman, it likewise gets away with mocking a Jewish female sex partner's actual wants, directions, and desires, simultaneously heralding Angel's sex star power and deflating it at the same time.

Angel's own play with the doll reroutes the Jewish smut joke as a postfeminist play with herself. One spliced video reel on her website shows the two figures side by side in a poolside montage. Angel makes light of her product and herself with shots of the two sunbathing and floating on rafts. Rendering the hangout entirely silly, Angel and her doll attempt to play catch. The doll's inability to catch the ball is, of course, its appeal. Angel's game reminds her male viewers that the doll won't catch or throw better than they do, it won't degrade or undermine them, and it won't even laugh back.

In showing the fun to be had with the doll outside of sex, Angel encourages the same kind of ironic laughter as the male intern does, but does it on her own terms. The difference between the jokes is the joker, most significantly, but also the address. The intern directs his attention to other sexually anxious men, while Angel makes fun of herself and her merchandise as a happy ploy that likely sells more dolls. Hers is another one-sided overpowering of the doll, but conceived through self-pleasuring time spent with herself. The masturbatory inference is a self-satisfying comic device and a nod to Angel's independence. Her body looks fleshy and alive in comparison to the plastic dummy, whose plastic parts may be the gimmicky reminder of just how real women really are (see figure 5.1).

In a parody sex scene with the doll called "Fuck Me and Not My Doll," action starts in a Burning Angel boardroom meeting, as queer porn luminary Jiz Lee introduces the marketability of a blow-up doll made in Angel's image. As she goes on, the camera cuts to a male actor holding a hand over one side of his mouth, as he not-so-subtly critiques the doll to his male colleagues, "A blow-up doll with tattoos? What's next, a dildo with a belly button piercing?" The men laugh, and when Angel looks hurt and confused, forcing them to answer seriously whether they find the doll exciting, the same guy says with increasing confidence and volume, "Um, not as exciting as . . . happy hour at motherfucking Applebee's!" The four men stand up, thrusting their office chairs back as they slap high fives and leave for a round at the corporate chain. Jiz Lee consoles her and says she thinks the doll is a great idea, saying she would fuck it on a lonely Saturday night. The two performers then have strap-on sex, overriding the lack of male interest (or interest in male interest) while queering the sex toy, too.

As much as Angel enjoys making lesbian scenes, she explained that they don't sell well with her fan base.[37] Research conducted through viewer surveys reveals that they prefer to see male-female penetration, and Angel strives to give them what they want, while also making what she likes and wants to see. She has considered making an additional site for queer porn, so that she doesn't alienate her straight male viewers, while continuing to work in the ways that excite her. This has been a challenge, especially when viewers have returned DVDs they bought but didn't like because, as Angel explained it, they couldn't identify the image on screen with the "dick in their hand."[38]

Figure 5.1: Joanna Angel and blow-up doll from burningangel.com. Copyright Joanna Angel.

As a result, Angel has folded same-sex scenes into larger film plots that feature guy-girl sex.

In the case of the scene with the doll and Jiz Lee, Angel included it as the first sex coupling in Angel's *Doppelganger* (2010), a three-hour compilation threaded together by the parody horror film plotline of a blow-up doll's evil antics. The film opens in the doll-manufacturing plant as a scientist in a white lab coat pours various liquids into the pelvic openings of the plastic dolls as if it is part of their assembly line production. When he leaves for lunch, a bored female worker finds herself aroused by the packaged dildos she had found so banal while on the clock moments before. While masturbating on the conveyer belt, she knocks over one of the bottles of liquid. Scrambling to cover up her error, she pours some of the "evil" fluid into the wrong beaker, making for a monstrous combination when the scientist returns to work. Haunting instrumentals accompany the next several sequences of the camera's close-up shots of the evil doll's face, as the blow-up toy presumably becomes the monster. Of course nothing changes in her looks, making the suspended moments watching her laughably amusing.

In the loose plot line that follows, the doll steals Joanna's clothes and her identity, engaging in a series of mischievous pranks that extend beyond the film. After sneaky attacks like shooting spitballs at the porn star's customers and locking doors, the possessed doll asphyxiates Joanna with a drier sheet, and Joanna passes out. The arms of the doll drag Joanna across the living room floor and out of the room. Later, the doll breaks free of the blue painter's tape that Joanna used to attach her to the bedroom dresser. When Joanna comes into her bedroom to change into her outfit for the next sex scene, the doll has escaped her taped trappings (see figure 5.2).

Next, as Joanna tries to get dressed, the doll knocks her out with a stiletto heel, a conspicuous camera trick made possible by the arm of an unseen actor moving inside the plastic skin like a puppeteer. The camera cuts to the doll inching its way on all fours out from behind the bedroom door and toward the male actor waiting in the living room. He doesn't notice the difference between the women, except to say during copulation that she's "not very wet." When Joanna comes to, she grabs a pair of scissors to wreak her final revenge, stabbing the doppelganger in the head and chest after a convincing physical struggle between porn star and doll that lasts several minutes. The last shot of the film cuts to the emptied plastic arm of the doll as it starts to reinflate. As the credits roll, giggling viewers will wonder what more this doppelganger will do on disk 2.

As the film sets up its horror plot, Angel plays on the joke of the evil twin double who wants to destroy the innocent porn star's world through a range of dangerous pranks. In this way, Angel draws on pop cultural references to similar themes in Hollywood that fuse unlikely monsters with the erotic and psychological thriller genres.[39] Predating *Black Swan* by one year, Angel's doppelganger parody draws on the related horror-humor of the repressed figure and in striking ways parallels the reflective lens of the Nina-Lily dyad. Copies of each other and projections that appear only in the monster's own mind, the doubling is made a cause of the troubled self: in each case a Jewish woman crazed by her own ambitions. But where *Black Swan* dramatizes the psychic breakdown of its protagonist (see chapter 4), Angel's film makes a horror-humor monster of herself, allowing her to mock her own image while comically wrestling with it. She kills off the doll, only for the monster to come back and haunt her again. All the while, no one else notices. Causing her cartoonish anxiety and confusion throughout an impossible plot, Angel only jokishly falls victim to her reflected image. In the context of Joanna Angel's success as porn star protagonist and director, the doll is the perfect projection of her own power and that which may

Figure 5.2: Joanna Angel in *Doppelganger* (2010). Directed by Joanna Angel.

always overpower her as she creates plots that both position and parody her place on top. She signals a comic awareness of the ways she is seen as a sex toy herself, offering the doppelganger horror as a kind of self-reflexive mediation of funniness and fatalism in the face of her own image.

HEEB MAGAZINE AND THE JEWISH CUTTING EDGE

The audiences for these various encounters with the blow-up doll are distinct. Whereas *Doppelganger* doesn't make any explicit reference to Jewishness, the Jewishness of the product is the full occupation of sites like *Heeb Magazine*. How the online magazine vets Angel's rise to fame is indicative of the New

Jewish generation it targets and helps shape, as well as its roles for Jewish women. An online and print magazine constructed as a site for "Jewishness without an agenda," *Heeb* creates a public Jewish platform that does not require membership. In this sense, it differentiates itself from porn sites, which rely on paying members, but more directly, it sets itself apart from other kinds of Jewish organizations like synagogues that depend on sustained Jewish membership. Named after the derogatory ethnic slur and abbreviation of Hebrew, the magazine celebrates and mockingly debases a Jewishness that has no agenda in the sense of traditional organized religion and cultural organizations that support specific Jewish causes.

Cultural studies scholar Barbara Kirshenblatt-Gimblett calls the population that *Heeb* targets the "unaffiliated" and "hardest to reach," in the sense that the eighteen- to thirty-five-year-old "New Jew" in the United States reflects unprecedented disaffiliation with traditional organizational models like synagogues.[40] The Brooklyn-based *Heeb* started in 2001 "as a take-no-prisoners zine for the plugged in and preached out," and it "has become a multi-media magnet to the young, urban and influential."[41] Major Jewish celebrities like Sarah Silverman, Seth Rogin, Jonah Hill, and Roseanne Barr have graced its pages, and the magazine throws popular annual parties in hip Palm Springs hotels. Reaching out to these jaded Jews appears to come with a price, however. Kirshenblatt-Gimblett accounts for an "anything goes for a lost cause" clause that allows *Heeb* to "bite the hand that feeds it," implying that the magazine's humor goes too far for its parents' generation.[42] *Heeb*'s editor in Chief from 2002 to 2010, Joshua Neuman, provides at least one critical reason why. Defending the magazine's vision, he writes, "We believe that in a world in which Jewish periodicals outdo themselves in attempting to highlight just how endangered Jews are, there should be one Jewish media outlet that actually makes its readers smile."[43] The generational gap, understood in this way, offers significant insight into the New Jew's use of joke-work to connect with a cultural identity whose dated rhetoric of self-preservation it distrusts.

An interview with Joanna Angel's mother at another online Jewish culture magazine reveals a similar generational gap, but as vetted through diverging stances on pornography. *Jewcy Magazine* blogger Arye Dworken asked Angel's Jewish mother if she was ashamed of her daughter's life work. "A long time ago, she knew she was doing something not nice" Angel's mother responded. "And she did whatever she could to not embarrass me, like change her name." Proud of her daughter for having worried about her mother, Angel's mom admits finally that Angel betrayed Jewish familial loyalty. Offering the Hebrew word *arzut metzach* as explanation, which means—in the mother's own words—that "you steal but you're proud of it," the justification for taking pride in something bad done without embarrassment "is not nice."[44] A Jewish mother being upset at her daughter exemplifies the gap Kirshenblatt-Gimblett describes between Jewish generations. The naughty ways in which Angel bites the hand that feeds her seem to sum up her honorary role as head of the *Heeb*-generation pack.

But if generational wars over boundaries of appropriate behavior are nothing new, according to Kirshenblatt-Gimblett the so-called New Jews are "new by virtue of the edge that they define and occupy." In her estimation, "they espouse an ethics and aesthetics of edge," which, she argues, "is *not* the same as margin or periphery." The Jewish edge is not "an involuntary disadvantage among those striving for the center," meaning that it is not an issue of structural and systemic dispossession. Instead, the Jewish edge is a "cutting edge, an edge in constant need of sharpening, a moving—a leading, even a bleeding—edge that resists the center."[45] Kirshenblatt-Gimblett argues:

If the historical edge, the outsider and marginal status of Diaspora Jews has dissipated, the New Jews have turned elsewhere for the energy—the stimulus—that comes from the margin: they have turned to subculture and counterculture, and to experimental contemporary art. They may have been born Jewish, but they consider themselves native to Hip Hop or reggae or punk, among others.[46]

The ever-adjusting edge outlined here articulates a postmodern culture-in-motion that departs from what the author calls diaspora Jews of the past. The nonaffiliation and postassimilation of today's New Jews break with any model that would claim a Jewish futurity of any kind. The "ethics and aesthetics of edge" cut across models of Jewish marginality in search of new stimuli. And in turning elsewhere for energy, they have reached to subcultures and countercultures that offer access to other identities more germane to hip-hop, reggae, and punk. Such a cutting off from Jewish pasts in search of more "native" new ones furthermore necessitates an edge in "constant need of sharpening." The process indicates a complex relationship between the New Jew that Kirshenblatt-Gimblett describes and the mechanisms through which that population sharpens its tools. If joking about Jewishness allows New Jews to move beyond generational concerns of their parents and grandparents, how can one explain the sharp turn to other native identities? And in what ways does Angel's punk porn help facilitate the move toward these new feelings and associations?

Burning Angel's contributions to a Jewish hard-core help sharpen the tools and the edges of contemporary Jewish identity in the US. Its female pornographer's perspective, directed from inside and outside the camera frame, choreographs the ways that the raunchy female body moves and how. The degree to which she may mediate her own Jewishness on camera, however, is less than totally clear, as it necessarily entangles intentional and less intentional aspects of bodily and narrative components. As her public persona likewise invites attention of all kinds on the subject of the convincingly sexy Jewish woman in America, Angel contends with any number of competing views that must confront, encourage, or criticize her position at the forefront of a Jewish female cutting edge.

Billed as "Not your Daddy's porn," Angel's branding distinguishes itself from the generation that raised her. As much as she has cut her own Jewish mother through the porn pursuits she proudly "steals," her business tactics acknowledge their departure from paternal controls as part of their mission. Having left the orthodoxy of her upbringing behind, the daddy she no longer regards is arguably a Jewish one where daddy stands in for a host of patriarchal traditions she has left behind. And yet in the context of porn, the epithet takes on additional meanings. Daddy's porn refers to the print magazines and adult films of a pre-Internet era. It is expressly not the Web technologies that proliferate ever more channels of professional and amateur images. For Angel's audience, likely born in the 1980s and after, daddy's porn is a bastion of the past. For some it symbolizes a soft sense of nostalgia, reminiscent of nudie magazines hidden under a father's bed. For others it is the less radical stuff of porn's preliberation, a throwback to unchecked misogyny in a mainstream man's world. In both cases, the concept configures the period it moves beyond as an unfortunate and passé one before the chauvinist pig was a woman and raunch was a Jewish girl's best friend.

The postfeminist promise of porn no longer made or monitored by daddy is helped by the punk aesthetics Angel also exaggerates, impersonates, appropriates, and commercializes. In addition to punk, she turns to hip-hop, participating in another set of the "native" roots Kirshenblatt-Gimblett describes. The next section looks closely at her first interracial film as a parody of race and race imagination as part of the strategy of new porn she makes and makes fun of at the same time.

THE GAME OF INTERRACIAL PORN AND JOANNA'S PHALLIC CHECKMATE

On the DVD cover of Burning Angel's first interracial video, *It's Big, It's Black, It's Inside Joanna* (2009), Angel wears hoop earrings, cornrows, a crop top, and baggy jeans and stands against a wall of graffiti (see figure 5.3). In it, she raps about sex with black men. The explicit lyrics become yet more visceral as they accompany a fully graphic sex scene with pornographer and persona Mr. Marcus. In this pairing of black impersonation and black desire, the interracial sex with a black man becomes an avenue by which Angel dresses herself up on the photo shoot in a kind of blackface. The aural and visual representations of a white female body with a black male sex partner may leave few scandalized in its continuance of long-standing threat-fantasies of interracial sex and its invocations of race miscegenation so ubiquitous in mainstream porn. Angel's play on the theme, however, partners a comic blackface with desire for black sex in ways that exceed those discussed in previous chapters.

In her marketing for the film, Angel writes in the promotional text that she tried to reverse stereotypes even though she admits some people might

Figure 5.3: DVD cover, *It's Big, It's Black, It's Inside Joanna* (2009). Directed by Joanna Angel.

find that racist. While the cover image of the video caricatures Angel as a stereotypical rap impersonator, the film plot features the black male as a nerdy
chess player. Readers may think here of *Broad City*'s play with similar reversals
in boyfriend Lincoln (Hannibal Buress), a dentist who tolerates Ilana's unfil-
tered promiscuousness, while she self-parodies as a clownish race appropri-
ator stylized in ghetto slang and garb (see "*Broad City*'s Bad Girls Getting Bi
In-Between" in chapter 3). Preceding *Broad City* by five years, Angel plays the
"gangster white chick" in ways that likewise exaggerate her Jewish femininity
as an identity play with black/white racial logic. Aiming to invert stereotypes

in this sense, Angel makes herself hard and him soft. The threat of a white-black sex act is thus parodied through its pacification of the racist predator stereotype and its companion, the wanting but passive white woman. As the gangster herself, Angel suggests a comment on her actual position on top, as film star and director producing the film, while her scene partner is but a pawn by comparison. But as the black-white sex sustains the imagination of the mainstream fetish category, it does little to alter the impact of its effect. Rather, in going to graphic sex, it ultimately rehearses the same scripts it means to rewrite.

The lyrics of a rap parody accompany the film, reiterating Angel's role in charge. "If it's big and it's black, Joanna's got to have it." Onscreen, Angel and her partner laugh, playing before sex with oversized chess pieces on a building rooftop. The phallic pawns read as black and white penises that will compete for Angel's attention. In the context of the accompanying song, the props take on racialized meaning. Justifying her desire for a black sex partner by way of putting down Jewish men, the lyrics explain: "My mama wanted me to grow up and marry a Jew / She set me up with a lawyer who wanted to sue / David Goldstein took me home at the end of the night / His pants came off and it was a scary sight." She sings of the insufficiency of Jewish men, based on the exaggerated trope of the inferior, castrated Jewish penis. The gangster white chick she impersonates here is a Jewish girl killing her mother twice over; first she refuses the rich Jewish guy and then she chooses a black man. Even in Angel's deliberate reversal of race and gender archetypes through her hard white woman and soft black nerd, she desexualizes Jewish men and hyper-sexualizes black men in the same old ways.

Angel's next lines spell out her pornographer's point of view. "I'll film it on the HD and get the perfect angle / Then I'll upload the whole thing onto Burning Angel." As the director able to get the perfect angle, she positions herself as a deliberate strategist, using the tools upon which she has built her career to capitalize on the racy event. Compared to the invocation of black-face by the performers in previous chapters, Angel's gangster white chick secures her position at the top of mainstream markets by way of graphic sex. As opposed to comic inference, the sex that Angel has "gotta have" happens on screen, inviting viewers to take it as they will. Titled with a similar refer-ence to going "inside Joanna," the black penis that Angel finally "has" like-wise extends the porn race premise. As she both has and becomes the black phallus that also gives her pleasure, Angel's jokes do more than invite white women out from behind closed doors. She outs repressed thinking, too, as the interracial chess fantasy plays out a game of impossible maneuvers to be the black man and be with him at the same time. The tangle of identification and desire resonates with Sandra Bernhard's address toward Roxanne in *Without You I'm Nothing* (see "Sandra Bernhard and the I/You Other" in chapter 3), but tellingly, Angel's film reveals no interracial sex between women, and neither does it problematize the black character's interest in her.

In talking with me about the film, Angel expressed a sense of remorse similar to Silverman's apology in the aftermath of the "Face Wars" episode. Never wanting the film to offend viewers, Angel noted specifically that she was aiming to reverse stereotypes, calling out how racist they are when unchecked. "All interracial porn likes to depict black guys as ghetto and white girls as innocent. In this movie I thought I would make a big statement by showing a girl being ghetto and having the black performers be accountants and doctors and chess players and stuff."[47] While working to revise porn's archetypal race roles, Angel added how comedy in general often plays up stereotypes as part of its public statements. "Comedy plays off of stereotypes and sometimes stereotypes have to do with race or gender and there is a delicate balance of how to show the pubic that you're doing something from a place of love and not from a place of hate."[48] The comment relates to one made by burlesquer Darlinda Just Darlinda, who defended the fact that the performance of stereotypes could create an exploitative dynamic on stage (see "'Polyester Feminism' and the Stakes of Self-Display" in chapter 1). The delicate balance Angel describes, however, is perhaps less a matter of intention than of address. Where the identity acts and impersonations of neoburlesque address the homosocial space of a women-centric circuit, the stereotypes Angel enacts play with a representational power that is always already public and therefore more susceptible to patriarchal logic. As Angel's characterizations aim to operate on the level of sexual fantasy more explicitly than does celebrity comedy, any formulation of their reception or impact necessarily engages porn's relationship to exploitative imagery, a subject for which perhaps there is no conclusive "there-there."

Wanting the interracial film to be seen in a positive light and as coming from "a place of love," Angel explained that the film "backfired," and people called her out online for her racist portrayals. Explaining that it was the first interracial movie that Burning Angel had made, and that she didn't want to make it, Angel said that the project was the result of all the sex scenes she had shot with black male actors and white female actors. She had come to find over time that only some of her viewers wanted to see interracial sex, and that customers often returned films that had sex they didn't like. "When you are dealing with people getting aroused, most of my fans don't want to jerk off to a black guy and white girl. I guess they can't relate." Angel continued, "I wish I didn't have to categorize my scenes like that in the first place, but everything has to be put in categories, in porn and everywhere else. When you buy clothes, when you buy music, that's what people need."[49] As Angel negotiates the demands of her market against the ways she is perceived "from the outside," she navigates the parameters these perspectives place both on her own desires around representation and her sense of what's permissible in porn.

Angel's interracial humor thus riffs on the racist structures of appropriation and exploitation that she means to avoid but that may be inevitable in her industry and beyond. Moreover, if the interracial video embodies the New Jewish edge through appropriated black vernaculars in ways that bring it into conversation with the Sexy Jewess schemes discussed in previous chapters, it does so alongside a self-conscious construction and critique of its own cutting agency. The comedic effect of this racialized chess game plays up its own exploitative potential in the name of shifting its terms, but finds itself losing out to more powerful social logics. Through such representational in-betweening, Angel satisfies only the small portion of fans who she says bought the film and kept it, marking the curious commercial limits of porn parody's ability to reverse stereotypes through reappropriating them.

CONCLUSION

Porn star and director Joanna Angel joins a growing movement of pornographers, advocates, scholars, and bloggers who understand themselves as impassioned defendants of the art form's sex-positive potential. They have taken on the anticensorship banners of second wave feminism to create ever-expanding genres of mainstream and subcultural niche markets that position women on top. Angel's leadership of Burning Angel exemplifies this postfeminist porn wave, figuring herself as the desiring subject rather than the object of desire. The liberatory crux of her postfeminist potential espouses a transgressive power, wherein the open enlisting of women viewers and the interaction with site visitors helps construct a progressive break with past porn practices. The idea that female site visitors are as hot as the models no doubt ups the thrill for Angel's fans.

As the company boasts its army of empowered hot punk chicks, Ariel Levy argues that the job description of sex film starlets costs more than it brings in. As pornography permeates all levels of female culture such that raunch appears as a full-time occupation, Levy writes that women outside, and perhaps even inside, the industry have become "female chauvinist pigs" who act "like men." In the Jewish case, this piggish appetite breaks with kosher traditions of all kinds. The pig, of course, is off limits for those who observe the religious dietary law. But as Angel leaves orthodoxy behind, her plays on Jewishness reveal sustained investment in cultural identity that she sources in her approach to XXX parody.

A Jewish female porn star makes good joke material for Jewish culture magazines like *Heeb*, in which Angel offers a way to identify with Jewishness that is rich, famous, and sex-soaked, whereas images of Jews in America have famously been self-deprecating, male, and meek. Speaking for a new generation of the religiously unaffiliated and hard-to-reach Jewish generations X and Y and millennials in the United States, *Heeb*'s coed audience still delivers on the old jokes. The thinking on sex splits between familiar images of effeminate, castrated men and Jewish women who can't be effectively commandeered, either because they are too princessy for the effort it entails or not pretty enough to entice men. The magazine props up Angel through misadventures with her blow-up doll, making fun of her and itself as representative of men who can't keep up with today's inflated women.

When it comes to homosexuality, the lack of sex between men in Angel's world takeover likewise fleshes out a vision for the future that, when viewed in the context of Jewish representational discourse, amounts to a significant recloseting of gay men. As Angel celebrates straight and lesbian female pleasure while ignoring that of homosexual men, she departs from a long tradition of Jewish female performance discussed in the previous two chapters who openly embrace gay men in a critique of compulsory heterosexuality. This may be more evidence of why Angel is left off the master list of feminist pornographers, despite her own sense of herself and her work.

Angel's selective depictions of sex intersect with her forays into ethnic and racial representation. Her Jewish content comes across through her use of comic appropriation and impersonation. Her holiday parody spoofs Hanukkah with flippancy similar to that of the Schlep Sisters and the Nice Jewish Girls Gone Bad, but goes bad all the way in a gang bang with Angel and eight men that skews straight sex to its hard-core extreme. Likewise, the oversized chess game of Angel's first interracial film aims to rework stereotypes through its power play of wits. The conscious game of black and white puts Angel squarely inside a national threat-fantasy of sex between white women and black men, while rendering Angel's Jewishness as a conscious position both inside and outside an American racial logic that allows her to play so scandalously with it.

But whether porn should or should not exist is less the question here than how it makes its moves and with what liberatory ethos. For the sake of this analysis, it is a given that the material selected for discussion intends to offend through social and sexual obscenities not meant to hurt, but to hurl acceptability on its head. These are the terms through which its hard-core porn humor performs its provocative and reiterative Jewish comment, and by which the gender, race, and ethnic aspects of its joke-work sell with unprecedented pig authority and alternative appeal.

Conclusion

Hello again, Gorgeous. You've made it to the end of the book, and here, in the vanity mirror of the bookend backstage, take another look. What do you see? Your funny face? Your gorgeous face? Look again. Stare back, and soften your gaze. Move your chin to the left a little to frame your best angle. Tilt your head down a bit; lift an eyebrow. Not enough light? Switch on the LED lights of your crafty candle flame headpiece and lean in a little closer. And now crack the glass with your piercing eyes. Laugh maniacally through the shards and lose yourself in the frame. Stab your reflection, peering back, until it stops mocking you, making fun of you, copycatting you. Pick up the mess and wipe down the counter, collecting yourself as you cut your finger. Stick it in your mouth and catch your double in the mirror daring you further. Flip your other finger up at her and watch her bite it off. Ouch!

Show your feelings on your face. First with your mouth, reaching one side of your lips all the way up. Drop the other end down and then switch, much slower. Get your eyebrows going asymmetrically and wiggle one ear at a time. Next, the nose. Make it move. Not just the nostrils, the whole thing. Lead with the bump. Notice it pulling you off balance. Tighten your sequined bra straps and go back to the beginning. Practice your technique. Keep working. Put a stage where the mirror was, and get out there! You've got this! You're living on the edge, but where are your pants? You notice your legs are stuck together, and are those fish scales? The anxiety is older than you. It connects you to your past. Send in the clowns! One wheels you into the spotlight, and no sound comes out when you start to sing. Instead, a frog hops out. You watch the amphibian prince leap and suspend mid jump, just to tell you something you can't quite hear. HELLLLOOOOOOO, you cry through a crackling microphone suddenly amplified too loud, and the tiny danseur crumbles into dust before you. You stare through its particles in the blinding spotlight and remember that it's show time. Hello, you smile, your teeth intact. Cue bucket of water. Banana peel.

In neoburlesque and stand-up comedy and mainstream and adult film, celebrities and lesser-known performers face their hysterical self-reflections as clownish projections that play with the ruse of representation and the fragmentation of a single, reconciled self. In skewed mirrors of self-display, they foreground the bodily conditions of their ethnic and gender differences to humorous and horrifying ends. With varying degrees of autonomy and access, they perform exaggerated versions of themselves and any others in their midst to wage social critiques that are distinct to American Jewishness as well as beyond its bounds. Embodying the worst of stereotypes and social extremes, often as harmful to themselves as others, performers enact reflexive, revisionist identities through reiteration of old modes with lighter and darker twists.

The performers discussed in each chapter of this book build on old and new corporeal dramas of identity politics as humor or horror material, arriving at competing and even contradictory ideas. They deliver their address through the body and talk in tune with genre-specific expectations. Like neoburlesque's Hanukkah pageant that ends without a winner, or even *Black Swan*'s ballet ambitions that promise no closure, a final synthesis points to their varied possibilities as reiterative representations of the Jewish woman in US pop culture. Significantly, this reiterative frame of the Sexy Jewess trope implies a certain kind of accumulative power that invests in its own continuity, its own preservation of traditions, at the same time that it creates the conditions for its interruption—its "undeterminedness" or "as to be determindness," as Judith Butler has called it.[1] In this sense, the assimilated "New Jew" that Barbara Kirshenblatt-Gimblett describes, with no ties to the synagogue, arguably reaffiliates with cultural contexts through performance, wherein it can attempt to identify and disidentify, do and undo.[2] When seen in this context, stereotypes staged again and again are less a matter of derivative self-disenfranchisements, internalizations of inferiority complexes, or status anxieties, than they are a way to reconnect to Jewishness when other channels no longer suffice. Disinvesting in traditional religiosity, cultural politics tied to Israel, status concerns with upward mobility, or other assimilatory attitudes that preceded them, contemporary Jewish female performers knowingly bite the hands that feed them, while animating new allegiances on their own terms.

Those terms reveal deliberately appropriative liberties taken by women who will not be tamed, whether as bosses of their own domains or as starring acts in their own shows. In content that aims to comment on itself, performers gaze, talk, and dance back at their critics. But for celebrity actors who take on mainstream roles, this emboldened female stance is just as readily subsumed. As in the case of ballet horror monsters, they may come to the surface as symbols of repressed identities only to hurt themselves. Whether expressly downwardly mobile as in the neoburlesque, or domesticated by the mainstream as in *Black Swan*, emboldened femininity faces its consequences, be they economic, ideological, or sensationally psychological.

The reiterative conventions of the Sexy Jewess take place in each case differently, and performers like to play within a repertoire of options that messing with familiar stereotypes provides. In the neoburlesque scene, such reiteration occurs through the course of a single night and by design of the annual event each year. The parameters of the genre (most often a song and a dance that follows the striptease score) meets the repeatability of the Hanukkah-themed acts (human menorahs, raunchy dreidels, general klutziness, and glamour). The pattern of it announces the good time to be had with the same joke-work performed by ever newer rosters of Jewish girls gone bad. The circuit knows itself best as a reaffirmative tradition, a way to go backward and forward at the same time. As it recollects what mattered in the past (a cohesive Jewish cultural identity), it tumbles forward toward an unknown future, gathering bits of current events and political discourses upon which practitioners admit it means not to tread too hard.

And yet even as burlesque's reiterative steps backward and forward solidify a performance tradition by way of repetition, such a performance practice allows a return to work that isn't yet finished. In this sense, the postassimilatory, postfeminist model this book proposes is a move further toward Jewish and gender freedoms as postmodern identities in flux. This is the proximal distance of reflexivity that a "post" frame provides. It is the "critical repetition with a distance" that Linda Hutcheon outlines as key to parody, funny and not.[3] It is also the "perspective on perspectives" that Kenneth Burke underlines as performative incongruity.[4] By naming that which it means to move beyond, the reiterative "post" is thus both freed and bound up by its stated breaks with the past. The "neo" of burlesque certainly makes this same case, as does the new "edge" of contemporary Jewish female comics, the "thrill" of Jewish female ballet monsters, and the "alt" of professional-amateur movements in Jewish female punk porn. All of these moves gesture toward the future while staking claim in the recuperative potential of their Jewish female pasts to open up a liberatory space for embodied social commentary.

On the level of physical technique, or at least the physicality of reiterative identity performance, any investment in repetition may be less a practice in perfection than a laboring for implicit and explicit premises dealing with the body and its signification. And yet physical repetition also covers over its work in the very act of its practice.[5] Once something is repeated enough, it becomes habit, muscle memory, known in the body at deep levels of somatic and cultural awareness. What repetition cannot accommodate is a clean break with the past; a cold turkey cut-off; an escape. If such a move could ever be plausible, it would entail the ends of an ideological episteme that would prove unrealistic. This is not the post's power, if even its aim.

So what then of reiterative identity performance in the context of Jewishness and gender, and the question of joke-work as progressive social commentary? Is there an effective liberatory potential of performing "Jewishly" as a means of broadening roles for women, for racial or sexual minorities, and for other marginalized figures? Across a range of spectacle embodiments, Jewish female performers, comic and not, reclaim what is deemed excessive about them in the name of a critical reappropriation. Performers demonstrate this process, spoken and unspoken, when they return to the very stereotypes for which they are criticized, or commodified, and play them up with self-empowering effect.[6] When it works, reappropriation provides a means for performers to talk and dance back at the ways they are seen as "different" or "same" in comparison to social norms and to reconstruct those identities as conflicting and coexisting points of access and agency to inspire a kind of representational change that excites and animates audiences. These reappropriative performances are most often self-reflexive, as they lean on the ethical and ethnic dimensions of Jewishness as avenues for social comment.

But when reappropriation fails, efforts to play up Jewish and female differences reaffirm a white (and Jewish) male perspective that puts them down or rehearse impersonations of other Others in damaging ways that repeat rather than interrupt racist, classist, or otherwise delimiting social logic. Reappropriation in these cases becomes misappropriation, in which performers meet violence with more violence and do so with differing degrees of self-consciousness and apology. In the most provocative cases, performers play with both of these outcomes (progressive or violent) as entangled facets of their reappropriative and misappropriative routines.

Rehearsing the defunct femininity of "funny girl" bodies through bawdry self-display, performers extend what it means to emphasize Jewish and female identities not only as joke material, but also as social and political leverage. From celebrity platforms and smaller stages, they do this with varying address and effect, mobilizing the progressive politics they preach, but just as often alienating their on-screen or off-screen audiences. This is where Jewish female joke-work meets its own limits and where the parodic citation of self as Other dives into the wreck of its own impossibility, whether because of the unmoving aspects of difference or the growing weight of white guilt. And it happens in different ways, depending on the genre and its shifting class bracket—namely, the upward or downward mobility that its joke-work makes possible.

Reiterating a host of roles in a repertoire most famous for its innocent or bawdry lack of filters, Jewish female performers continue to exaggerate themselves and other ethnic and racial Others, standing in for a near-universal position-in-excess, whereby jokes by and about Jewishness and gender have the power to transgress social values around men and marriage, sex and sexiness in ways that promise other Others can also. At the same time, the history of Jewish female performance has shown that funny girls egg on an increasingly uncertain fate through techniques of ironic incongruity and aggressive ambivalence in a postassimilatory, postfeminist era.

What the neoburlesque, comic, ballet horror, and porn genres have in common is their reiterative exaggeration of the Jewish woman as social misfit, inappropriate femme, and sexual deviant. Through different mechanisms, they condition the stage for Jewish women to maneuver through mainstream and subcultural markets, revealing different takes on the liberated woman. Across these contexts, I have wrestled with what this range of spectacle performers can do to upset larger social discourses of power when practical conditions of work or access are on the line.

Jewish female performance most often exaggerates "difference" as part of and in response to the postassimilatory, postfeminist contemporary period. Performance tropes most often negotiate white guilt complexes, in which rehearsals of ethnic and gender differences provide a means of destabilizing black/white racial logic by exaggerating it. In some contexts more than others, this premise is unconvincing in an era of privileged access and is too easily subsumed by commercial channels in search of content that will appear edgy but stops short of alienating white, male audiences. And yet even then, "difference" can never be a thing to be easily engaged or dismissed, now or in any other temporality; indeed, as is clear far beyond a Jewish female context, difference is a socioeconomic condition of excess that marks bodies under systems of real power and control. And yet just as difference cannot be dislodged from Jewish female bodies even after the thrust of race and class assimilation and women's lib movements, neither can "sameness" promise lasting pleasure or access to majoritarian acceptance. Spectacles of postassimilatory Jewish femininity show that such fixed entry into whiteness is tenuous. The effect of race impersonations can either render whiteness closer or more farfetched as it either exposes or covers up the social values to which it ascribes.

Even as whiteness cannot offer a fully achievable category for assimilatory Jews or other aspiring minorities, a consumptive white guilt occupies the shared social conscience of performances in the postassimilatory, postfeminist period. As performers play with an embodied, comic Jewface (and its related blackface and yellowface tropes), they enact and expose their entanglements in whiteness perhaps more than ever before. And still, Jewface parody offers a means for performers to talk and dance back at their own race and class privilege. In self-Othering exaggerations, the Sexy Jewess caricatures what is so "in-between" about her, when to be white is tied up in unwanted social hierarchies, and to deny its privileges is just as bad.

But white guilt also guides the Sexy Jewess to do social good while going bad. Susannah Perlman, the woman on the cover of this book, aptly named her show, *Nice Jewish Girls Gone Bad*, after this theme. Her cabaret of amateur comics has hit Jewish community centers and other embracing venues since the early 2000s to bring joy to crowds through life-sized dancing dreidels with funny sex appeal. The newest wave of neoburlesque now includes transwomen as a natural next step in the Hanukkah show. At the same time, *Broad City*'s Abbi Jacobson jams naked in her living room, assuredly "on the edge" of an unprecedented self-acceptance, and her companion Ilana Glazer arguably extends the edgiest effects of Sandra Bernhard and Sarah Silverman with a millennial sincerity, itself an ironic postmodern paradox. In great contrast, Natalie Portman's Nina Sayers is still far too good, and monstrously so as she grows obsessed with white perfection and its black alter ego. All the while, Joanna Angel mocks goodness altogether, even as she remains off as the most genuine of all these women in the end.

Whether good, bad, or both, Jewish women in popular culture are deliberately, appropriatively, and most often apologetically "in your face." This impact of Jewish female joke-work that is often brunt or brash finally returns to face-conscious embodiments of Jewish femininity and their histories of race and gender impersonation. What I have come to appreciate most about the women discussed in each chapter is how in-your-face they are, when to be there, up in someone's face or in the public's face, is so confrontational, so socially insensitive, so *problematic*.

For the bulk of the book's discussion, I have focused on the face and body issues of Jewish female performers that they reclaim through sexy ruse and comic self-display. I have made a point of foregrounding that what is so funny about funny Jewish girls is their self-conscious looks and internalized cultural anxieties about failing to fit in, when fitting in is trite and tiresome for emboldened women who would rather strive to be confidently eccentric. And yet this last point about comic female performers being so *in your face* is an aspect of funny power worth cherishing beyond an evaluation of the jokes as good or bad. In a book that prioritizes the face, this last point can look in new directions.

To say that one's humor, politics, or points of view are in your face is to imply that the person behind such antics lacks tact, good taste, and appropriate care for social etiquette. She disregards codes for how to be and behave or otherwise is a wild child who doesn't know them but is still to blame. But what if being in your face was less abrasive and more about moving closer to you? Facing you? Seeing you? Letting you see her? Is it at all possible that the choice to be in your face is a calling out to you, a movement toward you, and a way to see your face, too? A day in your life, in your face?

It doesn't quite work, I know. To find that something or someone is in your face is to connote a kind of unwanted attack on one's sensibilities, on one's private sphere. But even this is a matter of values and boundaries, again a matter of taste, personal, yes, but socially construed. Everything is in our faces all of the time, and yet it is not until something or someone violates some code of values that we label it so. For funny girls making careers as provocateurs, this in-your-face-to-face attention is raw creative power, wieldable for good or at least a good kind of bad.

Indeed, the sting of humor that is troublingly *face-ist* in the sense of literal, metaphorical, and embodied blackface, yellowface, or Jewface and other identity impersonation is damaging if it invisibilizes rather than visibilizes the Other it mocks. In order words, when it defaces rather than recognizes the actual and figurative faces of groups of people. And yet, the reappropriative capacity of in-your-face performance can also poke holes in the morality tales we tell ourselves about what's okay, and what's not, by provoking those very boundaries from the point of view of the performer and the audience. Performance can offend on purpose by triggering social sore spots, so long as those sore spots are the damaged egos of racist and sexist social norms that need to be bruised. "In your face" is also, after all, the big finish one friend or sibling might say to another when she's declaredly proven the other person wrong; that, and a colloquialism lifted into mainstream lingo once again from black urban aesthetics. Both possibilities speak to the appropriative license of Jewish female comedy that slides boldly between deliberately defensive and offensive gestures.

Reflexive performance, the kind that comments on itself, can allow performers and audiences to move in defensive and offensive ways with face, talk, and body, while making space for them to productively contradict themselves. I find that those contradictions are most generative when they suspend the limits on how performers may be seen and known. They may spiral between laughter and embarrassment, love and shame, or clownish antics and convincingly sexy moves, alternating between versions of themselves and who they want to be. As my own students like to remind me, the special thing about performance is that no one knows what is going to happen, and for the length of the dance, the set, the bit, the performer has the stage, has the mic. She sets the rules. I allow this idealism to sway me finally on the question of a performer's agency and her capacity to transgress social thinking about how bodies are read, how meaning is made. The trouble with representation, of course, is that it is never really right. Even so, for all of the readers who find themselves to be seen too often as too much, in your face, we have so much to learn.

NOTES

ACKNOWLEDGMENTS

1. Blanche Johnson, "Winona Ryder: My 30s Were a Little Bit Tough," *Fox News Entertainment*, July 28, 2016, http://www.foxnews.com/entertainment/2016/07/28/winona-ryder-my-30s-were-little-bit-tough.html.

INTRODUCTION

1. For a rich theorization of the "case" as category of study, see Lauren Berlant, "On the Case," *Critical Inquiry* 33, no. 4 (Summer 2007): 663–672. Berlant argues that the case represents a problem-event that has animated some kind of judgment. "Any enigma could do," she asserts. "And yet, although any case of *x* promises to generate an account of a situation that is recognizable enough that people can debate about it, one cannot produce a predictive account of the case as a communication action except for this: as an expressive form of expertise and explanation the case points to something bigger, too, an offering of an account of the event and of the world" (665). But what makes a case a case worthy of study? Berlant states: "It raises questions of precedent and futurity, of canons and contextualization, of narrative elucidation." Still, while always already marked by normative categories that classify it, the "case," as Berlant promises, "can incite an opening, an altered way of feeling thing's out, and of falling out of line" (665).

2. Harley Erdman, *Staging the Jew: The Performance of an American Ethnicity, 1860–1920* (New Brunswick, NJ: Rutgers University Press, 1997). Erdman explains the Belle Juive's ability to seduce gentile men, and indeed to side with them in various matters of narrative plot (betraying a Jewish father or patriarchal figure). She conjured a dangerous sexuality, a threat to and a fantasy for gentile men and audiences alike akin to the femme fatale, noble savage, and tragic mulatto myths of the day. By the early twentieth century, with growing xenophobia in response to Eastern European immigration, La Juive was increasingly domesticated and de-ethnicized, conquered and converted in sexual and Christian terms.

3. For further reading on postfeminism, see Ariel Levy, *Female Chauvinist Pigs: Women and the Rise of Raunch Culture* (New York: Free Press, 2005); Talia Modeleski, *Feminism Without Women: Culture and Criticism in a Postfeminist Age* (New York: Routledge, 1991); and Jennifer Baumgardner and Amy Richards, *Manifesta: Young Women, Feminism and the Future* (New York: Farrar, Strauss and Giroux, 2000).

4. "Postassimilatory" claims in Jewish cultural studies are discussed in Jon Stratton, *Coming Out Jewish: Constructing Ambivalent Identities* (London: Routledge, 2000); and Daniel Itzkovitz, "They Are All Jews," in *You Should See Yourself: Jewish Identity*

in *Postmodern American Culture*, ed. Vincent Brook (New Brunswick: Rutgers University Press, 2006).

5. While Derrida discusses the concept of iterability and citation in many texts, this logic is often attributed to his essay "Signature Event Context," in *Limited Inc.*, ed. Gerald Graff (Evanston, IL: Northwestern University Press, 1988).

6. Judith Butler, *Bodies That Matter: On the Discursive Limits of Sex* (London and New York: Routledge, 1993).

7. See anthropologist Victor Turner's *The Ritual Process: Structure and Anti-Structure* (Chicago: Aldine Publishing, 1969). See also Richard Schechner's foundational theory of restored behavior, which describes a reconstruction of realities whose origins are not and cannot be located in the events of performance but are "restored" by them. Richard Schechner, *Between Theater and Anthropology* (Philadelphia: University of Pennsylvania Press, 1985). Peggy Phelan addresses Turner's and Schechner's theories by reminding us of Freud's *Nachträglichkeit*, or "the retrospective account that reinterprets the past in such a way that what had been repressed by the unconscious can be joined with consciousness," in her introduction to *The Ends of Performance*, ed. Peggy Phelan and Jill Lane (New York: New York University Press, 1998), 6. Rebecca Schneider takes on this theme as it relates to feminist performance specifically, when she defines the "explicit body" in performance as "a mass of orifices and appendages, details and tactile surfaces" and "foremost a site of social markings, physical parts and gestural signatures of gender, race, class, age, sexuality—all of which bear ghosts of historical meaning, markings delineating social hierarchies of privilege and disprivilege." *The Explicit Body in Performance* (London and New York: Routledge, 1997), 2. Each of these ritualized, restored, and ghostly reconstructions of the past helps account for the kinds of reiterative citations that Jewish female performers rely on to render their identity plays legible to respective audiences, and for a variety of reasons, illegible to others.

8. Julia Foulkes, "Angels 'Rewolt!': Jewish Women in Modern Dance in the 1930s," in *American Jewish Women's History: A Reader*, ed. Pamela S. Nadell (New York: New York University Press, 2003), 209. In a larger discussion of the praised "emotional intensity" of Jewish female dancers so well suited for "universal" themes of human experience that vied with stereotypes of Jewish miserliness, Foulkes focuses on a celebrated capacity for "expressivity" that partnered well with the content of early modern dance, if not always with its whiter face. Though Foulkes does not interrogate the racial imagination of early modern dance outright, her invocation of this anti-Semitic moment reveals the Jewish female body at the center of more critical crises of ethnic and gender identification and visibility.

9. For this conceptualization, I especially thank Christine Leapman, a friend who half-jokingly referenced my "face issues" after sitting in on a dance class I was teaching. I understood her intention to tease and critique the expressivity of my face and its "issues" which we both recognized as quintessential to Jewish female identity. Among many examples of being cautioned about my face, I was advised while dancing in a friend's choreography to face away from the audience as much as possible so as not to cause them to laugh at the wrong parts. The same professor later explained that I'd never be "just a modern dancer," and I came to understand that my face exceeded the requisite neutrality of contemporary dance standards, no longer invested in the expressive Jewish character as they once had been. And yet, in another instance, on a flight coming home from an academic dance conference where I was asked in a contact improv workshop

why I was making a funny face, my former professor, Linda Tomko, seated in the same row, laughed with me kindly and said, "You'll always be performing on multiple registers that perhaps you won't even know." After confirming that she was talking about me, and not more generally, she added with a smile, "Your face is your self-reflexive capacity."

10. Sherill Dodds, "The Choreographic Interface: Dancing Facial Expression in Hip Hop and Neo-Burlesque," *Dance Research Journal* 46, no. 2 (2014): 38–56.

11. See also Sherill Dodds, "Embodied Transformations in Neo-Burlesque Striptease," *Dance Research Journal* 45, no. 3 (2013): 75–90; Sherril Dodds and Colleen Hooper, "Faces, Closeups and Choreography: A Deleuzian Critique of *So You Think You Can Dance*," *International Journal of Screendance* 4, no. 1 (2014): 93–113.

12. See chapter 4 for more on body-splicing Jewish ballet horror.

13. Eric L. Goldstein, *The Price of Whiteness: Jews, Race and American Identity* (Princeton, NJ: Princeton University Press, 2006), 12.

14. Ibid., 38.

15. For writing on Jewish dance in the United States, see Rebecca Rossen, *Dancing Jewish: Jewish Identity in Modern and Postmodern American Dance* (New York: Oxford University Press, 2014). Other influential works include Linda Tomko, *Dancing Class: Gender, Ethnicity, and Social Divides in American Dance, 1890–1920* (Bloomington: Indiana University Press, 1999); Julia Foulkes, "Angels 'Rewolt!'"; Naomi Jackson, *Converging Movements: Modern Dance and Jewish Culture at the 92nd Street Y* (Hanover, NH, and London: Wesleyan University Press, 2000); Ellen Graff, *Stepping Left: Dance and Politics in New York City, 1928–1942* (Durham, NC: Duke University Press, 1997); and Susan Manning, *Modern Dance, Negro Dance: Race in Motion* (Minneapolis: University of Minnesota Press, 2004) .Hannah Kosstrin, *Honest Bodies: Revolutionary Modernism in the Dances of Anna Sokolow* (New York: Oxford University Press, 2017) includes the author's beautiful readings of Anna Sokolow's work in incredible detail. See also Nina Haft, "36 Jewish Gestures," in *Moving Ideas: Multimodality and Embodied Learning*, ed. Mira-Lisa Katz (New York: Peter Lang, 2013); and Nina Haft, "Dancing Through a Jewish Lens," n.d., http://dancersgroup.org/author/nina-haft/.

16. Rossen, *Dancing Jewish*, 12.

17. Ibid., 12.

18. Ibid., 6. The metaphor likens dance to a Jewish preoccupation with nose jobs and other cosmetic manipulations. I would add breast reduction surgery in the case of more recent Jewish generations, though it is less openly discussed among Jews.

19. Barbara Kirshenblatt-Gimblett, "Corporeal Turn," *Jewish Quarterly Review* 95, no. 3 (2005): 451. See also Howard Eilberg-Schwartz, "The Problem of the Body for the People of the Book," in *People of the Body: Jews and Judaism from an Embodied Perspective*, ed. Howard Eilberg-Schwartz (Albany: State University of New York Press, 1992), 17.

20. Kirshenblatt-Gimblett cites especially the criticism of Hillel Halkin, "Feminizing Jewish Studies," *Commentary* 105 (February 1998): 39–45. For an alternative perspective see Matti Bunzl, "Jews, Queers, and Other Symptoms: Recent Work in Jewish Cultural Studies," *GLQ: A Journal of Lesbian and Gay Studies* 6, no. 2 (2000): 321–341.

21. Kirshenblatt-Gimblett, "Corporeal Turn," 449.

22. This configuration is distinct from but in necessary dialogue with the depiction of Israeli men as muscular Jews. A rich discussion of the militarization of the Israeli frontier during the period of state formation can be found in David Biale,

"Zionism as an Erotic Revolution," in *Eros and the Jews* (Berkeley: University of California Press, 1997).

23. Ann Pellegrini, *Performance Anxieties: Staging Psychoanalysis, Staging Race* (New York: Routledge, 1997), 18.

24. Ibid.

25. Riv-Ellen Prell, *Fighting to Become American: Jews, Gender, and the Anxiety of Assimilation* (Boston: Beacon Press, 1999), 44 and 207. See also Karen Brodkin, *How Jews Became White Folks and What That Says About Race in America* (New Brunswick, NJ: Rutgers University Press, 1998). Brodkin argues that as postwar suburbanization made space for middle- and upper-class Jews, stereotypes of the Jewish female circulated through mother-bashing humor and, by the 1970s, Jewish American princess jokes.

26. Brodkin, *How Jews Became White Folks*, 14.

27. This concept of "morphing" as an improvisational structure was taught to me by Los Angeles choreographer Susan Rose as an exercise in noticing what you are doing with a movement and then moving toward that, letting go of the last thing entirely. While the context in which Rose has dancers practice morphing has little to do with Jewishness or identity acts per se, she has encouraged me to use the task in the context of my own performance work, which for the length my research on this book has aided my understanding of how to unfix static ideas about identity (whether because of stereotypes or lack of imagination) through morphing ever forward through new ones.

28. Irving Howe, *World of Our Fathers* (New York: Harcourt Brace Jovanovich, 1976), is one of the first studies to document the prevalence of Jewish minstrelsy. He argues that Jews asserted Jewishness, not whiteness. Michael Alexander, *Jazz Age Jews* (Princeton, NJ: Princeton University Press, 2001), begins with a similar sympathetic assumption of Jewish blackface to discuss the popularity of black vernacular among Jews who continued to identify with marginalized Americans through an "exceptional Jewish liberalism" (1). Alexander argues that such cultural forms were less about assimilation or the desire to acculturate and more about marking oneself as different—by using a language familiar from centuries of being different—and imagining that one is a better American because of it.

29. Michael Rogin, *Black Face, White Noise: Jewish Immigrants in the Hollywood Melting Pot* (Berkeley: University of California Press, 1996), 29. See also Eric Lott, *Love and Theft: Blackface Minstrelsy and the American Working Class* (Oxford: Oxford University Press, 1995); and Annemarie Bean, James V. Hatch, and Brooks McNamara, eds., *Inside the Minstrel Mask: Readings in Nineteenth-Century Blackface Minstrelsy* (Hanover and London: Wesleyan University Press, 1996).

30. Joyce Antler, ed., "Jewish Women in Popular Culture," in *The Journey Home: Jewish Women and the American Century* (New York: The Free Press, 1997), 136–175. See also Antler's discussion of Tucker in "One Clove Away from a Pomander Ball: the Subversive Tradition of Jewish Female Comedians," *Studies in American Jewish Literature* 29 (2010): 129.

31. Lori Harrison-Kahan, *The White Negress: Literature, Minstrelsy, and the Black Jewish Imaginary* (New Brunswick, NJ: Rutgers University Press, 2011). Harrison-Kahan makes an important contribution to the scholarship through her focus on women. She calls for more attention to the ways in which interracial female-female relationships shed new light on a discourse of progressive era Jewish-black relations. She insists that interracial relations among black and Jewish women, particularly in the literary fiction of Zora Neal Hurston and Fanny Hurst, account for two-way interactions at least, if still "uneven" (3).

32. Manning, *Modern Dance, Negro Dance*, 10, 11, 21, 85, 118, 126, 193.
33. Marta E. Savigliano, *Tango and the Political Economy of Passion* (Westview: Boulder, 1995).
34. Ibid, 169.
35. Rossen, *Dancing Jewish*, 22. See also Erdman, *Staging the Jew*, 1–16.
36. Judith Butler, *Bodies That Matter: On the Discursive Limits of "Sex"* (London and New York: Routledge, 1993).
37. See Theodor Reik, *Jewish Wit* (New York: Gamut Press, 1962); Kalus L Berghan, "Comedy Without Laughter: Jewish Characters in Comedies from Shylock to Nathan," and Irving Saposnik, "The Yiddish are Coming! The Yiddish are Coming! Some Thoughts on Yiddish Comedy," in *Laughter Unlimited: Essays on Humor, Satire, and the Comic*, ed. Reinhold Grimm and Jost Hermand (London: University of Wisconsin Press, 1991), 3–26 and 99–105.
38. Sigmund Freud, *The Joke and Its Relation to the Unconscious*, trans. Joyce Chick (London: Penguin Books, 2003). Originally published as *Der Witz und seine Beziehung sum Unbewussten* (Leipzig: Deuticke, 1905).
39. Freud, *The Joke*, 106.
40. See Homi K. Bhabha, "Foreword, Joking Aside: The Idea of a Self-Critical Community," in *Modernity, Culture and "The Jew"*, ed. Bryan Cheyette and Laura Marcus (Stanford, CA: Stanford University Press, 1998), xx.
41. Mary Ann Doane explains Freud's theory in *Femmes Fatales: Feminism, Film Theory, Psychoanalysis* (New York: Routledge, 1991), 30.
42. Ibid., 215.
43. Freud, *The Joke*, 98. He writes that such animosity of jokes "turns into good account those ridiculous features in our enemy that the presence of opposing obstacles would not let us utter aloud or consciously."
44. Ruth Johnston, "Joke-Work: The Construction of Postmodern Identity in Contemporary Theory and American Film," in *You Should See Yourself: Jewish Identity in Postmodern America*, ed. Vincent Brook (New Brunswick, NJ: Rutgers University Press, 2006), 210. See also Jon Stratton, "Not Really White—Again: Performing Jewish Difference in Hollywood Films since the 1980s," *Screen* 42, no. 2. (Summer 2001): 142–146.
45. Linda Hutcheon, *A Theory of Parody: The Teachings of 20th Century Art Forms* (New York: Methuen, 1985).
46. Ibid., 75.
47. Studies of comic reliance on audience reception often make reference to Kenneth Burke, *Attitudes Toward History*, 3rd ed. (Berkeley: University of California Press, 1959). See also Hannah Ballou, "Pretty Funny: Manifesting a Normatively Sexy Female Comic Body," *Comedy Studies* 4, no. 2 (2013): 179–186; Lacy Lowery, Valerie R. Renegar, and Charles E. Goehring, "'When God Gives You AIDS . . . Make Lemon-AIDS': Ironic Persona and Perspective by Incongruity in Sarah Silverman's *Jesus Is Magic*," *Western Journal of Communication* 78, no. 1 (2014): 58–77.
48. Teresa de Lauretis, "Rethinking Women's Cinema," in *Figures of Resistance: Essays in Feminist Thought*, ed. and with an introduction by Patricia White (Urbana and Chicago: University of Illinois), 35.
49. Ibid., 34.
50. My use of "queer" encompasses the operative promise of gender and humor radicalism evidenced in the homosociality of neo-Jewish burlesque (chapter 1), the subversive performances of twentieth-century Jewish female comics (chapter 2), and an appropriative trope in the celebrity routines of more recent comedy (chapter 3). Queerness poses mixed promises in mainstream and adult film plots,

surfacing from its repressed realms in *Black Swan* (chapter 4) and meeting yet another uncertain fate in Burning Angel's conspicuous absence of gay male sex and limited airtime for lesbian scenes (chapter 5).

51. The scholarship on queer dance discourse is vast and increasing. For a range of queer definitions, dances, and methods, see Clare Croft, ed., *Queer Dance: Meanings and Makings* (New York: Oxford University Press, 2017); Kareem Khubchandani, "Snakes on the Dance Floor: Bollywood, Gesture, and Gender," *The Velvet Light Trap* 77 (2016): 69–85; Cindy Garcia, "Dancing Salsa Wrong," in *Salsa Crossings Dancing Latinidad in Los Angeles* (Durham, NC: Duke University Press, 2013), 43–65; Marta E. Savigliano, "Notes on Tango (as) Queer (Commodity)," *Anthropological Notebooks* 16, no. 3 (2010): 135–143; and José Esteban Muñoz, "Gesture, Ephemera, and Queer Feeling: Approaching Kevin Aviance," in *Cruising Utopia: The Then and There of Queer Futurity* (New York: New York University Press, 2009), 65–82.

52. Alana Kumbier, *Ephemeral Material: Queering the Archive*, Series on Gender and Sexuality in Information Studies, no. 4 (Sacramento, CA: Litwin Books, 2012).

53. A contrary case made for no such futurity has garnered critical attention for scholars who have questioned the reproductive tensions of futurity as a heteronormative conceptualization. Here I am referencing specifically the central arguments of José Esteban Muñoz, *Cruising Utopia: The Then and There of Queer Futurity* (New York: New York University Press, 2009); and Lee Edelman, *No Future: Queer Theory and the Death Drive* (Durham, NC: Duke University Press, 2004). In a paper presented at the UCLA Thinking Gender 2013 annual conference, "Which Child? Whose Queerness? On Situated Knowledges, Queer Embodiment and *No Future*," Jacob Lau positioned this death drive as a white gay male discourse in contrast to the 2008 occurrence of Thomas Beatie's transgender pregnancy, which queers the very possibility of reproductive futurity.

54. Sara Ahmed, *Queer Phenomenology: Orientations, Objects, Others* (Durham, NC, and London: Duke University Press, 2006).

55. Daniel Boyarin, Daniel Itzkovitz, and Ann Pellegrini, eds., *Queer Theory and the Jewish Question* (New York: Columbia University Press, 2003), 1.

56. Ibid., 5.

57. Ibid. See also Eve Kosofsky Sedgwick, *Epistemology of the Closet* (Berkeley: University of California Press, 1990).

58. Janet R. Jakobson, "Queers Are Like Jews, Aren't They? Analogy and Alliance Politics," in Boyarin, Itzkovitz, and Pellegrini, *Queer Theory and the Jewish Question*, 64–89.

59. Ibid., 9.

60. While queer Jewish studies is a growing field, to date there are still only a few scholarly texts on dance contexts specifically. Warren Hoffman offers a queer reading of Yiddish theater in *The Passing Game: Queering Jewish-American Culture: Judaic Traditions in Literature, Music and Art* (Syracuse, NY: Syracuse University Press, 2009); and Stacy Wolf presents a queer interpretation of the 1968 film *Funny Girl* in "Barbra's 'Funny Girl' Body," in Boyarin, Itzkovitz, and Pellegrini, *Queer Theory and the Jewish Question*; see also Nina Haft, "36 Jewish Gestures."

61. See José Esteban Muñoz, *Disidentifications: Queers of Color and the Performance of Politics* (Minneapolis: University of Minnesota Press, 2010). Muñoz defines disidentificatory performances as those that circulate in subcultural circuits and minoritarian counterpublic spheres that envision and animate new social relations (5). His understanding of performances that "work on and against"

dominant ideology helps position the queer potential of Jewish female performance that "neither opts to assimilate into such a structure nor strictly opposes it" (11).

CHAPTER 1

1. Under the alias Thirsty Girl Productions, Jen Gapay produces hundreds of music, burlesque, and variety shows (http://www.thirstygirlproductions.com/sign_up).
2. According to the Schlep Sisters' website, the two "have so much love, [they] schlep it all over the world" (http://schlepsisters.com/TheSchlepSisters/Welcome.html).
3. The *shamash* is the candle that lights all the others on Hanukkah. An online video of the signature opening act is available from a handheld camera at the 2008 Menorah Horah (http://www.youtube.com/watch?v=XQz8izazuf0).
4. The revival of burlesque is generally attributed to the opening of New York City's Blue Angel Exotic Cabaret in 1993. As a space created for strippers, acrobats, and aging musicians to do whatever they pleased, the Blue Angel became a popular venue for a mix of brand new burlesque that blended striptease and performance art. Amy Sohn, "Teasy Does It," *New York Magazine,* June 7, 2004, http://nymag.com/nymetro/nightlife/sex/columns/nakedcity/9210/.
5. At least two versions of the poster image circulated online announcing the December 2011 event. These include a Broadwayworld press release (http://music.broadwayworld.com/article/The-Schlep-Sisters-Thirsty-Girl-Prod-Present-5th-Annual-MENORAH-HORAH-20111129) and *Dose* (http://dose.clubzone.com/events/496826/new_york/The-5th-Annual-Menorah-Horah.html).
6. Since at least the Jewish invention of Barbie, this construct of the cream-colored American babe has fabricated a plastic Jewish promise of assimilatory success. Ruth Handler, wife of Mattel cofounder Elliot Handler, is credited as having tweaked the design of a German doll (not meant for children) and renamed it Barbie, after her preteen daughter. The toy was an instant success at the New York toy fair in 1959, rocketing the Jewish company to fame and fortune.
7. The Miss Exotic World Pageant and Striptease Reunion is an annual neoburlesque pageant and convention and is the showcase event and fundraiser for the Burlesque Hall of Fame, which moved from an abandoned desert goat farm in Helendale, California, to downtown Las Vegas. Over the course of a weekend of performances pageant competitors vie for the crown, which is quite seriously regarded as the top honor for a burlesque performance. A video of the Schlep Sisters performing "Chiribim, Zug es Mir, and Raindrops" is available at http://www.youtube.com/watch?v=BHZnAwOE7nI.
8. Phillip Roth, *Portnoy's Complaint* (New York: Random House, 1969). Readers familiar with Roth's portrait of Jewish American life may recall the scene in which Alex Portnoy defended his family's unkosher choice to eat shrimp and pork in Chinese restaurants because "to them we are not Jews but *white*—and maybe even Anglo Saxon" (90). See more on Jewish adoption of Chinese food as "Safe Treyf" in the context of urban American assimilation at Gaye Tuchman and Harry G. Levine, "New York Jews and Chinese Food: The Social Construction of an Ethnic Pattern," *Contemporary Ethnography* 22, no. 3 (1992): 382–407.
9. As noted burlesque scholar Robert C. Allen has argued, the subversive potential of burlesque's "awarish" self-displays since the late nineteenth century have enacted the power to upturn or upset patriarchal controls. Robert C. Allen, *Horrible Prettiness: Burlesque and American Culture* (Chapel Hill: University of North Carolina Press, 1991). See also Maria Elena Buszek, "Representing

'Awarishness': Burlesque, Feminist Transgression, and the 19th century Pin-Up,"
TDR 43, no. 4 (Winter 1999): 142; Sherill Dodds, "Embodied Transformations
in Neo-Burlesque Striptease," *Dance Research Journal* 45, no. 3 (December
2013): 75–90; and Natalie Marie Peluso, "High Heels and Fast Wheels: Alternative
Femininities in Neo-Burlesque and Flat-Track Roller Derby" (PhD diss., University
of Connecticut, 2010).

10. When I presented a paper on this subject at an academic dance conference, I stood
in an umbrella hat and a suit jacket hand-painted with a pattern of silver-blue
eyes. "Ever feel like all-eyes are on you?" I did my best to mimic the borscht belt
comedians of an earlier era for the conference room crowd, with all the lights up.

11. Laura Knowles, "Oy Vey, It's 'Nice Jewish Girls Gone Bad'!" *Lancaster Online*,
September 10, 2009, http://lancasteronline.com/features/entertainment/oy-vey-
it-s-nice-jewish-girls-gone-bad/article_e91dd3c6-b4e6-5718-9180-87131e16b89d.
html.

12. Darlinda Just Darlinda, "Feminist Neo-Burlesque Speech" (speech delivered at the
Feminist Neo-Burlesque Symposium at the Central School of Speech and Drama,
University of London, October 26, 2007), http://darlindajustdarlinda.com/darlinda-
just-darlinda-bio-and-press/feminist-neo-burlesque-speech-from-102607/.

13. Ibid.

14. Ibid.

15. Linda Williams defines postfeminism this way in"A Provoking Agent: The
Pornography and Performance Art of Annie Sprinkle," *Social Text* 37 (Winter
1993): 117–133.

16. Rossen, *Dancing Jewish*, 107.

17. Rogin, *Black Face, White Noise*, 29.

18. "Menorah Horah," *Highline Ballroom*, December 14, 2014, http://highlineball-
room.com/show/2014/12/14/menorah-horah-2/.

19. Phone interview with Zoe Ziegfeld, September 20, 2016.

20. Darlinda Just Darlinda, "Feminist Neo-Burlesque Speech."

21. Ibid.

22. See Freud, *The Joke*. See also Bhabha, "Foreword," xx.

23. Phone interview with Zoe Ziegfeld, September 20, 2016. She explained that while
a very limited number of artists live entirely off their work as neoburlesque performers, most maintain other jobs to pay their living expenses and costs of performance. The artist confirmed that at this phase, she is paying for performance
more than she is making, but she hopes for more and more opportunities to make
her performance life a viable source of income.

24. I even produced text copy upon request for a burlesquer's grant proposal and in
the process shared this analysis with performers themselves.

25. Interview with Minnie Tonka, New York City, July 21, 2016.

CHAPTER 2

1. This infamous line has made its way into the most quoted American movie history. Celebrity comics like Sandra Bernhard and Sarah Silverman make reference
to the scene in their own filmed stage shows, discussed at greater length in the
next chapter. As I argue in chapter 4, the terrorizing presence of mirrors in *Black
Swan* (2010) turns this legacy trope of Jewish female self-reconciliation into a
nightmarish cause for Natalie Portman's emotional breakdown.

2. *Playboy Magazine* 24, no. 10 (October 1977). Cover photo caption. http://barbra-
archives.com/bjs_library/70s/playboy.html.

3. Ibid., 148.

4. Impersonating Graham while joining her Jewish contemporaries, Brice famously cried out "Rewolt!" Foulkes, "Angel's 'Rewolt!'," 233–252. See also *Fanny Brice: The Original Funny Girl* (New York: Oxford University Press, 1992), 167.

5. Antler, *The Journey Home*, 150. Listen to *The Baby Snooks Show* episodes online at the Old World Radio, http://www.oldradioworld.com/shows/Baby_Snooks_Show.php.

6. Ann Van de Merwe, "My Man: The Vocal Signature of Fanny Brice," *The Phenomenon of Singing* 7 (2009): 139–141. http://journals.library.mun.ca/ojs/index.php/singing/article/view/907/785.

7. Sime Silverman, review of *Follies of 1916*, *Variety*, June 16, 1916. Brice as the dying swan harkened back to Mikhail Fokine's short ballet of the same name, choreographed for the esteemed Anna Pavlova to music from Camille Saint-Saens's *Carnival of the Animals*. The solo captures a swan in her last struggling moments of life, her supple upper body gliding over tiny steps called *pas de bourrée suivi*. Debatably a work of artistry and expressivity more than technical prowess, *The Dying Swan* was famously Pavlova's chance to dance with emotional abandon and heightened melodrama. A 1925 videorecording of her performance captures Pavlova's animated face. The furrow of her eyebrows matches the frown on her lips, as Pavlova projects her mortal fragility beyond the camera lens as if across a crowded auditorium. She was so identified with Fokine's work that the solo became the Russian ballerina's own swan song. Pavlova is known to have performed the work more than four thousand times, and legend has it that she called for her swan costume while on her deathbed.

8. Listen to a recording of Fanny Brice singing "Becky is Back in the Ballet" at https://www.youtube.com/watch?v=jj_dJ_It3PE.

9. Adapted from the 1964 musical *Funny Girl* and directed by William Wyler, the film recounts the story of Brice as an overnight stage success and a devastated romantic. In a movie-long flashback, protagonist Fanny reflects back on her turbulent life as the wife of gambler Nicky Arnstein, whose release from prison leads to a painful divorce. Among the musical and movie hit numbers, "Don't Rain on My Parade" is arguably the show's anthem, as the heartbroken star picks up her life again in a song reprise that allows her to realize and reconcile with her own belting power.

10. Brice performed the number live in the 1931 Ziegfeld Follies, just a year after *Be Yourself* came out in theaters.

11. "The Streisand Profile: The Nose," Barbra Streisand Archive library, http://barbra-archives.com/bjs_library/stories/nose_streisand.html. In the 1920s Fanny Brice did get a nose job in hopes of securing serious roles reserved for white women, though it didn't help her career. Audiences preferred her comic antics, and as Florenz Ziegfeld purportedly said, Brice's nose job was as foolish as "the clown who wants to play Hamlet." Karl K. Kitchen, unidentified clipping fragment from Boston newspaper, (probably the *Herald*) February 3, 1924, as quoted in Barbara W. Grossman, *Funny Woman: The Life and Times of Fanny Brice* (Bloomington and Indiana: Indiana University Press, 1992), 151.

12. Henri Bergson, *Laughter: An Essay on the Meaning of the Comic* (New York: Macmillan, 1914). Bergson contends that imitations of the most mechanical, most unconscious movements and gestures are as funny as the performance of stiffness. He describes stillness quite poetically as "when materiality succeeds in fixing the movement of the soul, in hindering its grace." Bergson emphasizes: "*The*

attitudes, gestures and movements of the human body are laughable in exact proportion as that body reminds us of a machine" (29).

13. Depending on the restaging, Odette drowns, disappears, or is otherwise doomed in the entrapped body of a swan by the betrayal of her prince, who mistakes her identity at the ball in act 3. Only in versions made largely for children or under the Soviet regime (the Mariinsky Ballet, then the Kirov, in 1950) do the two live happily ever after.

14. Wolf, "Barbra's 'Funny Girl' Body."

15. Ibid., 248.

16. For more discussion of queer swans, see Kent Drummond, "The Queering of Swan Lake: A New Male Gaze for the Performance of Sexual Desire," *Journal of Homosexuality* 45, nos. 2–4 (2003): 235–255; and Suzanne Juhasz, "Queer Swans: Those Fabulous Avians in the Swan Lakes of Les Ballets Trockadero and Matthew Bourne," *Dance Chronicle* 31, no. 1 (2008): 54–83.

17. Looking back to the years before the turn of the century, Pamela Brown Lavitt predates Tucker and Brice with Ziegfeld's earlier Jewess soubrettes, Anna Held and Nora Bayes. The first of the Red Hot Mamas and the stars of the previous generation, Held and Bayes ushered in an era of sexually expressed performance personages with public impact on and off stage. Held and Bayes enjoyed high public esteem. Both accompanied song and dance careers with chic personal lives telegraphed on a lavish, public scale. Held was known to bathe in milk and champagne, while Bayes, who took her name from the wreath of bay leaves she wore in her hair, modeled a habit for all-day lollipops that took hold among women across America. Held kept her humble Polish roots a mystery most of her life, while Bayes was more forthcoming about her Jewishness. But like Tucker and Brice, these entertainers intermarried and remarried, played up popular tropes, and set trends for how to be and look like the new American woman for Jews and non-Jews alike."First of the Red Hot Mamas: 'Coon Shouting' and the Jewish Question," *American Jewish History* 87. no. 4 (1999): 253–290.

18. Antler, *The Journey Home*, 140.

19. Torch songs are sentimental songs, often about unrequited love. What made Tucker's "hot" was her comic style of layering sexual content and context that made women the empowered subjects and not the victims of love.

20. Antler, *The Journey Home*, 140.

21. Ibid., 140 and 148.

22. Ibid., 136.

23. Brown Lavitt, "The First of the Red Hot Mamas."

24. Ibid. While Brown Lavitt refers to Jewish entertainers primarily, it is unclear whether Jewish women playing "everything" would have been received the same as other performers with similar identity acts.

25. Amelia Holdberg, "Betty Boop: Yiddish Film Star," *American Jewish History* 87, no. 4 (1999): 291–312.

26. In another Betty Boop cartoon that year called *I'll Be Glad When You're Dead, You Rascal* (1932), Betty is shown with dark skin. Bimbo and Koko the clown carry her across the rural African veldt to the sound of the live recordings of Louis Armstrong and his orchestra. Images of orchestra members and Armstrong himself become the ominous enemy tribe who capture Betty but eventually die in a volcanic eruption after Bimbo and Koko manage to free her and the natives chase her. Armstrong gets the last laugh as he ends the cartoon short, back with his ensemble, singing into the microphone the title line of the show: "I'll be glad

when you're dead, you rascal." Who finally wins is less than clear in this battle of cartoons and musicians, in which Betty can first darken up and then be captured and freed, and like a rascal, get away with it.

27. Josephine Baker's famous act for Folies-Bergère was her humorous and erotic dance in a banana skirt. The act spoke to the negrophiliac French love for black culture in the interwar period and evolved over time as Baker's playful costume went from rubber fruit phalluses to suggestive metal spikes. Read more about Baker's banana dance in Alicja Sowinski, "Dialectics of the Banana Skirt: The Dialectics of Josephine Baker's Self-Representation," *Michigan Feminist Studies* 19 (2005/2006): 51–72. Watch Betty Boop's rendition at http://www.youtube.com/watch?v=x_W-xsLfozU.

28. Despite an unfading fan base that reissues her image in endless merchandise, Betty reappears as a cartoon has-been a half century later in *Who Framed Roger Rabbit* (1988). Against Jessica Rabbit's lounge singer act, Betty looks like a forgotten vision of the past. Entirely upstaged by Rabbit's red-soaked stage performance of "Do Right," Betty appears in black-and-white, a nostalgic reminder of the Great Depression–era animation technologies that match the club scene. The first sexy cartoon pales so drastically in comparison to Jessica Rabbit that Betty's presence engenders a sympathetic sense of outmoded funny sex appeal no longer as viable as it once was. She tells the detective, "Work's been pretty slow since cartoons went to color, but I still got it Eddie, boop oop a doop." The cutesy curls of Betty's former fame, no matter how red they turned in her first color cartoon, *Poor Cinderella* in 1934, cannot compete with Jessica's glossier physique, no matter how sweet or assimilated.

29. For more on the Production Code of 1934 and its impact on representational culture, see Jenna Simpson, "Oh, Ya Got Trouble. Right Here in New York City! Or Gotta Find a Way to Keep the Young Ones Moral After School: The Boycott of Hollywood, March–July 1934," *Constructing the Past* 5, no. 1 (2004): 1–12. Simpson evidences a general Jewish support for the boycott of dirty film and questions whether it was a genuine interest in cleaning up content or a fear of increased anti-Semitism scapegoating Jews in the media (9).

30. Caties Lazarus, "Paying Homage to Comedy Matriarchs," *Forward*, September 9, 2005, http://forward.com/articles/2754/paying-homage-to-comedy-e2-80-99s-matriarchs/.

31. Giovanna P. Del Negro, "The Bad Girls of Jewish Comedy: Gender, Class, Assimilation, And Whiteness in Postwar America," in a *Jewish Feminine Mystique? Jewish Women in Postwar America*, ed. Hasia R. Diner, Shira Kohn, and Rachel Kranson (New Brunswick, NJ: Rutgers University Press, 2010), 144–159.

32. Ibid., 144.

33. Ibid., 150. Del Negro argues that the late night radicalism of transgressive, trickster-like figures of the 1950s and 1960s made the nightclub the site of liminality both in regard to the gray areas of adult indiscretion and the in-betweenness of Jewish female comics who called themselves weird. Refusing to hide at home, they sourced their weirdness by foregrounding repressed identities. Flagrant ethnic Jewishness and women's sexuality acted as weapons to mock social norms. As del Negro asserts, "these lusty, fleshy, obviously menopausal women in sequined dresses and painted-on eyebrows flaunted their girth to mitigate the threat of their jokes" (155).

34. The Kinsey Reports are two books on human sexual behavior published in 1948, written by Alfred Kinsey, Wardell Pomeroy, and Clyde Martin. The books were

immediately controversial in the eyes of the general public for their coverage of previously taboo subjects. Based on thousands of interviews with men and women, the reports found men to be more sexually active than women.

35. Watch the *Saturday Night Live* sketch at http://www.nbc.com/saturday-night-live/video/jewess-jeans/n8674. Watch the original 1979 Jordache Jeans commercial at https://www.youtube.com/watch?v=qAZP9i6MvSw.

36. Shuly Rubin Schwartz, "From Jewess Jeans to Juicy JAPs: Clothing and Jewish Stereotypes" (lecture presented at What to Wear event, March 11, 2012, Jewish Theological Seminary), available at http://www.youtube.com/watch?v=rZWz_XL_zWg&feature=youtube_gdata_player. See also Brodkin's reference to Radner's commercial in *How Jews Became White Folks*, 169, and Prell's discussion of the same in *Fighting to Become American*, 182. For more on why US Jewish female stereotypes were so limited to princess personifications, see also Joyce Antler, "Jewish Women on Television, Too Jewish or Not Enough?," in *Talking Back: Images of Jewish Women in American Popular Culture*, ed. Joyce Antler (Hanover: Brandeis University Press, 1998), 242–252.

37. Biographies of Radner describe the actor's ongoing battle with weight and self-image. *Making Trouble: Three Generations of Funny Women*, directed by Rachel Talbot (Jewish Women's Archive, 2006), .

38. Cited in Henry Bial, "How Jews Became Sexy, 1968–1983," in *Acting Jewish: Negotiating Ethnicity on the American Stage & Screen* (Ann Arbor: University of Michigan Press, 2005), 86–106. Bial's process-oriented chapter title makes clever reference to Brodkin's *How Jews Became White Folks*, and though he does not articulate the explicit connection, Bial focuses his argument on economic factors of "sexiness" in ways that fit well within Brodkin's discussion of ethnic whiteness as class mobility.

39. Bial, "How Jews Became Sexy," 86.

40. Ibid., 87.

41. Ibid., 92.

42. Linda Ellerbee, "Exclusive Interview with Barbra Streisand," *Live! Magazine* 1, no. 11 (1996), http://barbra-archives.com/bjs_library/70s/playboy.html.

43. *Blazing Saddles*, directed by Mel Brooks (Warner Brothers Pictures, 1974). View the saloon scene at http://www.youtube.com/watch?v=6-pmpgrYQgs&feature=player_embedded.

44. The hero is a black sheriff in an all-white town, The Count Basie orchestra plays "April in Paris" in the Wild West, and well-known cowboy radio Slim Pickens introduces the *Wide World of Sports*.

45. *Shiksa* is Yiddish for a non-Jewish, blond woman with all the attributes Jewish women purportedly lack. The jokish term "Shiks-appeal" was coined in season 9, episode 3 of *Seinfeld* (NBC, July 5, 1989 to May 14, 1998). Elaine says to a rabbi, "Rabbi, what am I going to do with my shiks-appeal?"; the rabbi answers back, "Oh Elaine, that's just an urban legend like the Yeti or its cousin, the sasquatch. Now, another interesting fact is that rabbis are allowed to date!"

46. For example: How do you know when a JAP has an orgasm? She drops her nail file.

47. Watch Midler's concert at https://www.youtube.com/watch?v=UOrzpQeJyKI.

48. "Hawaiian Oklahoma," (NBC, 1977), viewed at Paley Center for Media, Los Angeles. Available at https://www.youtube.com/watch?v=rolxQPogXqU.

49. *Diva Las Vegas*, directed by Marty Callner, written by Madalyn Minch, Bruce Vilanch, and Lom Weyland (Cream Cheese Films, Home Box Office, 1997), filmed at MGM Grand Garden Arena, Las Vegas. The one-time performance aired on

HBO on January 18, 1997. "Balls!" is available at http://www.youtube.com/watch?v=P_JlAx-TtXU&feature=related.

50. Wolf, "Barbra's 'Funny Girl' Body," 247. Wolf draws on articles from clippings housed at the Billy Rose Theater Collection of the New York Public Library that deal with reviewer responses to Streisand's looks. This phrase comes from American film critic and academic Judith Crist in a press release for *Funny Girl* (December 1977).

CHAPTER 3

1. Rogin, *Black Face, White Noise*. See also Lott, *Love and Theft*; and Bean, Hatch, and McNamara, *Inside the Minstrel Mask: Readings in Nineteenth-Century Blackface Minstrelsy* (Hanover and London: Wesleyan University Press, 1996).

2. We learn next from Bernhard's personal manager, Ingrid Horn (played by actress Lu Leopold), that the star has gotten "way out of hand" with her off-Broadway success. The disciplining tenor of Horn's remarks establishes the film's finger wagging at the comic in and out of character, an acknowledgment and admonishment of an out-of-hand humor that threads through the performances reviewed in this chapter. Moreover, Horn's reference to Bernhard's stage show, which did in fact precede the film by two years, sets up the blurring of truth and fiction that deliberately obscures the film's agenda throughout. Blurring these lines further, Horn narrates the incredible setup of the plot: a trip back to the black supper clubs of Los Angeles, where Bernhard presumably got her start.

3. The film's flamboyant scheme to fight racism is one Bernhard champions through a later homage to disco and funk that pays ultimate respect to her hero and major music celebrity, Sylvester.

4. Catherine Halley, "The Mouth That Launched a Thousand Rifts: Sandra Bernhard's Politics of Irony," *Iowa Journal of Cultural Studies* 14 (1995): 23–39, http://ir.uiowa.edu/ijcs/vol1995/iss14/4. Importantly, it is her face that Bernhard brings into focus in an interview outside of the film with Roseanne Barr for *Interview* magazine, when the two reminisce on Bernhard's life in the industry. Like the opening scene at the vanity mirror, Bernhard reflects on the dynamics of her career behind the scenes. "My whole point of view was, 'No matter what, you're going to respect me and love me the way I am, and I'm not gonna change.'" Noting what exactly she wouldn't change, she said, "I'm not gonna get a nose job. I'm not going to pretend I'm the girl next door. . . . But I do live in the neighborhood, so you better get used to me." Roseanne Barr, "Character Study: Sandra Bernhard," *Interview Magazine* (April 2012): 73.

5. "We'd gone through Roe v Wade. You know, I grew up, as you did, looking at that, and that was just part of our conversation as women. Like *Ms.* Magazine and Ms. Gloria Steinem. I was 12 years old. . . . I wanted to take it to a new place. 'It was post-feminist.'" Barr, "Character Study," 73, 148.

6. *Ms.* was launched as a "one-shot" sample insert in *New York* magazine in December 1971 (http://msmagazine.com/blog/about/). One of the magazine's founders, Gloria Steinem, was well known as a spokesperson for American feminism in the 1960s and 1970s and continues to tour internationally as an organizer and lecturer on issues of equality.

7. For the peak years of her fame and long before the Internet, Bernhard was rumored to have sustained a romantic relationship with Madonna. The actress has since exposed the media scandal as a ruse she and Madonna had fun playing out for the press effect.

8. See, for example, Andrea Dworkin and Catharine A. MacKinnon, *Pornography and Civil Rights: A New Day for Women's Equality* (Minneapolis, MN: Organizing Against Pornography, 1988), http://www.nostatusquo.com/ACLU/dworkin/other/ordinance/newday/TOC.htm.

9. Lott, *Love and Theft.*

10. bell hooks,"Eating the Other: Desire and Resistance," in *Black Looks: Race and Representation* (Boston: South End Press, 1992), 336–380; Ann Pellegrini, "You Make Me Feel (Mighty Real): Sandra Bernhard's Whiteface," in *With Other Eyes: Looking at Race and Gender in Visual Culture*, ed. Lisa Bloom (Minneapolis: University of Minnesota Press, 1999); and Lauren Berlant and Elizabeth Freeman, "Queer Nationality," *Boundary 2* 19, no. 1 (1992): 149–180. See also Elspeth Probyn, "Without Her, I'm Nothing," in *Sexing the Self: Gendered Positions in Cultural Studies* (London and New York: Routledge, 1993); Rebecca Schneider, "The Secret's Eye," in *The Explicit Body in Performance* (London and New York: Routledge, 1997); and Roberta Mock, "Without You I'm Nothing: Sandra Bernhard's Self-referential Postmodernism," *Women's Studies* 30, no. 4 (2001): 543–562.

11. hooks, "Eating the Other," 379.

12. Ibid.

13. Ibid.

14. Named only in the credits of the film, "Roxanne" is both Bernhard's foil and the subject-object of Bernhard's queer and racialized desire. When we see her before the ending scene, it's for moments that draw her in stark comparison to Bernhard: generally alone and outside the club, whether in shots walking through her Watts neighborhood or mid-experiment in a science classroom.

15. Pellegrini, "You Make Me Feel." Pellegrini writes that bell hooks estimates that what the striptease amounts to is yet another white female performance for a black male gaze of the club, which even in making fun of its failures to attract them erases black men completely. Pellegrini, however, argues that it is not the black male gaze that Bernhard is after through the film, but the black *female* gaze that the performer aims to entertain, blurring whether she wants to *be* Roxanne or *with* Roxanne (242).

16. Pellegrini, "You Make Me Feel," 242.

17. Ibid., 247.

18. Ibid., 246.

19. Ibid., 238.

20. Ibid., 241.

21. Ibid.

22. Dustin Bradley Goltz, "Ironic Performativity: Amy Schumer's Big (White) Balls," *Text and Performance Quarterly* 35, no. 4 (2015): 283.

23. Nick Marx, "Expanding the Brand: Race, Gender, and the Post-Politics of Representation on Comedy Central," *Television & New Media* 17, no. 3 (2016): 275.

24. "Face Wars," *The Sarah Silverman Program* (Comedy Central, episode 203), posted OctOber 17, 2007, at http://www.comedycentral.com/video-clips/ojqria/the-sarah-silverman-program-blackface-rally.

25. See Harrison-Kahan, *The White Negress*, 180–182; and David Gillota, "The New Jewish Blackface: African American Tropes in Contemporary Jewish Humor," in *Jews and Humor: Studies in Jewish Civilization* 22 (October 2009): 226–229.

26. Kelly Connolly, "Sarah Silverman Regrets Wearing Blackface for Sarah Silverman Program Joke," *Entertainment Weekly: Watch What Happens Live*, October 30, 2015, http://www.ew.com/article/2015/10/30/sarah-silverman-blackface- joke-regret.

27. Ibid.

28. "Amy Schumer Apologizes for 'Racist' Rape Joke About Hispanics: 'I Am Taking Responsibility'," *The Hollywood Reporter*, July 7, 2015, http://www.hollywoodreporter.com/news/amy-schumer-apologizes-racist-joke-807066.

29. Kia Makarechi, "'Girls' Reviews: New HBO Show and Lena Dunham Face Backlash on Racism and More," *The Huffington Post*, April 16, 2012, http://www.huffingtonpost.com/2012/04/16/girls-reviews-backlash-hbo-show_n_1429328.html?ref=entertainment?ref=entertainment&ir=Entertainment&ref=entertainment.

30. See "The Great Schlep," http://www.youtube.com/watch?v=AgHHX9R4Qtk.

31. *Jesus Is Magic*, directed by Liam Lynch, written and performed by Sarah Silverman (Black Gold Films, 2005).

32. A video clip is available at http://www.youtube.com/watch?v=Y_lUu_RyFpI.

33. Comic actress Rachel Feinstein makes a similar joke in her hour-long special for Comedy Central, *Only Whores Wear Purple* (2016). She explains that whenever she and her boyfriend "hook up," he asks her to do a sexy dance for him, for which she consents to wear lingerie, "but I'm not gonna do a jig. . . . I don't have a jazzy number for you, I'm sorry. This is not *America's Got Talent*." One time she "put on a bikini and did the Charleston above him," to which "he was disgusted . . . gently weeping." When she "finally gave him a lap dance," he found it confusing because she was "also singing a lot of Yiddish show tunes. . . . I sang a lot of songs from *Fiddler on the Roof*." As the crowd laughs and claps, she adds, "He was fully flaccid by the time the lap dance was complete." Watch the clip at http://splitsider.com/2016/04/how-rachel-feinstein-went-from-bombing-without-realizing-it-to-a-comedy-central-hour/.

34. *Blue Velvet*, directed by David Lynch (MGM, 1986). Silverman's sexy shtick takes on the "torch singer" tenor of Lynch's mysterious female lead, Dorothy Vallens (performed by Isabella Rossellini). Torch singers typically lament using lyrics of unrequited love, as they purport to "carry the torch" for someone who has forgotten them.

35. *Jesus Is Magic*.

36. Lowery, Renegar, and Goehring, "'When God Gives You AIDS," 58–77.

37. Ibid., 60.

38. Kenneth Burke, *A Grammar of Motives* (Berkeley: University of California Press, 1969).

39. Goltz, "Ironic Performativity," 266–285.

40. Emily Nussbaum, "Laverne & Curly: The Slapstick Anarchists of 'Broad City'," *New Yorker*, March 7, 2016, http://www.newyorker.com/magazine/2016/03/07/broad-citys-slapstick-anarchists.

41. Ibid.

42. Ibid.

43. Ibid.

44. Marx, "Expanding the Brand," 272–287.

CHAPTER 4

1. In her reading of the film, Ariel Osterweiss also discussed the central figure of the wereswan as a regendering of the werewolf trope. Reversing the horror of a boy becoming a threat to all by night, Osterweiss contends that *Black Swan*'s wereswan that is Odette-becoming-Odile is a threat only to herself. Osterweiss, "Disciplining Black Swan, Animalizing Ambition," in *The Oxford Handbook of Dance and the Popular Screen*, ed. Melissa Blanco Borelli (New York: Oxford University Press, 2014), 76–77.

2. One of the earliest Jewish mother figures in American popular culture was Molly Goldberg, portrayed by Gertrude Berg in the situation comedy *The Goldbergs* on radio (1929–1949) and television (1949–1955). Literary representations include Rose Morgenstern from Herman Wouk's 1955 novel *Marjorie Morningstar*, Mrs. Patimkin from *Goodbye, Columbus* by Philip Roth, and Sophie Ginsky Portnoy from *Portnoy's Complaint*, also by Roth. Sylvia Barack Fishman's characterization of Marjorie Morningstar and Sophie Portnoy is that each is "a forceful Jewish woman who tries to control her life and the events around her," who is "intelligent, articulate, and aggressive," and who does not passively accept life but tries to shape events, friends, and families, to match their visions of an ideal world. Fishman, "Introduction: The Faces of Women," in *Follow My Footprints: Changing Images of Women in American Jewish Fiction*, ed. Sylvia Barack Fishman (Hanover, NH: University Press of New England, 1992), 1–2, 30–32, 35.
3. Such an emotional cut between Jewish daughter and mother foreshadows the discussion of *Heeb*'s New Jews in chapter 5 and their break from their parents' generation.
4. Osterweiss refers to the *fouetté* turn as "the modern mark of female virtuosity in ballet from the late nineteenth century on" in "Disciplining Black Swan," 70.
5. Joann Kealiinohomoku personifies ballet as a set of Western aesthetic tropes in "An Anthropologist Looks at Ballet as a Form of Ethnic Dance," in *Moving History/Dancing cultures*, ed. Ann Dils and Ann Cooper Albright (Middletown, CT: Wesleyan University Press, 2001). She argues that recurring fairy-tale themes have come to seem so "acultural" that we forget to acknowledge their ethnic, geographic specificity in Western culture. For more on *Swan Lake* parodies, see Suzanne Juhasz, "Queer Swans: Those Fabulous Avians in the *Swan Lakes* of Les Ballet Trockadero and Matthew Bourne," *Dance Chronicle* 31 (2008): 54–83.
6. Robin Wood, "Introduction to the American Horror Film," in *Movies and Methods: An Anthology*, ed. Bill Nichols (Berkeley: University of California Press, 1985), 199. Wood defines the monster as the Other who is to be repressed, but never destroyed.
7. Matthew Saltmarsh, "Dior Fires John Galliano after Bigotry Complaints," *New York Times*, March 1, 2011; and "John Galliano: 'I Love Hitler' (VIDEO)" and "Natalie Portman 'Disgusted' by John Galliano Video," *The Huffington Post*, March 1, 2011, http://www.huffingtonpost.com/2011/03/01/natalie-portman-galliano-video-dior_n_829522.html.
8. Conversely, Dyer writes that passing as "white" allows one to play many roles, including ethnic ones. This is advantageous for white-looking actors, who have more options.
9. See Sander Gilman, *The Jew's Body* (New York: Routledge, 1991); and Ruth D. Johnston, "Joke-Work: The Construction of Jewish Postmodern Identity in Contemporary Theory and American Film," in *You Should See Yourself: Jewish Identity in Postmodern American Culture*, ed. Vincent Brook (New Brunswick, NY: Rutgers University Press, 2006), 207–229.
10. See online discussions of Portman, Ryder, and Kunis's nose jobs: "Natalie Portman Nose Job Before and After Photos," *Surgery Stars*, December 10, 2013, http://surgerystars.com/natalie-portman-nose-job-before-and-after-photos/; "Winona Ryder Nose Job," *Plastic Surgery Before After*, June 22, 2013, http://plasticsurgerybeforeafter.blogspot.com/2013/06/winona-ryder-nose-job.html; and "Mila Kunis Before and After," *Beauty Insider*, November 1, 2013, http://beautyeditor.ca/2013/11/01/mila-kunis-before-and-after/.

11. From *Seinfeld*'s tenure on TV to any number of recent films starring Ben Stiller, Adam Sandler, and Seth Rogen, a renaissance of updated *schlemiel* roles proliferates. Jewish and non-Jewish actors (think Steve Carell's *The 40 Year Old Virgin* [2005] and *Dinner for Shmucks* [2010]) play sexually inept, insecure dweebs, for whom a castrated but still lovable caricature extends to joblessness, wifelessness, and general male-less-ness.

12. Even as Fox's *Glee* features a Jewish American nose-conscious character desperately seeking Streisand, gone are the days of that singer's Hollywood heyday in *Funny Girl* and *Yentl* (1983), or even the more recent Fran Dresher on *The Nanny* (1993–1999).

13. "The 50 Sexiest Jewish Girls We Can't Passover [Photos]," *Coed Magazine*, April 18, 2011, http://coedmagazine.com/2011/04/18/the-50-sexiest-jewish-girls-we-cant-passover-photos/. Daniel Itzkovitz argues that these sites offer strange pleasures for Jewish and neo-Nazi groups alike, but does not entirely explain why, in "They Are All Jews," 230–252.

14. Susan Foster plays on this theme in her performative lecture, "The Ballerina's Phallic Pointe," contending that ballerinas are like penises. Access her text and video at http://danceworkbook.pcah.us/susan-foster/the-ballerinas-phallic-pointe.html.

15. In a rehearsal of the Black Swan pas de deux, Thomas criticizes Nina's prudish inability to perform the role's sex appeal, cuttingly asking her male dance partner, David, "Honestly, would you fuck this girl?" David, who plays the Prince in the film's ballet, is acted by Benjamin Millepied, the famous choreographer Portman married after making the film.

16. In fact, Lily (Mila Kunis) *is* faking the dancing here, as the camera allows only her upper body to be visible. As Lily then falls into a male cast member's arms unintentionally and laughs off her mistake, the point is driven home. Sex-inflected sensuality upstages dancing ability, such that dancing itself need only be assumed rather than seen.

17. For an account of early twentieth-century Jewish blackface, see Rogin, *Black Face, White Noise*. For a discussion of suburban Jews, see Brodkin, *How Jews Became White Folks*. See also David Roediger, "Whiteness and Ethnicity in the History of 'White Ethnics' in the United States," in *Race Critical Theories*, ed. Philomen Essed and David Theo Goldberg (Oxford: Blackwell, 2002), 325–334.

18. Osterweiss refers to the use of mirrors throughout the film as sites of both reflection and distortion, where the audience encounters the protagonist's self-scrutiny. Osterweiss writes that Nina's refection sometimes manifests as her own image and at other times as her doppelganger ("Disciplining Black Swan," 78). This potential of the mirror to reflect back the image of the threatening doppelganger adds a fascinating dimension to the parodied horror of Joanna Angel's blow-up double in chapter 5.

19. Jon Stratton, *Coming Out Jewish: Constructing Ambivalent Identities* (London: Routledge, 2000), 300.

20. Ibid., 12.

21. See Alexander Doty, *Making Things Perfectly Queer: Interpreting Mass Culture* (Minneapolis: University of Minnesota Press, 1993).

22. For more on the curious Jewish/queer connection, see Boyarin, Itzkovitz, and Pellegrini, *Queer Theory and the Jewish Question*.

23. Pas de chat translates from French as "step of the cat" and is the name of a ballet leap from one foot to the other in which the feet are drawn up and the knees

are bent so that the legs form a diamond. Used as a pun, the phrase plays on the female cattiness of the melodrama between Nina and Lily. The use of ballet innuendo to describe the nondance duet offers a significant blurring of the worlds of the characters on- and offstage.

24. According to Wood, the monster's "sympathetic" subjecthood defines the degree to which we ultimately accept or deny her "return" from the repressed, unseen margins ("Introduction to the American Horror Film," 205).

25. Perhaps Macaulay felt the pressure ABT's artistic director must also have experienced in remounting the ballet the month after the film came out in theaters. Perhaps he is just performing the very same snob that *Black Swan*'s demeaning director-character, Thomas, personifies without apology.

26. Alastair Macaulay, "A 'Swan' of Complex Shades," *New York Times*, February 14, 2011. Also, according to dance critic Luke Jennings of the London-based *Observer*, that city's infamous Royal Ballet received too many phone calls to count that winter of the film's release in hopes of securing tickets for Portman's performance of the Swan Queen. See Jennings, "Swan Lake – Review," *The Guardian*, January 29, 2011. https://www.theguardian.com/stage/2011/jan/30/swan-lake-royal-ballet-review.

27. Responding to claims that Portman didn't perform the majority of her on-screen dancing in her Oscar-winning role, Aronofsky released the following statement through studio Fox Searchlight: "Here is the reality. I had my editor count shots. There are 139 dance shots in the film. 111 are Natalie Portman untouched. 28 are her dance double Sarah Lane. If you do the math that's 80% Natalie Portman. . . . There are two complicated longer dance sequences that we used face replacement. . . . And to be clear Natalie did dance on pointe in pointe shoes. If you look at the final shot of the opening prologue, which lasts 85 seconds, and was danced completely by Natalie, she exits the scene on pointe. That is completely her without any digital magic. . . . And I don't want anyone to think that's not her they are watching. It is." In contrast to the director's defense of his actor, twenty-seven-year-old American Ballet Theater ballerina Sarah Lane told *Entertainment Weekly* that Portman only danced 5 percent of the full-body shots in the film. She also claimed that one of the film's producers asked her not to speak publicly about her work during Oscar season. "The shots that are just her face with arms, those shots are definitely Natalie," Lane says. "But that doesn't show the actual dancing." Lane admits that she was never promised a particular title for her six weeks of work on the film, though she was disappointed to see that she is credited only as "Hand Model," "Stunt Double," and "Lady in the Lane" (a brief walk-on role). Lane's comments were made after *Black Swan* choreographer and Portman's then fiancé and now husband, Benjamin Millepied, told the *L.A. Times* that Natalie did "85 percent" of the dancing in the film. Jean Linihan, "Benjamin Millepied on 'Black Swan,' Natalie Portman and His Dancing Future," *Los Angeles Times*, March 23, 2011. http://latimesblogs.latimes.com/culturemonster/2011/03/benjamin-millepied-on-black-swan-nataline-portman-and-his-dancing-future.html.

28. Even more so, the public hype surrounding the double seems to have pulled off its own set of stunts. Folded into the argument about who danced and how much is a debate about dance as a sphere of extreme practices and even unchecked horrors. In a film largely premised on the obsessive, monster-making work of dance, it is ironic that the public cries out for fair labor practices.

29. A focus group of seven male and female friends, visual artists, dancers, and PhD students in critical dance studies, history, anthropology, and ethnomusicology

screened and discussed the film on August 26, 2011. The group shared a unanimous sense of the film, and Portman's character in particular, as totally lacking in humor. One participant observed that the only gag moment is when the actor-dancer playing Von Rothbart walks past Nina backstage in the final scenes, and the viewer predicts this will scare Nina as yet another unsure hallucination, but instead we/she hear/hears von Rothbart say simply "hi" as he walks by with the corps members. Another participant suggested that the bits of laughing that punctured an otherwise deadly silent screening responded to the film's overall "badness," which he ascribed to the script, the acting, and the overall concept of the film. This notion of badness resonates with other responses to Portman's "bad" dancing.

30. Mikhail Bakhtin, "Epic and the Novel: Towards a Methodology for the Study in the Novel," in *The Dialogical Imagination: Four Essays*, ed. Michael Holquist (Austin: University of Texas Press, 1981), 23.

31. Phone interview with Susannah Perlman, August 20, 2011. See more discussion of the Nice Jewish Girls in chapter 1.

32. "Natalie Raps," *Saturday Night Live*, season 31, episode 14 (NBC, March 4, 2006), http://www.youtube.com/watch?v=VVPCz0W7Rm0.

33. It is worth mentioning here that the anxiety stems from the very component that makes blackface most legible: its ability to be taken off. The mega-famous hardcore punk group turned hip-hop group, the Beastie Boys, formed in 1981 in New York City, are doubtless the most popular and longest-running example of Jews who performed blackface via rap.

34. Ruth D. Johnston defines "Jewishness" as the secular set of self-reflexive concerns as opposed to a set identity ("Joke-Work," 208).

35. Stratton, *Coming Out Jewish*, 26.

36. Ibid., 5.

CHAPTER 5

1. The Suicide Girls (suicidegirls.com) features the online profiles, nude photographs, and blogs of heavily tattooed, punk women who commit "social suicide" by breaking away from societal norms (https://suicidegirlspress.com/faq/). For critical discussion of the Suicide Girls, see Shoshana Magnet, "Feminist Sexualities, Race, and the Internet: An Investigation of suicidegirls.com," *New Media & Society* 9, no. 4 (2007): 577–602.

2. Joanna Angel, telephone interview, September 19, 2016.

3. Angel opens her essay ". . . On Being a Feminist with a Porn Site" with a similar sentiment:"There are two kinds of sluts in this world: the kind I used to be, and the kind I am now. The former sleeps with guys for attention. . . . The latter sleeps with guys because she really genuinely likes having sex." In *Naked Ambition: Women Who Are Changing Pornography* (New York: Carroll & Graf Publishers, 2005), 233–244.

4. The US Supreme Court established the *Miller* test in 1973, by which judges and juries determine whether matter is obscene. The three-pronged test is described in detail on the official website of the US Department of Justice, at https://www.justice.gov/criminal-ceos/citizens-guide-us-federal-law-obscenity.

5. Robin Morgan, *Going Too Far: The Personal Chronicle of a Feminist* (New York: Vintage Books, 1978), 169.

6. Constance Penley, Celine Parreñas Shimizu, Mireille Miller-Young, and Tristan Taormino, "Introduction: The Politics of Producing Pleasure," in *The Feminist*

Porn Book: The Politics of Producing Pleasure, ed. Tristan Taormino, Celine Parreñas Shimizu, Constance Penley, and Mireille Miller-Young (New York: The Feminist Press at the City University of New York, 2013), 10.

7. Porn star and registered nurse Nina Hartley had begun producing and starring in sex education films for Adam and Eve. The shift in the industry signaled an acknowledgment of female desire and a market for it, even if it was still limited by mainstream preferences. For example, independent, lesbian-produced lesbian porn grew at a slower pace, but gained traction through the mid-1990s, and the openly lesbian Sprinkle made the first porn film to feature a trans man.

8. Pro-am is a category of professional-amateur or semiprofessional films that pairs amateur performers with professionals.

9. "AVN Awards," Burning Angel, http://www.burningangel.com/en/avn-2016.

10. "What Are the Feminist Porn Awards?," Feminist Porn Awards, http://www.feministpornawards.com/what-are-the-feminist-porn-awards/.

11. Angel was one of six performers in Tristan Taormino's *House of Ass*, produced by Adam and Eve Studios in 2005. Inspired by reality TV, the film takes place in the mountains on a secluded weekend. Shot in Taormino's signature "gonzo" style, performers have their own camcorder cameras to shoot each other's scenes. *House of Ass*, Feminist Porn Awards, http://www.feministpornawards.com/house-of-ass/.

12. Phone interview with Joanna Angel, September 19, 2016.

13. Angel, ". . . On Being a Feminist with a Porn Site," 234.

14. Ibid., 234.

15. Levy, *Female Chauvinist Pigs*.

16. Ibid., 4.

17. Ibid., 3.

18. Ibid., 4.

19. Ibid., 93.

20. Ibid., 74.

21. Ibid., 30.

22. "There is something twisted about using a predominantly sexually traumatized group of people as our erotic role models," Levy argues. "It's like using a bunch of shark attack victims as our lifeguards" (ibid., 180).

23. It is worth pointing out that "pig" is most often a derogatory term directed at men who sleep around or otherwise ignore the binding contracts of their relationships. These may or may not be the same men who leave their rooms as pigsties, which is most commonly seen as the fault of their mothers, who spoiled them and now no longer live close enough to clean up after them. Pigpens for women are the rooms of social rebels, whether the result of drugs and alcohol, unmedicated mental health issues, or deliberately unkempt teen years—to be a female pig ignores the rules of well-tended spaces and relationships, too, as both reflect on bad rehearsals for life. As practice spaces of obligatory domesticity, piggish rooms and promiscuity raise the hairs of parents and sex-censoring social police. Of course, women are called pigs for eating too much, a slap made worse when women use the label to name and shame themselves.

24. Levy, *Female Chauvinist Pigs*, 184.

25. Ibid., 31.

26. Jane Ward, "Queer Feminist Pigs," in Taormino, Shimizu, Penley, and Miller-Young, *The Feminist Porn Book*, 130–139.

27. Readers can consider Ward's point in the context of Minnie Tonka's similar argument in the end of chapter 1 of this book, when the burlesque performer reminds us that what people find sexy is up to them and need not follow any formula.

28. Ward concludes her essay with her "Queer Pig Manifesta" in five key points. "I get off on porn smartly and mindfully," she writes, staying interested in her desire, which does not presume to be natural, static, or predictable. "I do not take my 'self' as a viewer too seriously." She adds that she does not feel any need to conform to expectations of marketers, her communities, or herself. "I am responsible for the impact of my sexual desires and sexual consumerism on others and myself," she states, noting that she will mind where and to whom she directs her gaze with attention to consent and dehumanization. She will "cultivate a private, internal space where [she] can honor and observe the complexity of [her] sexuality as it evolves," trusting herself to work "queerly and feministly" with her desire. Finally, Ward promises to "praise those who aim to dismantle racism and melt heteropatriarchy with their art, their porn." Closing by saying she is "bored by patriarchy," Ward writes that, "sexuality breathes life into the revolution." A diverse reality of sexualities and bodies can serve as models for what our bodies can do and be, she reiterates: an idealist premise uncompromised by personal tastes for the mainstream.

29. "Why Burning Angel Rules," Burning Angel, http://www.burningangel.com/forum/thread/2022/why-burning-angel-rules.

30. Niels van Doorn, "Keeping It Real: User-generated Pornography, Gender Reification, and Visual Pleasure," *Convergence: The International Journal of Research Into New Media Technologies* 16, no. 4 (2010): 414. See also Susanna Paasonen, "Labors of Love: Netporn, Web 2.0 and the Meanings of Amateurism," *New Media & Society* 12, no. 8 (2010): 1297–1312.

31. "About Joanna Angel," Joanna Angel, http://www.joannaangel.com/en/about.

32. Phone interview with Joanna Angel, September 19, 2016.

33. "Porn Hub," Porn Hub Network, http://www.pornhub.com/view_video.php?viewkey=1696556116.

34. Phone interview with Joanna Angel, September 19, 2016.

35. Laura Kipnis, *Bound and Gagged: Pornography and the Politics of Fantasy in America* (New York: Grove Press, 1996), 128.

36. Ibid., 129.

37. Phone interview with Joanna Angel, September 19, 2016.

38. Ibid.

39. Think *Frankenstein* (1931) meets *Single White Female* (1992).

40. Barbara Kirshenblatt-Gimblett, "The 'New Jews': Reflections on Emerging Cultural Practices" (paper presented at Re-thinking Jewish Communities and Networks in an Age of Looser Connections Conference, Wurzweiler School of Social Work, Yeshiva University and Institute for Advanced Studies, Hebrew University, New York City, December 6–7, 2005), 1.

41. "About Heeb," *Heeb Magazine*, http://heebmagazine.com/about/.

42. Kirshenblatt-Gimblett, "New Jews," 2.

43. Joshua Neuman, "So Much for Controlling the Media," *Heeb Magazine*, August 26, 2010, http://heebmagazine.com/so-much-for-controlling-the-media/19154. The article announced the suspension of the magazine's print form, and the new editor in chief, Erin Hershberg.

44. Arye Dworken, "Kiss Your Mother with That Mouth? PART 1," *Jewcy Magazine*, November 2006, 15 http://www.jewcy.com/post/kiss_your_mother_mouth_part_i#sthash.i0XgW97g.dpuf.

45. Kirshenblatt-Gimblett., "New Jews," 3.

46. Ibid.

47. Joanna Angel, email to author, September 19, 2016.

48. Phone interview with Joanna Angel, September 19, 2016.
49. Ibid.

CONCLUSION

1. Butler, *Bodies That Matter.*
2. Kirshenblatt-Gimblett, "New Jews."
3. Hutcheon, *Theory of Parody*, 75.
4. Burke, *A Grammar of Motives.*
5. Peggy Phelan, "The Ontology of Performance: Representation without Reproduction," in *Unmarked: The Politics of Performance* (London and New York: Routledge, 1993).
6. Muñoz, *Disidentifications.*

BIBLIOGRAPHY

"About." Thirsty Girl Productions. http://www.thirstygirlproductions.com/sign_up.

"About Heeb." *Heeb Magazine.* http://heebmagazine.com/about/.

"About Joanna Angel." Joanna Angel. http://www.joannaangel.com/en/about.

Ahmed, Sara. *Queer Phenomenology: Orientations, Objects, Others.* Durham, NC, and London: Duke University Press, 2006.

Alexander, Michael. *Jazz Age Jews.* Princeton, NJ: Princeton University Press, 2001.

Allen, Robert C. *Horrible Prettiness: Burlesque and American Culture.* Chapel Hill: University of North Carolina Press, 1991.

Angel, Joanna. ". . . On Being a Feminist with a Porn Site." In *Naked Ambition: Women Who Are Changing Pornography,* edited by Carly Milne, 233–244. New York: Carroll & Graf Publishers, 2005.

Antler, Joyce. "Jewish Women on Television, Too Jewish or Not Enough?" In *Talking Back: Images of Jewish Women in American Popular Culture,* edited by Joyce Antler, 242–252. Hanover, NH: Brandeis University Press, 1998.

Antler, Joyce. *The Journey Home: Jewish Women and the American Century.* New York: Free Press, 1997.

Antler, Joyce. "One Clove Away from A Pomander Ball: The Subversive Tradition of Jewish Female Comedians." *Studies in American Jewish Literature* 29 (2010): 129.

"AVN Awards." Burning Angel. http://www.burningangel.com/en/avn-2016.

Ballou, Hannah. "Pretty Funny: Manifesting a Normatively Sexy Female Comic Body." *Comedy Studies* 4, no. 2 (2013): 179–186.

Barr, Roseann. "Character Study: Sandra Bernhard." *Interview Magazine,* April 2012, 73.

Baumgardner, Jennifer, and Amy Richards. *Manifesta: Young Women, Feminism and the Future.* New York: Farrar, Straus and Giroux, 2000.

Berghan, Kalus L. "Comedy Without Laughter: Jewish Characters in Comedies from Shylock to Nathan." In *Laughter Unlimited: Essays on Humor, Satire, and the Comic,* edited by Grimm, Reinhold, and Jost Hermand, 3–26. London: University of Wisconsin Press, 1991.

Bergson, Henri. *Laughter: An Essay on the Meaning of the Comic.* New York: Macmillan, 1914.

Berlant, Lauren. "On the Case." *Critical Inquiry* 33, no. 4 (Summer 2007): 663–672.

Berlant, Lauren, and Elizabeth Freeman. "Queer Nationality." *Boundary 2* 19, no. 1 (1992): 149–180.

"Bette Midler—Continental Baths Concert" (1971). YouTube video, 54:50. Posted April 29, 2014. https://www.youtube.com/watch?v=UOrzpQeJyKI.

Bhabha, Homi K. "Foreword, Joking Aside: The Idea of a Self-Critical Community." In *Modernity, Culture and "The Jew"*, edited by Bryan Cheyette and Laura Marcus, xv–xx. Stanford, CA: Stanford University Press, 1998.

Bial, Henry. *Acting Jewish: Negotiating Ethnicity on the American Stage & Screen*. Ann Arbor: University of Michigan Press, 2005.

Biale, David. *Eros and the Jews*. Berkeley: University of California Press, 1997.

Blazing Saddles. Directed by Mel Brooks. Warner Brothers Pictures, 1974.

Blue Velvet. Directed by David Lynch. Toronto: De Laurentis Entertainment Group, 1986.

Boyarin, Daniel, David Itzkovitz, and Ann Pellegrini, eds. *Queer Theory and the Jewish Question*. New York: Columbia University Press, 2003.

Brodkin, Karen. *How Jews Became White Folks and What That Says about Race in America*. New Brunswick, NJ: Rutgers University Press, 1998.

Brown Lavitt, Pamela. "The First of the Red Hot Mamas: 'Coon Shouting' and the Jewish Question." *American Jewish History* 87, no. 4 (December 1999): 253–290.

Bunzl, Matti. "Jews, Queers, and Other Symptoms: Recent Work in Jewish Cultural Studies." *GLQ: A Journal of Lesbian and Gay Studies* 6, no. 2 (2000): 321–341.

Burke, Kenneth. *Attitudes Toward History*. 3rd ed. Berkeley: University of California Press, 1959.

Burke, Kenneth. *A Grammar of Motives*. Berkeley: University of California Press, 1969.

Buszek, Maria Elena. "Representing 'Awarishness': Burlesque, Feminist Transgression, and the 19th century Pin-Up." *TDR* 43, no. 4 (Winter 1999): 141–162.

Butler, Judith. *Bodies That Matter: On the Discursive Limits of "Sex"*. London and New York: Routledge, 1993.

"Citizen's Guide to U.S. Federal Law on Obscenity." United States Department of Justice. Last modified July 6, 2015. https://www.justice.gov/criminal-ceos/citizens-guide-us-federal-law-obscenity.

Connolly, Kelly. "Sarah Silverman Regrets Wearing Blackface for Sarah Silverman Program Joke." *Entertainment Weekly: Watch What Happens Live*, October 30, 2015. Accessed July 3, 2016. http://www.ew.com/article/2015/10/30/sarah-silverman-blackface-joke-regret.

Croft, Clare, ed. *Queer Dance: Meanings and Makings*. New York: Oxford University Press, 2017.

Darlinda Just Darlinda. "Feminist Neo-Burlesque Speech." Presented at the Feminist Neo-Burlesque Symposium at the Central School of Speech and Drama, University of London, October 26, 2007. http://darlindajustdarlinda.com/darlinda-just-darlinda-bio-and-press/feminist-neo-burlesque-speech-from-102607/.

Darlinda Just Darlinda. "Menorah Trio." YouTube video. Posted October 26, 2009. http://www.youtube.com/watch?v=XQz8izazuf0.

De Lauretis, Teresa. "Rethinking Women's Cinema." In *Figures of Resistance: Essays in Feminist Thought*, edited and with an introduction by Patricia White. Urbana and Chicago: University of Illinois Press, 2007.

Del Negro, Giovanna P. "The Bad Girls of Jewish Comedy: Gender, Class, Assimilation, and Whiteness in Postwar America." In a *Jewish Feminine Mystique? Jewish Women in Postwar America*, edited by Diner, Hasia, Shira Kohn, and Rachel Kranson, 144–159. New Brunswick, NJ: Rutgers University Press, 2010.

Diva Las Vegas. Directed by Marty Callner. Written by Madalyn Minch, Bruce Vilanch, and Lom Weyland. Filmed at MGM Grand Garden Arena, Las Vegas. Cream Cheese Films/Home Box Office (HBO), 1997.

Doane, Mary Ann. *Femmes Fatales: Feminism, Film Theory, Psychoanalysis.* New York: Routledge, 1991.

Doty, Alexander. *Making Things Perfectly Queer: Interpreting Mass Culture.* Minneapolis: University of Minnesota Press, 1993.

Drummond, Kent. "The Queering of Swan Lake: A New Male Gaze for the Performance of Sexual Desire." *Journal of Homosexuality* 45, no. 2–4 (2003): 235–255.

Dworken, Arye. "Kiss Your Mother with That Mouth? PART 1." *Jewcy Magazine*, November 2006. http://www.jewcy.com/post/kiss_your_mother_mouth_part_i#sthash.i0XgW97g.dpuf.

Dyer, Richard. *White: Essays on Race and Culture.* London: Routledge, 1997.

Edelman, Lee. *No Future: Queer Theory and the Death Drive.* Durham, NC: Duke University Press, 2004.

Eilberg-Schwartz, Howard. "The Problem of the Body for the People of the Book." In *People of the Body: Jews and Judaism from an Embodied Perspective*, edited by Howard Eilberg-Schwartz, 17–46. Albany: State University of New York Press, 1992.

"Face Wars." *The Sarah Silverman Program*, episode 203, October 17, 2007. Comedy Central. http://www.comedycentral.com/video-clips/ojqria/the-sarah-silverman-program-blackface-rally.

"50 Sexiest Jewish Girls We Can't Passover, The." *Coed Magazine*, April 18, 2011. http://coedmagazine.com/2011/04/18/the-50-sexiest-jewish-girls-we-cant-passover-photos/.

Fishman, Sylvia Barack. *Follow My Footprints: Changing Images of Women in American Jewish Fiction.* Hanover, NH: University Press of New England, 1992.

Foulkes, Julia. "Angels 'Rewolt!': Jewish Women in Modern Dance in the 1930s." In *American Jewish Women's History: A Reader*, edited by Pamela S. Nadell, 201–218. New York: New York University Press, 2003.

Freud, Sigmund. *The Joke and Its Relation to the Unconscious.* Translated by Joyce Chick. London: Penguin Books, 2003. Originally published as *Der Witz und seine Beziehung sum Unbewussten*. Leipzig: Deuticke, 1905.

Garber, Marjorie. "Moniker." In *Quotation Marks*, 121–146. New York: Routledge, 2003.

Garcia, Cindy. "Dancing Salsa Wrong." In *Salsa Crossings: Dancing Latinidad in Los Angeles*, 43–65. Durham, NC: Duke University Press, 2013.

Gillota, David. "The New Jewish Blackface: African American Tropes in Contemporary Jewish Humor." In *Jews and Humor: Studies in Jewish Civilization*, edited by Leonard J. Greenspoon, 226–229. West Lafayette, IN: Purdue University Press, 2009.

Gilman, Sander. *The Jew's Body.* New York: Routledge, 1991.

Glasscastle. "Sexy Sabra Sluts Spell DANGER, Will Robinson." Dowbrigade. July 20, 2005. http://blogs.law.harvard.edu/dowbrigade/2005/07/20/sexy-sabra-sluts-spell-danger-will-robinson/.

Goldstein, Eric L. *The Price of Whiteness: Jews, Race and American Identity.* Princeton, NJ: Princeton University Press, 2006.

Graff, Ellen. *Stepping Left: Dance and Politics in New York City, 1928–1942.* Durham, NC: Duke University Press, 1997.

Haft, Nina. "36 Jewish Gestures." In *Moving Ideas: Multimodality and Embodied Learning in Communities and Schools*, edited by M. Katz, 139–156. New York: Peter Lang, 2013.

Halley, Catherine. "The Mouth That Launched a Thousand Rifts: Sandra Bernhard's Politics of Irony." *Iowa Journal of Cultural Studies* 1995, no. 14 (1995): 23–39.

Harrison-Kahan, Lori. *The White Negress: Literature, Minstrelsy, and the Black Jewish Imaginary*. New Brunswick, NJ: Rutgers University Press, 2011.

Hawaiian Oklahoma. NBC, 1977. Viewed at Paley Center for Media, Los Angeles. Available at https://www.youtube.com/watch?v=rolxQPogXqU.

Heilman, Uriel. "Bernie Sanders Hires Outspoken Critic of Occupation as Jewish Outreach Director." *Forward*, April 12, 2016. http://forward.com/news/338492/bernie-sanders-hires-outspoken-critic-of-occupation-as-jewish-outreach-dire/.

Hoffman, Warren. *The Passing Game: Queering Jewish American Culture; Judaic Traditions in Literature, Music and Art*. Syracuse, NY: Syracuse University Press, 2009.

Holdberg, Amelia. "Betty Boop: Yiddish Film Star." *American Jewish History* 87, no. 4 (December 1999): 291–312.

hooks, bell. "Eating the Other: Desire and Resistance." In *Black Looks: Race and Representation*, 336–380. Boston: South End Press, 1992.

"House of Ass." Feminist Porn Awards. http://www.feministpornawards.com/house-of-ass/.

Howe, Irving. *World of Our Fathers*. New York: Harcourt Brace Jovanovich, 1976.

Hutcheon, Linda. *A Theory of Parody: The Teachings of Twentieth Century Art Forms*. New York: Methuen, 1985.

"Israeli Defense Forces." *Maxim Magazine*, July 9, 2007. http://www.maxim.com/girls-of-maxim/israeli-defense-forces.

"Israeli Soldier Girl Doing Strip Dance in Army Tent." Xhamster. Posted September 1, 2011. http://xhamster.com/movies/829707/israeli_soldier_girl_doing_strip_dance_in_army_tent.html.

"It's Big, It's Black, It's Inside Joanna!!!" Comment by Punk Porn Princess, Xoxojoannaangel. Posted on July 28, 2009. http://xoxojoannaangel.com/2009/07/this-is-just-a-test/.

Itzkovitz, Daniel. "They Are All Jews." In *You Should See Yourself: Jewish Identity in Postmodern American Culture*, edited by Vincent Brook, 230–252. New Brunswick, NJ: Rutgers University Press, 2006.

Jackson, Naomi. *Converging Movements: Modern Dance and Jewish Culture at the 92nd Street Y*. Hanover, NH, and London: Wesleyan University Press, 2000.

Jakobson, Janet R. "Queers Are Like Jews, Aren't They? Analogy and Alliance Politics." In *Queer Theory and the Jewish Question*, edited by Daniel Boyarin, Daniel Itzkovitz, and Ann Pellegrini, 64–89. New York: Columbia University Press, 2003.

Jennings, Luke. "Swan Lake – Review." *The Guardian*, January 29, 2011. https://www.theguardian.com/stage/2011/jan/30/swan-lake-royal-ballet-review.

Jesus Is Magic. Directed by Liam Lynch. Written and performed by Sarah Silverman. Black Gold Films. 2005.

"John Galliano: 'I Love Hitler' (VIDEO)" and "Natalie Portman 'Disgusted' by John Galliano Video." *Huffington Post*, March 1, 2011. http://www.huffingtonpost.com/2011/03/01/natalie-portman-galliano-video-dior_n_829522.html.

Johnston, Ruth D. "Joke-Work: The Construction of Jewish Postmodern Identity in Contemporary Theory and American Film." In *You Should See Yourself: Jewish Identity in Postmodern American Culture*, edited by Vincent Brook, 207–229. New Brunswick, NJ: Rutgers University Press, 2006.

Juhasz, Susanne. "Queer Swans: Those Fabulous Avians in the Swan Lakes of Les Ballet Trockadero and Matthew Bourne." *Dance Chronicle* 31 (2008): 54–83.

Kealiinohomoku, Joann. "An Anthropologist Looks at Ballet as a Form of Ethnic Dance." In *Moving History/Dancing Cultures*, edited by Ann Dils and Ann Cooper Albright, 33–43. Middletown, CT: Wesleyan University Press, 2001.

Kipnis, Laura. *Bound and Gagged: Pornography and the Politics of Fantasy in America.* New York: Grove Press, 1996.

Kirshenblatt-Gimblett, Barbara. "Corporeal Turn." *Jewish Quarterly Review* 95, no. 3 (Summer 2005): 447–461.

Kirshenblatt-Gimblett, Barbara. "Feminizing Jewish Studies." *Commentary* 105 (February 1998): 39–45.

Kirshenblatt-Gimblett, Barbara. "The 'New Jews': Reflections on Emerging Cultural Practices." Paper presented at Re-thinking Jewish Communities and Networks in an Age of Looser Connections Conference, Wurzweiler School of Social Work, Yeshiva University and Institute for Advanced Studies, Hebrew University, New York, NY, December 6–7, 2005.

Knowles, Laura. "Oy Vey, It's 'Nice Jewish Girls Gone Bad'!" *Lancaster Online*, September 10, 2009. http://lancasteronline.com/features/entertainment/oy-vey-it-s-nice-jewish-girls-gone-bad/article_e91dd3c6-b4e6-5718-9180-87131e16b89d.html.

Kosofsky Sedgwick, Eve. *Epistemology of the Closet.* Berkeley: University of California Press, 1990.

Kosstrin, Hannah. *Honest Bodies: Revolutionary Modernism in the Dances of Anna Sokolow.* New York: Oxford University Press, 2017.

Kumbier, Alana. *Ephemeral Material: Queering the Archive.* Series on Gender and Sexuality in Information Studies, no. 4. Sacramento, CA: Litwin Books, 2012.

Lau, Jacob. "Which Child? Whose Queerness? On Situated Knowledges, Queer Embodiment and *No Future*." Paper presented at UCLA Thinking Gender 2013 annual conference, Los Angeles, California. February 1, 2013.

Levinas Reader, The. Edited by Sean Hand. Oxford: Blackwell, 1989.

Levine, Harry G., and Gaye Tuchman. "New York Jews and Chinese Food: The Social Construction of an Ethnic Pattern." *Contemporary Ethnography* 22, no. 3 (1992): 382–407.

Levy, Ariel. *Female Chauvinist Pigs: Women and the Rise of Raunch Culture.* New York: Free Press, 2005.

Linihan, Jean. "Benjamin Millepied on 'Black Swan,' Natalie Portman and His Dancing Future." *Los Angeles Times*, March 23, 2011. http://latimesblogs.latimes.com/culturemonster/2011/03/benjamin-millepied-on-black-swan-nataline-portman-and-his-dancing-future.html.

Lott, Eric. *Love and Theft: Blackface Minstrelsy and the American Working Class.* Oxford: Oxford University Press, 1995.

Lowery, Lacy, Valerie R. Renegar, and Charles E. Goehring. "'When God Gives You AIDS . . . Make Lemon-AIDS': Ironic Persona and Perspective by Incongruity in Sarah Silverman's *Jesus Is Magic*." *Western Journal of Communication* 78, no. 1 (2014): 58–77.

Macaulay, Alastair. "A 'Swan' of Complex Shades." *New York Times*, February 14, 2011. Page C1 of the New York edition.

Magid, Shaul. "Butler Trouble: Zionism, Excommunication, and the Reception of Judith Butler's Work on Israel/Palestine." *Studies in American Jewish Literature* 33, no. 2 (2014): 237–259.

Magnet, S. "Feminist Sexualities, Race, and the Internet: An Investigation of suicide-girls.com." *New Media & Society* 9, no. 4 (2007): 577–602.

Mahler, Jonathan. "Howard's End: Why a Leading Jewish Studies Scholar Gave Up His Academic Career." *Lingua Franca* (March 1997): 51–57.

Manning, Susan. *Modern Dance, Negro Dance: Race in Motion.* Minneapolis: University of Minnesota Press, 2004.

Mclean, Adrienne L. *Dying Swans and Madmen: Ballet, the Body and Narrative Cinema*. New Brunswick, NJ: Rutgers University Press, 2008.

Midgelow, Vida L. *Reworking the Ballet: Counter Narratives and Alternative Bodies*. London: Routledge, 2007.

Mock, Roberta. "Without You I'm Nothing": Sandra Bernhard's Self-Referential Postmodernism. *Women's Studies* 30, no. 4 (2001): 543–562.

Modeleski, Talia. *Feminism Without Women: Culture and Criticism in a Postfeminist Age*. New York: Routledge, 1991.

Morgan, Robin. *Going Too Far: The Personal Chronicle of a Feminist*. New York: Vintage Books, 1978.

Most, Andrea. "Gilda Radner 1946–1989: From Dancing Lessons to *Saturday Night Live*." Jewish Women's Archive. http://jwa.org/discover/infocus/comedy/radner.html.

Muñoz, José Esteban. *Cruising Utopia: The Then and There of Queer Futurity*. New York: New York University Press, 2009.

Muñoz, José Esteban. *Disidentifications: Queers of Color and the Performance of Politics*. Minneapolis: University of Minnesota Press, 2010.

"Muskeljudentum." *Judische Turnzuitung* (June 1900): 10–11.

"Natalie Portman Nose Job before and after Photos." *Star Surgery*, December 10, 2013. http://surgerystars.com/natalie-portman-nose-job-before-and-after-photos/.

Neuman, Joshua. "The Making of the First Ever Jewish Swimsuit Calendar." *Heeb Magazine*, July 28, 2008. http://heebmagazine.com/the-making-of-the-first-ever-jewish-swimsuit-calendar/3392.

Neuman, Joshua. "So Much for Controlling the Media." *Heeb Magazine*, August 26, 2010. http://heebmagazine.com/so-much-for-controlling-the-media/19154.

"1979 Jordache Jeans commercial" (1979). YouTube video, 0:30. Posted October 24, 2010. https://www.youtube.com/watch?v=qAZP9i6MvSw.

Osterweiss, Ariel. "Disciplining Black Swan, Animalizing Ambition." In *The Oxford Handbook of Dance and the Popular Screen*, edited by Melissa Blanco Borelli, 68–82. New York: Oxford University Press, 2014.

Paasonen, Susanna. "Labors of Love: Netporn, Web 2.0 and the Meanings of Amateurism." *New Media & Society* 12, no. 8 (2010): 1297–1312.

Pellegrini, Ann. *Performance Anxieties: Staging Psychoanalysis, Staging Race*. New York: Routledge, 1997.

Pellegrini, Ann. "You Make Me Feel (Mighty Real): Sandra Bernhard's Whiteface." In *With Other Eyes: Looking at Race and Gender in Visual Culture*, edited by Lisa Bloom, 237–250. Minnesota: University of Minnesota Press, 1999.

Penley, Constance, Celine Parreñas Shimizu, Mireille Miller-Young, and Tristan Taormino. "Introduction: The Politics of Producing Pleasure." In *The Feminist Porn Book: The Politics of Producing Pleasure*, edited by Tristan Taormino, Celine Parreñas Shimizu, Constance Penley, and Mireille Miller-Young, 9–22. New York: The Feminist Press at the City University of New York, 2013.

Phelan, Peggy. "The Ontology of Performance: Representation without Reproduction." In *Unmarked: The Politics of Performance*, 146–166. London and New York: Routledge, 1993.

"Porn Hub." Porn Hub Network. http://www.pornhub.com/view_video.php?viewkey=1696556116.

Prell, Riv-Ellen. *Fighting to Become American: Jews, Gender, and the Anxiety of Assimilation*. Boston: Beacon Press, 1999.

Probyn, Elsbeth. "Without Her, I'm Nothing." In *Sexing the Self: Gendered Positions in Cultural Studies*, 138–164. London & New York: Routledge, 1993

Reik, Theodor. *Jewish Wit*. New York: Gamut Press, 1962.

Reilly, Jill. "They Really Are Dangerous Curves: Heavily Armed and Bikini-clad Female Israeli Soldiers 'Mingle' with Beachgoers." *Daily Mail*, July 13, 2012. http://www. dailymail.co.uk/news/article-2173050/Do-NOT-steal-woman-s-towel-Heavily-armed-bikini-clad-female-Israeli-soldiers-mingle-Tel-Aviv-beachgoers.html.

Rettman, Tony. "Racist Rock: An Overview of White Supremacy in Punk and Metal." *Noise Creep*, August 20, 2012. http://noisecreep.com/white-power-punk-hardcore/.

Rivera-Servera, Ramón. *Performing Queer Latinidad*. Ann Arbor: University of Michigan Press, 2012.

Roediger, David. "Whiteness and Ethnicity in the History of 'White Ethnics' in the United States." In *Race Critical Theories*, edited by Philomen Essed and David Theo Goldberg, 325–343. Oxford: Blackwell Publishing, 2002.

Rogin, Michael. *Blackface, White Noise: Jewish Immigrants in the Hollywood Melting Pot*. Berkeley: University of California Press, 1996.

Rossen, Rebecca. *Dancing Jewish: Jewish Identity in American Modern and Postmodern Dance*. New York: Oxford University Press, 2014.

Roth, Phillip. *Portnoy's Complaint*. New York: Random House, 1969.

Saltmarsh, Matthew. "Dior Fires John Galliano after Bigotry Complaints." *New York Times*, March 1, 2011. http://www.nytimes.com/2011/03/02/fashion/02dior. html.

Saposnik, Irving. "The Yiddish Are Coming! The Yiddish Are Coming! Some Thoughts on Yiddish Comedy." In *Laughter Unlimited: Essays on Humor, Satire, and the Comic*, edited by Reinhold Grimm and Jost Hermand, 99–105. London: University of Wisconsin Press, 1991.

"Sarah Silverman and the Great Shlep." YouTube Video. Posted September 28, 2008. http://www.youtube.com/watch?v=AgHHX9R4Qtk.

Savigliano, Marta E. "Notes on Tango (as) Queer (Commodity)." *Anthropological Notebooks* 16 (2010): 135–143.

Savigliano, Marta E. *Tango and the Political Economy of Passion*. Westview: Boulder, 1995.

"Schlep Sisters & Thirsty Girl Prod Present 5th Annual MENORAH HORAH, The." *Broadway World*, November 29, 2011. http://music.broadwayworld.com/article/The-Schlep-Sisters-Thirsty-Girl-Prod-Present-5th-Annual-MENORAH-HORAH-20111129.

"Schlep Sisters & Thirsty Girl Productions Present the 8th Annual Menorah Horah! Hanukkah Burlesque Show, The." Highline Ballroom. http://highlineballroom. com/show/2014/12/14/menorah-horah-2/.

"Schlep Sisters Chiribim, Zug es Mir, and Raindrops." YouTube video. Posted March 23, 2010 by Darlinda Just Darlinda. http://www.youtube.com/ watch?v=BHZnAwOE7nI.

Schneider, Rebecca. "The Secret's Eye." In *The Explicit Body in Performance*, 88–125. London and New York: Routledge, 1997.

Schwartz, Shuly Rubin. "From Jewess Jeans to Juicy JAPs: Clothing and Jewish Stereotypes." Presented at What to Wear event, Jewish Theological Seminary, March 11, 2012. http://www.youtube.com/watch?v=rZWz_XL_zWg&feature=youtube_gdata_player.

Silverman, Sime. Review of *Follies of 1916*. *Variety*, June 16, 1916.

Simpson, Jenna. "Oh, Ya Got Trouble, Right Here in New York City! Or Gotta Find a Way to Keep the Young Ones Moral After School: The Boycott of Hollywood, March–July 1934." *Constructing the Past* 5, no. 1 (2004). http://digitalcommons.iwu.edu/cgi/viewcontent.cgi?article=1032&context=constructing.

Sohn, Amy. "Teasy Does It." *New York Magazine*, June 7, 2004. http://nymag.com/nymetro/nightlife/sex/columns/nakedcity/9210/.

Sowinski, Alicia. "Dialectics of the Banana Skirt: The Dialectics of Josephine Baker's Self-Representation." *Michigan Feminist Studies* 19. (Fall 2005/2006): 51–72.

Stratton, Jon. *Coming Out Jewish: Constructing Ambivalent Identities.* London: Routledge, 2000.

Stratton, Jon. "Not Really White—Again: Performing Jewish Difference in Hollywood Films since the 1980s." *Screen* 42, no. 2 (Summer 2001): 142–146.

"Streisand Profile, The: The Nose." Barbra Streisand Archive Library. http://barbra-archives.com/bjs_library/stories/nose_streisand.html.

"Susan Foster, Three Performed Lectures: The Ballerina's Phallic Pointe." *Dance Workbook*, March 21, 2011. http://danceworkbook.pcah.us/susan-foster/the-ballerinas-phallic-pointe.html.

Tomko, Linda. *Dancing Class: Gender, Ethnicity, and Social Divides in American Dance, 1890–1920.* Bloomington: Indiana University Press, 1999.

Tonka, Minnie, interview by Hannah Schwadron, New York City, July 21, 2016.

Van de Merwe, Ann. "My Man: The Vocal Signature of Fanny Brice." *Phenomenon of Singing* 7 (2009): 139–141.

Van Doorn, Neils. "Keeping It Real: User-Generated Pornography, Gender Reification, and Visual Pleasure." *Convergence: The International Journal of Research Into New Media Technologies* 16 (2010): 4.

Villett, Michelle. "Mila Kunis, Before and After: What the World's Sexiest Woman (According to FHM) Looked Like Before She Got Famous." *Beauty Editor*, November 1, 2013. http://beautyeditor.ca/2013/11/01/mila-kunis-before-and-after/.

Ward, Jane. "Queer Feminist Pigs." In *The Feminist Porn Book: The Politics of Producing Pleasure*, edited by Taormino, Tristan, Celine Parreñas Shimizu, Constance Penley, and Mireille Miller-Young, 130–139. New York: The Feminist Press at the City University of New York, 2013.

"Was bedeutut Turner fur uns Juden?" *Judische Turnzeitung* (July 1902): 109–112.

"Welcome." Schlep Sisters. http://schlepsisters.com/TheSchlepSisters/Welcome.html.

"What Are the Feminist Porn Awards?" Feminist Porn Awards. http://www.feminist-pornawards.com/what-are-the-feminist-porn-awards/.

"Why Burning Angel Rules." Burning Angel. http://www.burningangel.com/forum/thread/2022/why-burning-angel-rules.

Williams, Linda. *Hard Core: Power, Pleasure, and the Frenzy of the Visible.* Berkeley: University of California Press, 1989.

Williams, Linda. "A Provoking Agent: The Pornography and Performance Art of Annie Sprinkle." *Social Text* 37 (Winter 1993): 117–133.

"Winona Ryder Nose Job." *Plastic Surgery Before and After*, June 22, 2013. http://plasticsurgerybeforeafter.blogspot.com/2013/06/winona-ryder-nose-job.html.

Wolf, Stacy. "Barbra's 'Funny Girl' Body." In *Queer Theory and the Jewish Question*, edited by Daniel Boyarin, Daniel Itzkovitz, and Ann Pellegrini, 246–265. New York: Columbia University Press, 2003.

Wood, Robin. "Introduction to the American Horror Film." In *Movies and Methods: An Anthology*, edited by Bill Nichols, 2:195–219. Berkeley: University of California Press, 1985.

INDEX

Page numbers followed by *f* indicate figures. Numbers followed by n indicate notes

dirty films, 177n29
dirty jokes, 17
disidentificatory performances, 172n61
Doane, Mary Ann, 171n41
Dodds, Sherill, 7–8, 169n11, 174n9
do-it-yourself scheme, 46–48
domestication, 112
"Don't Rain on My Parade," 175n9
Doppelganger (2010), 147–149, 149f
doppelgangers, 159–160
    Black Swan, 123–124, 123f–124f,
        131, 183n18
    Jewish, 144–148
Doty, Alexander, 120, 183n21
doubled female subject, 16–19
downward mobility, 29, 46
Dr. Suzy's Porn and Purim DVD
    Bacchanal, 144
Dresher, Fran, 114, 183n12
Drummond, Kent, 176n16
Dude, Am I a Slut?, 137
Dunham, Lena, 93
Dworken, Arye, 150
Dworkin, Andrea, 180n8
"the Dying Swan," 55–56
The Dying Swan, 175n7
dynamic positioning, 9

Edelman, Lee, 172n53
edginess, 159–160
    "Abbi on the Edge of Glory" (*Broad
        City*), 104–106, 105f
    Jewish cutting edge, 149–152
Edwards, Leo, 54–55
egalitarianism, 138
Eilberg-Schwartz, Howard, 10, 169n19
Ellerbee, Linda, 69–70
emboldened femininity, 160–161
emo porn, 133
emotional intensity, 168n8
entertainment, 48
Entertainment Weekly, 93
Erdman, Harley, 167n2
Essman, Susie, 101
ethnicity, open, 62, 75
exoticism, 15
explicit body, 168n7
exploitation, gender, 45
expressivity, 168n8

face issues, 6–8, 85–86, 159–160, 168n9
    funny face performance, 7
    "in your face," 164–165
    Jewish noses, 6, 113–114, 128–129,
        143, 169n18, 175n11, 182n10
"Face Wars" (*The Sarah Silverman
    Program*), 91, 91f, 92f, 93, 107
facial expression, 7–8
fashion, 113
Feinstein, Rachel, 181n33
female body
    bawdy bodies, 60–64, 162
    Hustler body, 144
    Jewish body, 7
female chauvinism, 135, 138–140, 156
female chauvinist pigs (FCPs), 139–140
female comedy, 4–5, 51–108, 154–155,
    160–162. *See also specific performers*
female monsters, 109–110, 113–119,
    126–128
female performance, 163
femininity, emboldened, 58, 160–161
feminism, 69–70, 137–139
    polyester, 38–46
    raunch, 139
    second wave, 40
feminist activism, 136
"Feminist Neo-Burlesque Speech"
    (Darlinda Just Darlinda), 38–40
Feminist Porn Awards, 137
Femme Productions, 136
Fields, Totie, 82
Fishman, Sylvia Barack, 182n2
Fleisher, Dave, 62
Florida, 93–94
Fokine, Mikhail, 55, 175n7
Foster, Susan, 183n14
Foulkes, Julia, 168n8, 169n15
"Four Women" (Simone), 82, 83f
Freeland, Thornton, 55
Freud, Sigmund, 16, 45, 168n7, 171n43
"Fuck Me and Not My Doll" (Angel), 146
funny face performance, 7
Funny Girl (1968), 51, 57–60, 58f, 65–66,
    75, 130–131, 175n9
    "Don't Rain on My Parade," 175n9
    queer interpretation of, 172n60
funny girls, 51–76, 86, 120. *See also
    specific performers*

futurity, 172n53

Galliano, John, 113
gangster white chicks, 153–154
Gapay, Jen, 173n1
Garcia, Cindy, 172n51
gender exploitation, 45, 162
Gillota, David, 180n25
Gilman, Sander, 182n9
girl power, sex-positive, 3
Girls Gone Wild, 138
glamour, 46
Glazer, Ilana, 5–6, 78, 99–104, 102*f,*
    107, 121–122, 164
Glee, 114, 183n12
Goehring, Charles E., 98–99, 171n47
The Goldbergs, 182n2
Goldman, Herbert, 53
Goldstein, Eric L., 8–9
Goltz, Dustin Bradley, 99
Goodbye, Columbus (Roth), 182n2
"Gorgeous to Be Graceful," 56
Graff, Ellen, 169n15
Graham, Martha, 53
Grease, 6–7
"The Great Schlep" (Silverman),
    93–94, 181n30

Haft, Nina, 169n15
hag stereotype, 2
Halkin, Hillel, 169n20
hamantaschen, 144
Handler, Elliot, 173n6
Handler, Ruth, 173n6
Hanukkah, 143, 161
"Hard Hearted Hannah," 12–13
Harrison-Kahan, Lori, 14, 170n31, 180n25
Hartley, Nina, 186n7
Hatch, James V., 170n29, 179n1
Hawaiian Oklahoma (NBC), 72
Hays Code, 64
Heeb Magazine, 135, 145, 149–152,
    156–157, 187n43
Held, Anna, 176n17
Hershberg, Erin, 187n43
Hershey, Barbara, 109, 111–112, 130
Hershlag, Natalie, 111–112
Herzstein, Barbara, 111–112
Highline Ballroom, 46

Hill, Jonah, 150
"Hinei Ma Tov," 85
Hoffman, Warren, 172n60
Holberg, Amelia, 62–63
Hollywood, 69
home, 141–144
homophobia, 20
homosexuality, 119, 121
hooks, bell, 86, 89, 108, 180n15
Hooper, Colleen, 169n11
horah, 27–28
Horowitz, Winona, 111–112
horror, 126–129
House of Ass (2005), 186n11
Howe, Irving, 13–14, 170n28
humor. *See also* comedy
    blue, 60–61, 65
    cartoons, 62–63
    interracial, 153–156
Hurst, Fanny, 170n31
Hurston, Zora Neal, 170n31
Hustler body, 144
Hutcheon, Linda, 18, 161
hypersexuality, 110–111, 113, 117–118,
    120–121, 134, 144, 154

"I Ain't Takin Orders from No One," 60–61
idealism, feminist, 139
identity acts, 12–16
identity politics, 101
I'll Be Glad When You're Dead, You Rascal
    (1932), 176n26
imitations, 175n12
impersonation, 12–16
    racial, 14, 106
improvisation, 170n27
interracial porn, 153–156
interracial relations, 170n31
Interview Magazine, 81–82
"in your face" faces, 164–165
irony, 99
Israel, 169n22
Israeli men, 169n22
It's Big, It's Black, It's Inside Joanna
    (2009), 152–156, 153*f,* 157
It's My First Time 2 (2015), 137
Itzkovitz, Daniel, 20, 167n4,
    183n13, 183n22
I/you other, 80–90